Basics in Psychology

1

Basics in Psychology

Barbara Woods

Hodder & Stoughton
A MEMBER OF THE HODDER HEADLINE GROUP

Orders: please contact Bookpoint Ltd, 39 Milton Park, Abingdon, Oxon OX14 4TD. Telephone: (44) 01235 400414, Fax: (44) 01235 400454. Lines are open from 9.00 - 6.00, Monday to Saturday, with a 24 hour message answering service. Email address: orders@bookpoint.co.uk

British Library Cataloguing in Publication Data
A catalogue record for this title is available from The British Library

ISBN 0 340 64360 9

First published 1995
Impression number 10 9 8 7 6 5
Year 2004 2003 2002 2001 2000 1999 1998

Typeset by Greengate Publishing Services, Tonbridge, Kent.
Printed in Great Britain for Hodder & Stoughton Educational, a division of Hodder Headline Plc, 338 Euston Road, London NW1 3BH by The Bath Press, Bath.

Contents

Introduction ix

Section A Ways of explaining human action 1

1 The influences of inborn characteristics 3
Instincts • Reflexes • Maturation • Sensitive period • Heredity and the nature or nurture debate • Twin studies

2 The role of learning in shaping behaviour 8
Classical conditioning • Operant conditioning • Social learning

3 Social and cultural influences 14
Affiliation • Social norms • Social roles • The environment and the nature or nurture debate • Cross-cultural studies

4 The influences of thinking and perception 19
Transduction • Processing information • Mental representation

Section B Psychological methodology 27

5 Discovering and testing psychological knowledge 29
Research methods • Types of study

6 Carrying out and reporting practical research 39
Aim of the research • Design of study • Sampling • Controlling the variables • Collecting data • Presenting data • Drawing conclusions from the data • Practical report checklist

7 Ethics in psychological research 56
Why are ethics important?

Section C Social and anti-social relationships 59

8 Making attachments to others 61
What is an attachment and how does it develop? • How do we know when an attachment has developed? • How do attachments vary? • Why do attachments vary like this? • Why are attachments important? • John Bowlby's ideas • Theory of monotrophy – a single early attachment? • Maternal deprivation – what exactly is it? • What is the effect of divorce on children?

9 Widening social relationships **76**
How do children develop relationships with their peers? • How do patterns of friendship change as children develop? • What attracts one person to another? • How do other people affect our behaviour? • Putting the theories together

10 Prejudice **91**
What is prejudice and why is it important? • Psychodynamic explanations of prejudice • Cognitive-information explanations of stereotyping and prejudice • Social learning explanations of stereotyping and prejudice • What is the difference between prejudice and discrimination? • How can prejudice and discrimination be reduced?

11 Aggression **105**
What is aggression? • Ethological explanations for aggression • Psychodynamic explanations for aggression • Learning theory explanations for aggression • What effect do child rearing styles have on aggression? • Are there ways of reducing aggression?

Section D Individuality and identity **119**

12 The development of personality **121**
What is personality and how does it develop? • Psychodynamic explanations of personality development • Radical behaviourist explanations of personality development • Social learning explanations of personality development • Temperament as an explanation of personality development

13 Intelligence **133**
What is IQ and how is it calculated? • How have IQ tests been used? • What are the limitations of IQ testing? • What is the hereditarian view of intelligence? • Does research support the hereditarian view? • What is the environmental view of intelligence? • Does research support the environmental view? • What is the outcome of the nature or nurture debate on intelligence?

14 The development of gender **148**
What is gender? • What is gender concept and how does it develop? • Children's behaviour and its relationship to gender • Psychodynamic explanations for the acquisition of gender • Social learning explanations for the acquisition of gender • Cognitive-developmental explanations for the acquisition of gender • Gender schema explanation • What evidence is there for gender differences? • How are gender differences promoted and reinforced?

15 Towards a concept of self 163
What is a concept of self? • Self-image • Self-esteem • How do social roles contribute to an individual's self-concept? • The self-fulfiling prophecy • Labelling

Section E Cognitive and social competence 179

16 Cognitive development 181
Piaget's stages of cognitive development • How do children progress through these stages? • What influence have Piaget's ideas had? • The development of visual perception • Evidence for the hereditarian view of the development of visual perception • Evidence for the environmentalist view of the development of visual perception • How can we decide between the influences of heredity and environment? • So what conclusions can we come to?

17 The development of moral behaviour and moral judgements 200
What are moral behaviour and moral judgements? • Psychodynamic explanation for moral development • Learning theory explanations of moral development • Cognitive-developmental explanations of moral development • How does pro-social reasoning develop in most children? • How is the individual's moral development and behaviour related to others?

18 Pro-social behaviour 214
What is pro-social behaviour? • How does empathy develop in children? • What is altruism? • What have psychologists found out about altruism? • Bystander intervention – when do we help others? • How may social norms affect pro-social behaviour?

19 Construction of social reality 228
How do we form overall impressions of others? • How do internal mental processes act as personal filters of information? • How do social filters of information work?

Glossary 241

Index 248

Acknowledgements

I would like to thank Richard and my mother for their continuing support and encouragement and Ann Searle for practical ideas and humour. Thanks also to Miriam Thomas and Mary Inness for advice and to Tim Gregson-Williams and Louise Tooms at Hodder & Stoughton for their help and efficiency.

The author and publisher would like to thank the following for permission to use photographs: Popperfoto, Fig. 5.5; Bubbles/F Rombout, Fig. 8.1; Angela Hampton Family Life Pictures, Figs. 8.2, 17.1, 17.3, 19.2; Collections/Sandra Lousada, Figs. 8.3, 12.3; Mike Abrahams/Network, Fig. 8.4; Bubbles/Loisjoy Thurston, Fig 8.5; Bubbles/J Lamb, Fig. 9.1; Range/Bettmann/UPI, Fig. 9.4; Telegraph Colour Library, Fig. 9.8; J Allan Cash, Figs. 10.1, 19.1; Maggie Murray/Format, Fig. 10.2 left; Topham Picturepoint, Fig. 10.2 right; Rex Features, Fig. 10.3; Brenda Prince/Format, Fig 10.4; Associated Press/Topham Picturepoint, Fig. 11.1; Bubbles/Jacqui Farrow, Fig. 11.2; Esaias Baitel/Frank Spooner Pictures, Fig. 11.4; Paul Lowe/Network, Fig. 11.5; Nicola Sutton/Life File, Fig. 12.2; Rob Nelson/Katz Pictures Ltd, Fig. 13.3; Cyril Letourneur/GLMR/Colorific!, Fig. 14.2; ™ © LWTP 1992/1993/1994/5, Fig. 14.4; Gary John Norman/Impact, Fig. 15.1; Collections/Anthea Sieveking, Figs. 15.2, 16.2, 16.3, 18.1; Ronald Grant Archive, Fig. 15.5; NYT Pictures, Fig. 16.1; Sally & Richard Greenhill, Fig. 16.4; Sarah Lenton/Practical Parenting/Robert Harding Syndication, Fig. 17.2; Paul Nightingale/Frank Spooner Pictures, Fig. 18.2; PA News, Fig. 18.3; Arthur Jumper/Life File, Fig. 18.4; Peter Jordan/Network, Fig. 19.3

The author and publisher would also like to thank the following: *Scientific American* for permission to reproduce the Fantz bar chart (Fig. 16.5), adapted from R. Fantz (1961) 'The origin of form perception', *Scientific American*, **204**(5), 66–72; Lawrence Erlbaum Associates Inc. for permission to reproduce Fig. 9.7 The causes and results of deindividuation' from E. Diener (1980) 'Deindividuation: the absence of self-awareness and self-regulation in group members', in P. B. Paulus (ed.) *The Psychology of Group Influence*; Ann Searle for permission to reproduce Fig. 5.3, 'The fat lady on a bicycle'; Dr Janet Collis and Blackwell Publishers for permission to reproduce Fig. 5.4, from J. Collis *et al.* (1995) 'The British Army recruitment battery goes operational', *International Journal of Selection & Assessment*, **3**(2); Academic Press for permission to reproduce Tables 9.1 and 16.1, 'Completion times' from B. Schmidt (1986) 'Mere presence and social facilitation', *Journal of Experimental Social Psychology*, **22**,3; Table 16.1 is a summary of the results from two studies: B. Schwarz, A. Campos and E. Baisel (1973) 'Heart rate results on the visual cliff, *Journal of Experimental Child Psychology*, **15**, 86–9 and J. Campos, A. Langer and A. Krowitz (1970) 'Heart rate results from the visual cliff, Science, 196–7; Yale University Press for permission to reproduce Table 19.1, from A. Luchins (1957) 'Primacy-recency in impression formation', in C. Hovland (ed.) *The Order of Presentation in Persuasion*; the authors and publishers of R. Rosenthal and L. Jacobson (1966) 'Teachers' expectancies: determinants of pupils' IQ gains', Psychological Reports, 19, 115–18, © 1966 Southern Universities Press; the American Educational Research Association for permission to reproduce Fig. 15.3 adapted from Witken *et al.* (1977) 'Field dependent and field independent cognitive styles and their educational implications', *Review of Educational Research*, **47**, 164. While every effort has been made to trace copyright holders, this has not been possible in all cases; any omissions brought to our attention will be remedied in future printings.

Index compiled by Frank Merrett, Cheltenham, Gloucester

Introduction

Although *Basics in Psychology* will be of interest to those studying topics such as child-care or education, it is primarily written for students studying the new GCSE Psychology syllabus. It has four aims:

1 to be interesting and easy to read.
2 to cover information which you need to know for the exam. At the end of each chapter are a few exercises to test or extend your understanding. These are similar to the kind of questions you might be asked in the exam.
3 to help you write your practical report. Details are in Chapter 6, but throughout the book there are examples from actual psychological research which will illustrate these details.
4 to help you understand how the core topics in the syllabus are integrated into the optional sections. Where core topics appear in the optional sections they are printed in green and are identified by small symbols as well.

The book is divided into five sections which are the same as the SEG Psychology syllabus. The first two sections relate to the **core topics**. Section A covers four ways of explaining human action (comprising Chapters 1–4). Section B is on methodology (comprising Chapters 5–7). At the beginning of each of these sections there is an explanation of how to use the symbols and the terms printed in green.

These **core topics** keep reappearing in the **optional** sections. Section C comprises four chapters covering aspects of social and anti-social relationships, Section D consists of four chapters on individuality and identity and Section E has four chapters on cognitive and social competence.

Words in **bold type** show you that these are key terms in the optional topics. The Glossary gives definitions of many of the green or **bold** terms. If they do not appear there, look in the Index at the back which will direct you to the right page. Names of psychologists are also printed in **bold** type.

I hope that this book succeeds in its four aims, and that it also stimulates your interest in psychology.

TO THE TEACHER

Basics in Psychology acts as a guide to the new GCSE syllabus from SEG, and provides enough material to cover both the Foundation and Higher tiers of entry. You may wish to extend the information for Higher tier standards, so there are some ideas for further reading at the end of each chapter. However they are only a tiny selection of possible sources and many other texts should meet your needs equally well.

Below is a list of all the texts mentioned in this book.

General reading

Atkinson R, Atkinson R, Smith E and Bem D (1993) *Introduction to Psychology* (11th ed), Orlando, Harcourt Brace Jovanovich
Gross R (1992) *Psychology – The Science of Mind and Behaviour* (2nd ed), London, Hodder & Stoughton
Hayes N (1994) *Foundations of Psychology*, London, Routledge

Specific reading

Attachment

Rutter M (1981) *Maternal Deprivation Reassessed*, Harmondsworth, Penguin

Developmental

Sylva K and Lunt I (1982) *Child Development – A First Course*, Oxford, Basil Blackwell Ltd.
Bee H (1992) *The Developing Child* (6th ed), New York, Harper Collins

Methodology

Coolican H (1995) *Introduction to Research Methods and Statistics in Psychology*, London, Hodder & Stoughton

Sex differences

Nicholson J (1984) *Men and Women – How Different are they?*, Oxford University Press

Social

Deaux K, Dane F and Wrightsman L (1993) *Social Psychology in the 90s* (6th ed), Pacific Grove, Brooks/Cole

Details of some studies referred to in this book

Gross R (1992) *Key Studies in Psychology* (2nd ed), London, Hodder & Stoughton
Hook R (1992) *Forty Studies that Changed Psychology*, Englewood Cliffs, Prentice-Hall

The book has been planned so that which ever two of Sections C–E you choose to cover, they will provide a good range of examples of methodology and links with core topics. The way you approach the syllabus, and therefore how you use this book, is up to you. You might, for example, start with material from Section D and then move back to Sections A and B for core topic explanations as you come across them. Alternatively, you could start with core topics but pull in material from later in the book which exemplifies a particular point as you work through the topics. The book is designed to help both teacher and student to move easily backwards and forwards, and my hope is that by doing this, students gain greater confidence in using ideas and evidence.

Barbara Woods

WAYS OF EXPLAINING HUMAN ACTION

SECTION A

Introduction

In this section we will be looking at some of the important psychological ideas which have been put forward to explain what humans do and why they do it.

The ideas in this section are core topics and appear again at other places in this book. For example, in Chapter 1 you can read an explanation of instincts. In later chapters you will see how instincts may be related to aggression, or to attachment.

To help you make the link between these core topics and the places where they appear later, you will find a symbol. Here is a list of the chapters in this section, which says what the chapters are about and shows their symbols.

Chapter 1	**The Influences of Inborn Characteristics** This chapter describes some of the abilities we are born with.	I
Chapter 2	**The Role of Learning in Shaping Behaviour** This chapter describes theories which explain how humans learn from their environment.	L
Chapter 3	**Social and Cultural Influences** Here we look at some of the ways that other people affect us.	S
Chapter 4	**The Influences of Thinking and Perception** This chapter describes some aspects of cognition – how we see and make sense of the world we live in.	C

Look for these symbols throughout the book when you want to find where examples of the ideas in this section appear in later chapters. The key terms used in this section are also printed in green throughout the book, for example instincts or social norms.

When you see one of these symbols, or a term printed in green, this reminds you that they refer to core topics. You can turn back to this section for an explanation.

Chapter 1

The Influences of Inborn Characteristics

If characteristics are described as inborn, then we are born with them. For example, all babies are born with a 'rooting' reflex: touch a baby only a few hours old on the cheek and it will turn its head towards the touch. This reflex makes the newborn baby turn its head towards the nipple and start sucking. The key fact here is that the baby does not learn to do this: it is born with the ability to do it. We say this behaviour is innate.

This chapter introduces you to some characteristics that we are born with, such as instincts, reflexes and how development unfolds in a fixed pattern – maturation. We will also see how these characteristics contribute to our development, our abilities and our behaviour.

Instincts

The term instinct has been used rather loosely but is now taken to mean a need, and the drive to satisfy that need, which we are born with. Hunger is an instinct.

Instincts drive behaviour: they need to be satisfied or acted upon. If you are hungry this will make you do something to satisfy your hunger. An instinct, therefore, is one of the things that makes us behave in certain ways, although it is not the *only* thing which motivates behaviour. If we are hungry and eat, the instinctive drive is *reduced* for a while because it has been satisfied. However the drive to satisfy our hunger will build up again; if the instinct is *not* satisfied then the build-up of drive can cause severe problems.

One example of the part which instincts play in psychology comes from **Sigmund Freud**'s psychoanalytic theory. He said we have several instincts, such as those for food or sex. He said these instincts operate at the unconscious level so that we are not aware of them and much of our behaviour is aimed at satisfying them. If they are not satisfied, then the energy which drives them builds up in us. This creates pressure which *has* to be released, or there will be serious consequences for the individual. The difficulty for humans is that we have to find ways of releasing this energy that are *acceptable* – both to ourselves and others. Freud said we have life-enhancing instincts (the libido) and destructive instincts (the death wish). These instincts form the basis for Freud's explanation of the development of personality, moral and gender development.

There are several explanations for human behaviour which include the notion of instincts. Here are examples of two more.

LINKS

- **the bonding instinct** – the infant has an inborn need to stay close to its mother, and the mother's instinct makes her care for her infant (Chapter 8)
- **the aggressive instinct** is an innate response to particular objects, actions or situations (Chapter 11)

Reflexes

Reflexes are automatic physical responses. If a puff of air is blown close to your open eye, you blink. This is an automatic, innate response to a stimulus; you do not *learn* to do it, you cannot stop yourself from doing it, so you have no control over it.

Reflexes are important for survival. For example the rooting reflex enables the child to feed as soon as it is born. But according to some psychologists reflexes are the basis for the development of behaviour and understanding.

Jean Piaget said a child's understanding of its world (its cognition) starts from reflexes such as sucking and grasping. From this early understanding its knowledge becomes increasingly richer.

Reflexes also form the basis for some learned behaviour. A reflex like the eye-blink response can become associated with something quite different, such as the sound of a bell so that when the bell sounds, the eye blinks. This is called classical conditioning and is explained in Chapter 2. Other responses, such as anxiety or fear, can be classically conditioned and this is how some psychologists have proposed that children learn right from wrong, for example.

LINKS

- **reflexes in cognitive development** – the basis of schemas (Chapter 16)
- **reflexes in classical conditioning** – its relationship to punishment (Chapter 17)

Maturation

Maturation is the genetically programmed progression of changes, leading to full development, which is common to all humans. For example puberty is a period of rapid physical change. This change is 'programmed' into the genes – it is inborn so it is not caused by experience. A one-year-old does not have to be *taught* to walk, it seems to *know* what to do with its legs. That ability is inborn: it is genetically programmed to occur at a particular stage in the child's development, it is part of a sequence. That sequence is the same for all humans – for example children do not walk until they are first able to sit up by themselves.

Maturation is important in the development of basic skills such as perceiving, walking and talking. It is also important in the development of children's understanding. Maturation is of interest to psychologists because the changes which are due to maturation will affect the individual's behaviour and may change the way a child interacts with and understands its world.

When we look at human development, maturation refers to that part of development that is due to nature. This provides a framework, but the environment in which a child grows up will also affect its development. One of the difficulties for psychologists is how to find out how much of a behaviour is due to maturation or to some other factor.

It is important to know what stage of maturation the child has reached in order to provide the child with an appropriate environment and be able to help if there are difficulties in development.

LINKS

- **Piaget's cognitive developmental theory** – as children mature they understand their world in different ways (Chapter 16)
- **visual perception** – depends to some degree on the maturation of the visual system (Chapter 16)

Sensitive period

During a sensitive period part of the maturation process is particularly responsive to a certain experience or influence.

The sensitive period is important because if the right experience is available during the sensitive period, then development will take place successfully. If it is *not* available then the ability may develop poorly, or not at all. If the right experience is only available *after* the sensitive period has finished, then it will be much more difficult for the individual to benefit from it.

The notion of a sensitive period has been used mostly for *physical* development, but **John Bowlby** said it was important for *emotional* development too. He claimed that a good **attachment** between a baby and its mother could only occur within the first two to three years of life. After that age, attachment would be very difficult. Bowlby was therefore saying that the first two to three years of life are the sensitive period for attachment.

LINKS

- **attachment** – must it occur during the first three years of life? (Chapter 8)
- **visual perception** – vision develops rapidly during the first few weeks after birth (Chapter 16)

Heredity and the nature or nurture debate

Heredity refers to anything we inherit through our genes. This includes things humans have in common – maturation sequences for example – and characteristics which are specific to the individual, such as eye colour.

Heredity is important to psychologists because they want to find out what causes particular behaviour or abilities and what can be done to change or improve them. Physical characteristics which we inherit may be easy to see, such as long fingers or red hair. It is not so easy to find out how much intelligence or personality is determined at birth. If intelligence is as 'fixed' as long fingers are, then there is little that can be done to change it.

Knowledge of which abilities are inherited contributes to the nature or nurture debate. If psychologists showed that intelligence *was* fixed at birth then this would have implications for many areas of our lives – education and health care for example. Earlier this century some psychologists claimed that intelligence was inherited and that those with lower intelligence were the cause of many social problems and should therefore be discouraged from having children.

Few psychologists today see intelligence as fixed and some see it as underdeveloped. But because we still know very little about our intellectual functions and abilities there is still debate about how much effect heredity has on intellectual development. Does heredity provide a *limit* on the extent to which intelligence can develop? This is an important question because, if heredity plays a major part in the individual's intellectual development, then the role of the environment is not very important.

LINKS

- **intelligence** – how, and how much, can we affect intelligence? (Chapter 13)
- **temperament** – what effect does it have on personality? (Chapter 12)

Twin studies

There are two types of twins. Identical twins are those which develop from a single egg. They are called monozygotic (MZ) twins because monozygotic means 'one egg'. MZs are genetically the same because once the egg is fertilised, it splits into two. This results in two genetically identical humans.

It is different when *two* eggs are fertilised at the same time. Twins who develop from two different eggs are called dizygotic (DZ) twins because dizygotic means 'two egg'. Genetically these children will be as alike as brothers and sisters are. However, because they have the same experiences in the womb and are the same age as they develop, their environment is likely to be more similar than that of children who are three or four years apart in age.

Twin research is important because it is a way of comparing the parts that heredity and the environment play in human behaviour. Psychologists want to find out how much of our behaviour and abilities are due to what we inherit and how much to what we experience. Because we cannot just take children and rear them in special surroundings, psychologists have looked for ways of comparing children who are identical genetically but have been reared in *different* environments. In other words, we are interested in studying separated MZ twins, to see if we can find out how much a different environment affects their development.

For example, if MZs (identical twins) are reared apart in a different family, perhaps in a different city, and if they grow up to be very similar in their personality, health and intelligence then we could conclude that the environment has very little impact. These results would show our abilities and behaviour are genetically determined. If these twins become quite *different,* this suggests that our environment is what determines our abilities and behaviour.

Psychologists have also studied **temperament** by comparing MZs with DZs when there has been no separation. If identical twins (MZs) reared together have very similar temperaments, and fraternal twins (DZs) reared together do *not* have similar temperaments, then the reason for this could be that MZs have identical genes. This could point to **temperament** being genetically determined.

LINKS

- **temperament** – comparing MZs with DZs to see whether temperament is genetic (Chapter 12)
- **intelligence** – comparing separated MZs to see whether intelligence is genetic (Chapter 13)

EXERCISES

1. Define instinct and give an example of an instinct from later in this book. Show how this instinct might affect someone's behaviour.
2. Give an example of a reflex and describe how it contributes to learning.
3. Show why maturation is important by describing an example from later in this book.
4. Define 'sensitive period' and describe how it has been used to explain an aspect of development.
5. Say, in your own words, what is meant by the nature or nurture debate. Briefly describe the importance of heredity to the debate.
6. Briefly describe a study of twins and relate its conclusion to the nature or nurture debate.

Chapter 2

The Role of Learning in Shaping Behaviour

L

IMAGINE THAT TWO BOYS ARE SHOWN A VIDEO OF ANOTHER CHILD DAMAGING A TOY. AFTERWARDS EACH BOY IS GIVEN THE SAME TYPE OF TOY, AS WELL AS SOME OTHERS, TO PLAY WITH. ONE BOY DOES THE SAME THING TO THE TOY AS THE CHILD IN THE VIDEO, THE OTHER DOES NOT. WE KNOW THAT THE BOY WHO DAMAGES THE TOY HAS LEARNED THAT BEHAVIOUR BECAUSE WE CAN SEE HIM PERFORMING THE BEHAVIOUR.

IN PSYCHOLOGY, PEOPLE WHO HAVE STUDIED LEARNING HAVE LOOKED AT BEHAVIOUR AS EVIDENCE OF LEARNING, AND THEY ARE CALLED BEHAVIOURISTS. LEARNING CAN BE DEFINED AS A RELATIVELY PERMANENT CHANGE IN BEHAVIOUR WHICH IS DUE TO EXPERIENCE. BEHAVIOURISTS SAY THAT WE LEARN THROUGH THE PROCESSES OF CLASSICAL CONDITIONING AND OPERANT CONDITIONING. HOWEVER, MORE RECENTLY THESE IDEAS HAVE BEEN DEVELOPED TO TAKE ACCOUNT OF HOW THE CHILD LEARNS IN ITS SOCIAL SETTING. THIS TYPE OF LEARNING IS CALLED SOCIAL LEARNING.

Classical conditioning

WHAT IS CLASSICAL CONDITIONING?

Classical conditioning is showing an automatic response to a previously unrelated stimulus. It sounds complicated, but the best way to understand it is to know how it occurs. Early work in classical conditioning was done in the 1900s by a Russian, **Ivan Pavlov**. His work with dogs showed him that they salivated (they produced saliva) even when they saw an *empty* food dish. Salivation is a reflex, it is innate behaviour over which the animal has no control. At first the dogs salivated when they were given a dish of food. Gradually they learned to associate the dish itself with food, and this is why they salivated when the empty dish was presented. They had become classically conditioned to salivate when they saw the dish.

Pavlov called the food the unconditioned stimulus. This means that food *automatically* stimulated the salivation in the dogs. He called their salivation the unconditioned response because they had no control over it.

When food is presented *with* the dish, the dish is called the conditioned stimulus: if these two are presented together many times the dog learns to associate them. Eventually the dish (the conditioned stimulus) by itself will make the dog salivate, which is the conditioned response.

You can see that although the dog salivates after both stimuli, the salivation is called by two different names. When it is caused by the 'natural' stimulus of food, the salivation is the unconditioned response. When it is caused by the *associated* stimulus it is called the conditioned response.

Pavlov found that dogs could also be conditioned to salivate to a bell or a buzzer or a rotating object. Each trial involved pairing the food with the stimulus.

HOW IS CLASSICAL CONDITIONING RELATED TO HUMAN BEHAVIOUR?

Pavlov's ideas have been tested using human subjects. For example, our emotions may be classically conditioned. In 1920 **J. B. Watson and R. Raynor** conditioned an 11-month-old boy (known as 'Little Albert') to show fear. He played quite happily with a white rat, then a metal bar was struck close by him while he played with the rat. The noise frightened him: the noise was the unconditioned stimulus, his fear the unconditioned response. But he learned to associate the rat with his fear, and eventually when he was given the rat he showed fear of it. The rat had become the conditioned stimulus and his fear the conditioned response.

If something embarrassing happens to you in a shop, you may feel anxiety (conditioned response) whenever you return to the shop (conditioned stimulus).

In classical conditioning then, the involuntary response (or reflex) to a particular stimulus becomes associated with a new stimulus. The two stimuli have to be presented *together* before this learning can take place.

LINKS

- **aggression** – stimuli such as weapons can trigger aggression (Chapter 11)
- **punishment** – the anxiety associated with punishment may be conditioned (Chapter 17)

Operant conditioning

WHAT IS OPERANT CONDITIONING?

Operant conditioning is learning which occurs as a result of reinforcement or punishment. In operant conditioning (also called instrumental conditioning) it is what happens *after* a particular behaviour which determines whether or not it is learned. This way of learning became known as operant conditioning because it is concerned with the way animals operate on their environment. In contrast, Pavlov's dogs *responded* automatically to their environment. The ideas in operant conditioning started from work done by **E. L. Thorndike,** who was working at the same time as Pavlov; the ideas were developed by **B. F. Skinner.**

THORNDIKE'S LAW OF EFFECT

Thorndike thought that the *consequences* of our actions determined whether or not they were learned. Thorndike put a hungry cat in a specially made box, which had a lever or catch to open it. When the cat was able to open the box and escape, it could reach the fish which was outside the box. At first the cat ran around the box until it pressed the lever accidentally and escaped. But after several trials the animal would press the lever as soon as it was placed in the box. At first then, the cat pressed the lever as a result of trial and error, but because the *effect* of pressing the lever was satisfying (escape and fish!) it eventually learned to press the lever to escape.

Thorndike's Law of Effect states that a particular stimulus will lead to a particular response if that response brings satisfaction. He also showed that if there is no satisfaction then the response stops – it is extinguished

REINFORCEMENT AND PUNISHMENT

These ideas were developed further by **B. F. Skinner**, who became a major figure in psychology. He was keen to make psychology much more scientific and precise. For example, in the Law of Effect, how did Thorndike know the animal gained 'satisfaction' and how could you measure 'satisfaction' anyway? Skinner was not concerned with *why* things were done, because he said you could not measure what was going on in the minds of animals or humans.

Using similar techniques to **Thorndike,** he devised the 'Skinner box' which allowed the animal to press a lever to release a pellet of food. **Skinner**'s aim was to see the exact relationship between 'satisfaction' and learning. He noted things like the number of trials before a rat learned to press the lever straight away or the number of times a rat pressed the lever when *no* pellet dropped.

Skinner concluded that 'behaviour is shaped and maintained by its consequences'. What did he mean? He meant that what happens *after* a particular behaviour will affect whether or not it is likely to be repeated. In particular he investigated ways of strengthening behaviour (positive and negative reinforcement) and weakening behaviour (punishment). Let us look at each of these in turn.

Strengthening behaviour through reinforcement

Skinner found that if consequences were rewarding they made behaviour more likely to happen – the behaviour was strengthened or reinforced. He noted two types of reinforcement – positive and negative.

- Positive reinforcement is when a pleasant result follows a particular behaviour (this is a rewarding consequence). When the rat accidentally pressed the lever it received a food pellet. After several trials the rat pressed the lever as soon as it was put in the box. Its 'lever pressing' behaviour was strengthened.
- Negative reinforcement is when an unpleasant experience is stopped (this is also a rewarding consequence). An electric current was passed through the rat's cage. When the rat pressed the lever the current stopped. After several trials the rat pressed the lever as soon as the current started, its behaviour was strengthened.
- Reinforcement has the effect of energising behaviour and if the reinforcement stops, then gradually the behaviour is extinguished. However if the reinforcement is partial (only given after some responses), then extinction takes much longer. Reinforcement is most effective when it occurs immediately after the behaviour.

Positive reinforcement and humans

There is evidence of positive reinforcement all around us, but the strongest examples relate to children. For example, if a child puts her toys away, the parent may say 'well done' or give a hug. This is rewarding for her and makes it more likely that she will put away her toys in the future – her behaviour will be strengthened or reinforced; it has been energised by the reinforcement.

The hug is a reinforcer because it strengthens behaviour. Other reinforcers are smiles, 'well done', gold stars, sweets or other treats. These are called secondary reinforcers because they do not satisfy basic instincts. Food and drink (to satisfy the basic instincts of hunger and thirst) are called primary reinforcers.

An example of partial reinforcement in adults is in gambling. The gambler will not win very often, but will keep gambling because he or she knows that *at some point* there will be a win. Behaviourists argue that we can use this pattern of reinforcement with children. Partial reinforcement leads to behaviour which takes much longer to extinguish, and of course it is much less work!

Secondary reinforcement

Negative reinforcement and humans

An example of negative reinforcement is when a child who wants its own way screams and kicks. If the parent gives in, the child stops. Because the unpleasantness stops when the parent gives in, giving in is negatively reinforcing for the parent (it has a pleasant consequence) and he or she is more likely to give in next time the child makes a fuss.

Weakening behaviour through punishment

Skinner also said that if the consequences were unpleasant, then the behaviour would be *less* likely to happen – it would be *weakened*. For his rats, Skinner found that if they were given an electric shock after they pressed a lever, they were *less* likely to press the lever again. Any consequence which weakens behaviour is called punishment

Punishment and humans

If you ask your teacher for help and he or she snaps back, you will be less likely to ask for help again. Your behaviour is weakened because of the punishment you experienced.

There is a problem if punishment is used on purpose to weaken behaviour, because it shows only the behaviour which is *not* desirable. The purpose of punishment is to de-energise the behaviour, to reduce the energy which makes it happen. It is difficult to reduce this energy, so punishment may reduce a particular behaviour but the energy may create *another* behaviour as an outlet. A two-year-old may stop hitting her newborn baby brother when she is punished, but may start hitting the dog. Punishment does not show what the undesirable behaviour should be replaced with. In contrast, positive reinforcement shows which behaviour *is* desirable.

Let me just summarise the three processes in operant conditioning before we look at some links from later in the book.

- positive reinforcement *strengthens* behaviour because it is rewarding
- negative reinforcement *strengthens* behaviour because it stops an unpleasant experience
- punishment *weakens* behaviour because it is unpleasant

LINKS

- **positive reinforcement** – encourages the development of gender (Chapter 14)
- **negative reinforcement** – its effect on moral development (Chapter 17)
- **punishment** – its relationship to aggression (Chapter 11)

Social learning

WHAT IS SOCIAL LEARNING?

Social learning is learning from others. Social learning theory differs from classical and operant conditioning because it is concerned only with *human* behaviour, and in addition it is also interested in human *understanding.*

HOW DOES LEARNING TAKE PLACE?

Social learning theorists agree that people learn by reinforcement and punishment, but say they also learn by watching others – which is why social learning is also called observational learning. For example you can watch a three-year-old child telling off his teddy bear in exactly the same words and tone as his parent has used with him. Social learning theorists would argue that this behaviour is not learned through reinforcement. The child learns it through observing the parent, and then reproduces what he has seen and heard. This is called modelling, and in this example the parent is the model.

Albert Bandura is a leading social learning theorist and he has proposed that children are more likely to model themselves on people who are **powerful, nurturing** or **similar.** For example, a cartoon character may be powerful, a teacher may be nurtring, a friend of the same sex would be similar. A parent of the same sex will probably be *all* of these! They are also more likely to copy the behaviour which they see reinforced and less likely to copy behaviour which is punished. This learning through models is called vicarious learning.

Social learning theory takes account of what people see and hear of others, and also what they think about, understand and remember. These are cognitive abilities. These factors in turn affect what people are able (and want) to reproduce. So our three-year-old has heard what his parent says, and remembered it very accurately. Not only *can* he reproduce the behaviour, but he *wants* to. We say he is motivated to reproduce it.

Children and adults may not model the behaviour they see because they make judgements about whether it is *appropriate* for them (perhaps the model is of the opposite sex), or whether the *circumstances* are right for them (you don't try out new swear words in front of your parents).

Bandura found that although a child may not *perform* certain behaviours she has seen, she may still have *learned* them. Bandura explained that seeing the behaviour provides the individual with information on how to behave and what the probable outcomes will be. This is also how individuals learn to produce the behaviour in the appropriate settings. Social learning theory stresses the influence of parents, peers, siblings, teachers and the media in providing models and outcomes for behaviour.Individuals' success in modelling the appropriate behaviour in the appropriate setting, in a way which they find rewarding, enables people to feel they have control over their lives and increases what Bandura called **self-efficacy.**

LINKS

- **aggression** – the role of television (Chapter 11)
- **gender acquisition** – same sex modelling (Chapter 14)

EXERCISES

1 Give an example of a conditioned emotional response from a later chapter in this book.

2 Imagine you once ate some food which made you very ill. Whenever you smell that food now, you feel ill. According to classical conditioning, what are the terms you would use to describe what happened to you? Fill in the gaps.

When you ate the food, the food was the ....
the smell was the ....
being ill was the ....

Now the smell is the ....
feeling ill is the ....

3 Give an example of positive reinforcement which a teacher may use. Say why it is rewarding.

4 Describe your own example of negative reinforcement.

5 What is the difference between negative reinforcement and punishment?

6 Watch a children's cartoon on television. Describe it briefly then explain why one of the characters is likely to be modelled. Choose another character, who is not likely to be modelled, and explain why not.

Chapter 3
Social and Cultural Influences

S

FROM BIRTH THE HUMAN INFANT IS ABLE TO DISTINGUISH BETWEEN HUMANS AND NON-HUMANS AND THE INFANT QUICKLY DEVELOPS THE ABILITY TO RECOGNISE AND RESPOND TO OTHERS AND TO LEARN HOW TO INTERACT WITH THEM. IT SEEMS THAT WE NEED OTHERS FOR SECURITY AND TO HELP US UNDERSTAND OURSELVES AND OUR WORLD.

THIS CHAPTER INTRODUCES YOU TO SOME OF THE REASONS WHY OTHERS ARE IMPORTANT TO US AND HOW THEY INFLUENCE US, OFTEN IN WAYS THAT WE ARE NOT FULLY AWARE OF.

Affiliation

Affiliation is the need to be in contact with others and it seems to be an important factor in our behaviour. We vary in the degree to which we need others – psychologists say we have a high or low affiliative need. However, we all seem to need others *some* of the time. When we seek the company of others because we *like* them, this is called **attraction.**

There seem to be several reasons why affiliation is important. Here are some of them.

RELIEVING DISTRESS

When we feel concerned, or fearful, or shocked or distressed then we seek the company of others. If we cannot be with people we know, just being with strangers will help. We prefer, however, to be with those who can understand our distress rather than those who cannot. It seems that being with others reduces our anxiety and may provide support or information in interpreting our experience.

PROVIDING INFORMATION

When we are not sure what is happening, or what to do about something, we look to others to help us make sense of things. If you are in a shop and suddenly everyone starts to leave quickly, you want to ask someone why. This would probably be an emergency situation but we seek the opinions of others in less important circumstances, for example on films we have seen, or items on the news or an explanation of a friend's behaviour.

FOR COMPARISON

We seek out others so we can compare ourselves with them and this is one source of our **self-esteem.** If you find some homework really difficult, you will want to know how others found it. If they struggled too, then you know that it was because the work was difficult, and you can regain some self-esteem.

SENSE OF BELONGING

We need to feel we belong so we are likely to conform to the norms of the group we belong to. By doing this we strengthen the group *and* show we belong to it. Our desire to belong to a group may lead us to adopt the style of dressing, behaviours and attitudes which others in the group show. Most of us belong to several groups; the family is a group, as are teenagers, or women or Italians. The *importance* of a group to us will vary, and sometimes we do not realise how important a group is to us until we are outside it, but most people need to feel that they are affiliated with a group.

SENSE OF IDENTITY

We need others to give us our identity. If people do not respond to us, then it is as though we do not exist. However, we play different parts (roles) in our lives, and we need to be with others in order to see their reactions to us. If they respond in accordance with the role we are playing then this confirms our self-identity for us.

A BASIS FOR CLOSER RELATIONSHIPS

Even the newborn infant responds to others, and this need is the basis for our important relationships. For the infant and carer it is the basis for **attachment;** as we develop it is the basis for friendships and sexual relationships. Psychologists have proposed that people with high affiliative needs will be more active in seeking out others.

So we need others to help us make sense of our world and to make sense of ourselves. Often other people influence us in ways we have no control over.

LINKS

- **bystander behaviour** – the way we respond in an emergency is affected by how many other people are present, and by what they do (Chapter 9)
- **self-esteem** – its relationship to social comparison (Chapter 15)

Social norms

Social norms are the rules, expectations, obligations, rights and behaviours which members of a group are expected to show. They are largely unspoken and are learned through interaction with others in the group. The group may be small – people working together in an office, or large – a religious or national group.

Social norms may influence and explain our behaviour in several ways. People tend to conform with the social norms of their group for some of the reasons we looked at under affiliation, for example needing approval from others or wanting to be accepted as part of a group. We may also conform in order to maintain predictability and stability in our social environment.

Another reason for conforming is that when we are new to a group, we are unsure how to behave so we look to other members. Thus we are likely to do what they do and indeed this is how we learn social norms. For example, a child who has realised that it will always be female starts to pay more attention to what *other* females do. This may be because she wants to feel she belongs to the group.

So social norms influence our behaviour by making us want to conform to expectations. We feel uncomfortable if we do not conform. If we want to explain another's behaviour, it is helpful to look at the group they feel part of, or want to belong to.

LINKS

- **conforming to group norms** – judging line lengths (Chapter 9)
- **pro-social behaviour** – the influence of social norms (Chapter 18)

Social roles

Social roles are the 'parts' we play in society. They are the behaviours and attitudes which relate to a particular position we hold at any one time. We all have several roles – such as student, brother, mother, footballer, pedestrian, friend and so on. A social role provides us with a predictable set of expectations about how to behave.

Other people expect us to conform to the role we are playing, and we expect them to treat *us* according to our role. A student needs a teacher in order to perform his student role and a doctor needs a patient in order to perform her doctor role. In these role relationships both parties need each other, and need each other to behave according to role *expectations*. If you go to your doctor and she doesn't ask what is wrong with you, or starts to tell jokes, or completely ignores you she is acting out of role. You are unable to play the patient role. How would you deal with this situation?

According to **Irving Goffman**, we learn about roles by watching others, for example in real life or through the media. We tend to 'act' our roles when we are new to them, but gradually the role behaviour becomes so familiar that we **internalise** it. This means that we perform it unconsciously and feel it is part of us. This is why an individual's sense of who they are (their **self-concept**) is developed partly from the social roles they occupy. Even quite young children will say they are a sister or a pupil in school, or a member of a football team.

Our relationships with others may change as we take on new roles. Your relationship with your parents changes if you become a parent yourself. Your relationship with your workmates changes if you are promoted. The relationship between two people changes as their roles change. The role of your teacher has more power than your role as a student. However, your relationship changes at the end of the day if you take on your role as a car driver and you offer him a lift, so he takes on the passenger role.

Some roles are more clearly defined than others; for example a doctor's role carries a more predictable set of expectations than a car passenger's role. A uniform is a way of defining a role, and has been shown to have considerable influence on a person's behaviour.

LINKS

- **scripts** – affected by the roles people play (Chapter 19)
- **roles affect behaviour** – we act in accordance with the uniforms we wear (Chapter 15)

The 'environment' and the nature or nurture debate

When psychologists talk about the environment, they mean the things that make up our world – our experiences, our surroundings, what we eat, the type of people we interact with, what we hear, how others treat us and so on.

The nature or nurture debate is about which factors are most important in making us the people we are. We saw in Chapter 1 that the nature side says that we are born with certain inherited characteristics which largely determine how we develop. The nurture side accepts that biological factors such as maturation play an important part in development. However, it says our environment is more important because we need to act on it in order to allow characteristics to develop, and also our environment can modify or alter those characteristics.

You can see that psychologists who think that nurture is the most important influence on our development will be very interested in the individual's environment. For instance they will look at how a child is treated, what type of stimulation it gets, and cultural factors such as what are the expectations of its society, what skills are valued, and what behaviour is discouraged. By providing opportunities for individual actions and thoughts, these experiences will enable the child to use and develop its abilities.

How can the environment influence our development? At a basic level it provides food for the development of bones, muscles and so on, as well as opportunities for physical activity so they can develop. The environment also seems to affect the development of visual perception because, for example, the abilities of animals reared in darkness do not develop properly.

When a child is ready to move to the next stage of development, a good environment can speed up development but more importantly it may *enhance* the development beyond that which it would reach with a poor environment. This has been found with IQ levels in orphans who were brought up in an unstimulating environment and then given stimulation. A good environment includes a wide range of social and cultural experiences to enrich development.

You can see how heredity and the environment are *both* important factors in human development and behaviour. Both are involved in the explanation of psychological development, although they differ in importance in each explanation. Psychologists are no longer looking at which has the most influence on the development of human abilities and behaviour. They are looking instead for answers to questions such as:

- How do we understand our social world?
- How do the experiences of others affect our behaviour?
- How do hereditarian and environmental influences interact?

Here are some examples, from later in the book, which attempt to answer these three questions.

LINKS

- **moral development** – the child's understanding of social and moral rules (Chapter 17)
- **divorce** – its effect on parents and therefore on children (Chapter 8)
- **temperament** – how it affects the way others treat us (Chapter 12)

Cross-cultural studies

Studying other cultures provides some answers in the nature or nurture debate. It helps us to identify which aspects of human development are inherited and which are the result of our environment, and how they interact. For example, if there are differences between cultures, then this suggests that the environment in which the individual is raised causes the differences. If there are *few* differences between cultures, then this suggests that behaviour or ability are inherited because they are similar *regardless* of environment. Language is a good example. It develops in a very similar way across many cultures; children start to speak at about the same age and they seem to learn about various aspects of language in the same stages. This is the case *whatever* language they hear around them. However, the language they *speak* depends on their environment.

Studies of other cultures (cross-cultural studies) also enable psychologists to discover *which* aspects of the environment may cause different effects. One way to do this is to look at how people from other cultures behave in the same situations. For example, we can look at how many carers a very small child has and see what effect it seems to have on their development.

LINKS

- **temperament** – different responses in different cultures (Chapter 12)
- **visual perception** – Segall's research (Chapter 16)

EXERCISES

1. Find evidence from later in this book of an individual looking to others for information.
2. Find evidence from later in this book that other people influence our behaviour.
3. Give an example of one way in which a social norm might influence behaviour.
4. Give an example of one way in which a social role may explain behaviour.
5. In your own words say what is meant by the nature or nurture debate. Briefly describe the importance of the environment to this debate.
6. Find another study from later in this book which has identified a difference between two cultures.

Chapter 4

The Influences of Thinking and Perception

C

THIS CHAPTER INTRODUCES YOU TO SOME OF THE WAYS IN WHICH PSYCHOLOGISTS TRY TO EXPLAIN OUR COGNITIVE ABILITIES – HOW WE SEE AND MAKE SENSE OF OUR WORLD AND WHAT WE DO WITH THIS INFORMATION. IN THE FIRST SECTION WE WILL LOOK AT HOW OUR BRAIN MAKES SENSE OF THE INFORMATION IT RECEIVES. THEN WE WILL LOOK AT HOW WE PROCESS INFORMATION AND FINALLY WE WILL LOOK AT HOW WE REPRESENT IT TO OURSELVES.

Transduction

Sensory information is information that we receive through our senses. For example, the information that comes in through our eyes is in the form of light waves, yet we can *recognise* a familiar face or pick our way to an empty seat in a dark cinema. How do we do this? The first stage in understanding how this happens is called transduction (which means changing information) and we will look at what happens in the eye.

Light enters the eye and strikes the retina, which contains several types of cells. The receptor cells change the information coming in to the eye (in this case the information carried by the light waves) into electrical impulses, because the brain can only recognise information in the form of electrical impulses. There are two types of receptor cells: rods and cones. Rods respond to dim light and are very sensitive; they are in the part of the retina nearest the lens. Cones are located near the centre of the retina and respond to bright light and colours.

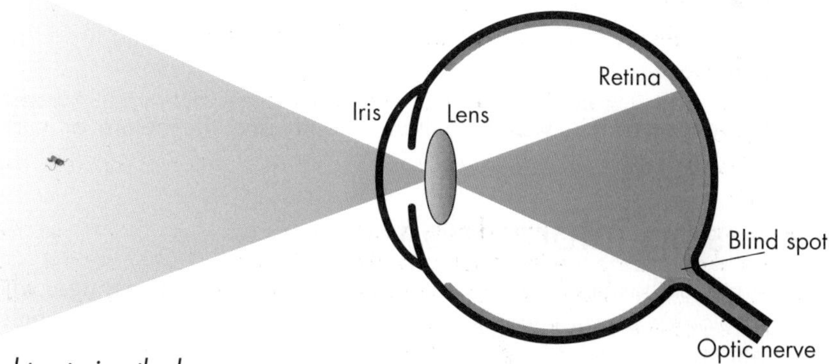

Fig. 4.1 Light entering the human eye

The receptor cells contain chemicals which react to the light. This reaction results in an electrical impulse which is passed on to other cells called ganglion cells. These have long branches which carry the impulses to the brain. The branches are bunched together to form the optic nerve, and you can see from Figure 4.1 that there is a place where the optic nerve leaves the eye. There are no receptor cells in that part of the eye, so we are 'blind' to light which falls there. You can find your own blind spot from the picture below.

Fig. 4.2 Test for your blind spot

Find your blind spot by closing your right eye and putting the book about 30 cm in front of you. Stare at the *upper* cross and move the book around until the big circle disappears. This is when the circle is projected on to your blind spot. Keep the book still and look at the *lower* cross. The gap in the lower line should disappear. You can see how your visual system *compensates* for the gap by automatically filling it in, so that you are not aware of it.

So the ganglion cells take the electric impulses to the part of the brain which analyses them. Different parts of the brain respond to impulses from different sense organs: the visual cortex analyses information coming from the eye.

There are various types of cells in the visual cortex and information from a simple cell is passed to a higher cell which integrates the simple information. These cells are organised in patterns in the brain and certain cells relate to particular functions – such as responding to colour or to information from *one* eye. Given this degree of organisation, it seems possible that we may have an innate mechanism for recognising some of the visual information we receive.

LINKS

- **visual perception** – visual abilities at birth and the nature or nurture debate (Chapter 16)

Processing information

Once information has been transformed into something we can manage, what happens next? Psychologists propose that first we select information, then we organise it for storage so that we can use it later. This way of looking at our cognition as a series of processes is called the information processing approach.

SELECTION OF INFORMATION

Of all the things we can hear or see or feel, how do we only select *some* for attention? We do this by scanning our environment and it seems that much of what we take in is automatically processed. This means we are not consciously aware of it. For example you may not be aware that you notice the colour of your friend's eyes, but if the colour was to change one day, then you would be aware of it. By noticing your friend's eyes you are selecting information to attend to.

What sort of things do we select for attention? **Ulrich Neisser** proposed that we are active in our selection and will look for anything which will be important or relevant to us. Because our situations and our needs are always changing, we will select different things at different times. Information will be selected if it is:

- **self-related** – because anything related to us is important. You will hear someone speak your name, even in a very noisy room
- **distinctive** – because it will 'stand out' in contrast to what we expect. Anything new or unusual, such as your friend's change of eye-colour, will take your attention. The more effort we make to understand new information the more likely it is that we will remember it
- **schema-related** – because our schemas prime us to look for certain types of information (see page 24 for an explanation). **Susan Fiske and Steven Neuberg** have proposed that we immediately categorise people. If we cannot do this from the first piece of information we select, then we will select some other aspect. The *basis* on which we categorise will depend on our schemas though. If the information is new it may be incorporated into our schemas: in this way it is it is organised and stored in memory
- **vivid** – because it will 'hit' us. For example, something which makes us angry or fearful may focus our attention so that we notice information directly related to it, but we are then unable to attend fully to other aspects of the situation

As you can see from the last point, psychologists suggest there is a limit to how much we can attend to at one time. It seems that we have to *learn* what to attend to as well, because young children often notice *irrelevant* information but by about 11 years old they can select the right things much more accurately. This could be one explanation for the way children's understanding appears to change at different ages

LINKS

- **personal constructs** – what we look for to construct our own reality (Chapter 19)
- **self-concept** – selection of information related to the self-schema (Chapter 15)

ORGANISATION OF INFORMATION

Once we have selected information it is in our short-term or working memory while we make sense of it, often by using information from long-term memory. You would do this to compare your friend's 'new' eye colour. Working memory is not very large – we quickly forget information held here unless we can link it into long-term memory.

How is our long-term memory organised? We seem to store related information together but *why* it is related depends to some extent on an individual's knowledge and experience. We will be looking at three proposals for how we organise information when we look at mental representation in the next section. However, the schema is particularly relevant here.

A schema is a mental framework, that is, a way of organising information based on our experience. We combine knowledge of others, ourselves, emotions, expectations and so on in our schemas. We have a schema for buying birthday cards and a schema for going to the dentist. If you can quickly think of many words which you associate with dentist this suggests you have a 'dentist' schema.

Another way of organising information is by category. For example 'dentist' is also in a 'job' category, as 'apple' is in 'fruit' and 'hammer' is in 'tool'. We know that people organise by category, because if we are given long lists of words to remember we recall many more if we can associate them by category.

There is a model of memory which explains how we can remember 'dentist' whether it is stored in our schema or by category. This is the associative network model and it proposes that we store each 'idea' (for example 'dentist') as a node, and it is linked to other nodes. The more associations there are between nodes the easier it is to access the idea from memory. In addition the more often we *associate* two things, the stronger the association between the two nodes is. According to this model, 'dentist' is linked to some nodes because they are part of the same schema, and it is linked to another network of nodes because it is part of a category

The more associations we have, the better we will be able to remember information. For example, we remember more information when asked to form an impression of someone than if we are just asked to remember what they do. This could be because when we **form impressions** we use associations which are stored in long-term memory. We can generate (infer, see below) more information about people as well. But we can remember even more about them if we are asked to **empathise** with them. This suggests emotions create even stronger links with information stored in long-term memory.

This model suggests that the way we organise information is flexible, and shows how our own experience affects the way we associate information in memory.

LINKS

- **impression formation** – applying individual stereotypes when forming impressions (Chapter 19)
- **stereotyping** – its relationship to prejudice (Chapter 10)

INFERENCE

Making an inference is making a deduction. If someone walks into the room dripping wet, I would infer that it is raining. Our tendency to make inferences – to fill in the gaps – seems to be automatic. Your brain automatically filled in the gap when you checked on your blind spot at the start of this chapter. Inferences enable us to create more information, and act upon it, when knowledge is incomplete. We will look at some situations in which we make inferences and some of the reasons why our inferences might be wrong.

Schemas

We have already seen how we select and organise information – and the result of these processes enables us to make inferences. Our schemas enable us to make inferences, because we have stored schema-related information and when we trigger one part of the schema the rest follows automatically. When I see an elderly man I infer from my 'elderly person' schema that he is hard of hearing and will speak loudly to him. This makes it unlikely that I will discover if he is *not* hard of hearing. My stereotype (group schema) for old people leads me to make a wrong inference, which I am unlikely to correct.

We tend to seek information which confirms what we *think* we know, with the result that we look for supporting evidence and ignore contradictory information. If we think people are friendly, then we will infer from their behaviour that they *are* friendly and discount information which suggests they are not.

Distorting memory

The way we organise information in memory may lead us to recall wrong information. Work on eyewitness testimony by **Elizabeth Loftus** found that when people were asked about cars which they had seen 'hitting' or 'smashing into' each other, the word distorted their memory. They inferred that a smashed car was going faster than one which was hit for example. People also remembered more broken glass from the 'smashed' car when in fact there was none!

Illusory correlation

We tend to associate two things that are unrelated (variables) because both are particularly distinctive, or we assume two things are more closely related than they are because they occur together. An example would be a report in the media that a member of a minority group has committed a crime. We might infer, wrongly, that members of this group are more likely to commit such crimes, simply because their group membership was mentioned.

Categorising

We tend to categorise things on the basis of similarity, so we infer that those who are attractive have attractive personalities for example. Also, if the information we select suggests two things are similar, we will infer that they are *more* alike than they really are. Equally if the information we select suggests two things are *dissimilar,* then we are likely to infer that they are *more* different than they really are. This is evident in the way we categorise people into ingroups and outgroups.

LINKS

- **ingroup-outgroup categorisation** – stereotyping (Chapter 10)
- **impression formation** – the halo effect (Chapter 19)

Mental representation

A mental representation is something in our minds which stands for something else. It is a way of storing information and we will look at schemas, mental images and forming concepts

SCHEMAS

We have already touched on the idea of the schema (page 22). A schema is a mental structure, which represents our knowledge about something. A schema simplifies our world; it enables us to extract information from the world around and store it so we can respond faster and more accurately. As schemas are adjusted and modified, we adapt our behaviour and learn from it. We can make inferences from schemas, but as we have just seen we can also make mistaken inferences.

Our schemas are built up from experience and form the basis for cognitive development according to **Jean Piaget.** He said we develop and create ever more complex schemas, which are our internal representation of our experiences. We can apply these representations to the solution of new problems.

The way schemas explain how we understand social experiences is an example of social cognition. For example, psychologists have proposed that we have self-schemas, group schemas (stereotypes), event schemas (scripts) and role schemas. We have schemas for emotional experiences too. **John Bowlby** said that a child develops an internal working model of **attachment** because it learns to expect what will happen, and how people will respond, on the basis of its attachment experiences.

LINKS

- **schemas** – their relationship to cognitive development (Chapter 16)
- **social scripts** – filters of information (Chapter 19)

MENTAL IMAGES

These are 'pictures' which we can create internally which we can refer to as we would a photograph or film. If I ask whether Bristol is closer to Glasgow or London, how would you work out the answer? You may create a mental image of a map of the British Isles and 'see' the relative distances.

Mental images are also the way we can store information. Visual information is very influential, and we use the appearance of others as the first method of categorising people we do not know. Research shows that people who form vivid mental images of others also have more accurate memory for characteristics and behaviour. We can consciously create mental images to help us remember things. If you want to recall something when you are taking an exam, create a mental image of the classroom where you learnt it.

LINKS

- **stereotyping** – prejudice (Chapter 10)
- **impression formation** – the primacy effect (Chapter 19)

CONCEPT FORMATION

We form a concept when we group or classify things. A concept builds up with experience and it has defining features. In everyday life concepts are not always very clear so that it seems impossible to find defining features. Notions of the fuzzy concept have developed and this means that a concept cannot be clearly defined, but some characteristics will be better examples of it than others.

Much of the work on concept formation was done in artificial laboratory situations, and results suggested that there are two ways we can learn a concept:

- **exemplars** – a child learns the name for a particular thing, say a cat. The child then notes certain features of this exemplar (example) and tries to find more examples. So a dog may be called a cat because it has four legs. Or a rabbit may be called a cat because it is black. The child learns by this trial and error process until it understands the concept of cat and can describe the features that make the animal a cat.
- **hypothesis testing** – this is when we look for a set of common features of objects and hypothesise that these are what defines that concept. We then test this definition against new objects. In doing this we think at a more abstract level

Our thinking develops from concrete (what we see) to abstract (what we can imagine) according to **Piaget**, so exemplars are evidence of children's early understanding because they are based on what they *see.* When the child is able to extract rules and apply them this is evidence of hypothesis testing, in other words of abstract thinking.

LINKS

- **cognitive development** – when does thinking becomes abstract (Chapter 16)
- **gender concept** – how the child develops a more accurate idea of what gender is (Chapter 14)

EXERCISES

1. Describe a study which suggests that visual abilities are largely innate.
2. Watch some advertisements on television and find one which attracts your attention because it has a 'distinctive' feature. Describe the advertisement and say why this feature is distinctive.
3. Briefly describe your schema for either a) a visit the dentist or b) buying a birthday card.
4. In your own words describe one of the errors that might occur when we make an inference. How might it affect our behaviour?
5. Think of your own example of the formation of a concept which shows a child's understanding has moved from the concrete to the abstract.

PSYCHOLOGICAL METHODOLOGY

SECTION B

Introduction

In this section we will look at ways in which psychologists find out about people. For instance, they may look at what people do, listen to what they say, then develop explanations for what is happening. They will read what other psychologists have found, and may test their explanations to see how good they are. You will see that there are a number of different methods they can use, and all of the methods have some strengths and some weaknesses. The information on methods appears in Chapters 5 and 6.

In Chapter 6 you can also find out how to plan and write up your own research in a practical report. When you do this you too will be acting as a psychologist would, so you need to think about some of the things a psychologist would consider and to write up what you have done in a way which is easy for someone else to understand. We also consider the psychologist's duty to respect and protect the people they are studying. This is called ethics and is covered in Chapter 7.

Throughout this book you will see examples of the topics which are covered in this section. In order to help you make the link between terms when they are used in this section and where they appear later in the book, these terms are printed in green because they relate to a core topic. So for example you will come across terms such as experiment, subjects or consent later in the book. They are printed in green to remind you that they are terms related to a core topic and also to remind you that you can turn back to this section – Section B – Methodology – for an explanation.

Chapter 5

Discovering and Testing Psychological Knowledge

HUGH COOLICAN (SEE FURTHER READING ON PAGE 37) SAYS THERE ARE THREE MAJOR WAYS IN WHICH PSYCHOLOGISTS GET INFORMATION ABOUT PEOPLE: 'YOU ASK THEM, WATCH THEM OR MEDDLE.' IN THIS CHAPTER WE ARE GOING TO LOOK AT THE WAYS IN WHICH PSYCHOLOGISTS ASK, WATCH AND MEDDLE. IN OTHER WORDS, WE ARE GOING TO LOOK AT RESEARCH METHODOLOGY.

Research methods

CASE STUDY

The case study is a detailed study into the background of one person or a small group of people. It involves looking at past records (health, school, etc.), asking other people about the subject's past or present experiences and behaviour, and asking the individual, in a clinical interview, about the present and past. In the clinical interview, the interviewer usually starts by asking specific questions, but the questions which follow will depend on how the subject answers. This method is often used for investigating people who show unusual abilities or difficulties.

- **advantages** are that it gives a detailed picture of the individual which is useful in treating individual problems; it helps in discovering how a person's past may be related to the present; it can form the basis for future research; by studying those who are *unusual*, psychologists can discover more about what is usual
- **disadvantages** are that it relies on memory or records which may be poor, or distorted; it can only tell you about one person so you cannot generalise the information to others; it relies on participants telling the truth; a clinical interview is difficult with children because of their limited language; the interviewer may be biased because he or she is looking for certain information

OBSERVATION

When psychologists observe, they watch people's behaviour. An observational study is a way of finding out how people behave in everyday life. Psychologists might do an observational study on children's aggressive behaviour in a playground. The children may be videoed (for analysis later) or the observers may make written records of their behaviour as it happens. A study which observes behaviour as it occurs naturally is often called a naturalistic observation study.

Because of the complexity of behaviour, and the possibility of bias in the observer, it is usual to have more than one observer. Observers need to be trained in how to analyse and measure behaviour so that they all interpret the behaviour in the same way. This is called inter-observer reliability. They will have practised observing the type of behaviour they are interested in, and will note the behaviour on an observation schedule. This is how they keep track of everything that is going on. Here is a simple schedule for observation of pro-social play, with each of the subjects given a number.

Subject	Number of times subject				
	gave object	smiled at other	physically assisted other	agreed to help	encouraged other
1					
2					
3					
4					
5					

Fig. 5.1 Example of an observation schedule

An observational study can be used as a starting point for further research. As a result of what they find, researchers may devise an experiment to find out if one *particular* thing causes more aggressive behaviour, for example.

In contrast to the observational *study*, observation is also used as a *method* of research. It is frequently used with children or in social psychology research, and may be one of several methods which a psychologist uses in one investigation.

Sometimes the observational method is part of an experiment, and takes place in a controlled setting. **Bandura's** research into children's aggression involved observing each child's play after watching an adult model. But researchers have also used the observational method in more natural settings as part of an experiment. The **Piliavin** study (see Chapter 18) is one example.

- **advantages** are that observations enable the researchers to see people behaving naturally; the observations can form the basis for further research
- **disadvantages** are that observations can be expensive, because they require several specially trained people and analysis can take a long time; if subjects are aware they are being observed they may not behave naturally; it is difficult for observers to be completely objective; researchers are not able to control the variables in a natural setting and they may affect the subject's behaviour and so distort the results; it is difficult to record *all* behaviour

SURVEY

A survey asks people questions, either through a written questionnaire or face-to-face interviews. The questions must be carefully prepared so that they are clear, and do not persuade the participant to answer in a particular way. The psychologist needs to make sure that people understand the questions and find them fairly straightforward to answer. The psychologist might first do a pilot study. This means that the psychologist gives the questions to a few people and asks for their comments. If there *are* problems, then the questions can be changed or re-written.

An example of a questionnaire is the social distance questionnaire, which is related to investigation of **prejudice.** An extract is given in Fig. 5.2.

Please complete the questionnaire by following these instructions.
Using the scale of 1 to 5, write in each box in the table the number of the statement that agrees most closely with your feelings about being in each situation with a member of each group.

1 I'd actively encourage it.
2 It's alright with me.
3 I'm neutral.
4 I'd avoid it if I could.
5 I'm strongly opposed to it.

Social situation	White	Black	Catholic	Muslim	Jew
Be my friend					
Be my closest friend					
Work with me					
Work under me					
Be my boss					
Live next door					
Visit my home					
Date me or a member of my family					
Marry me					
Go to school with my child					
Totals					

Scoring: Add up the numbers in each column. The maximum possible is 50. The lower the score, for each group, the greater the participants willingness to interact with a member of that group. The higher the score, the more the participant is reluctant to interact.

Fig. 5.2 Extract from a social distance questionnaire (from M. Birmbaum et al., 1983)

In a survey questions may be closed (offering one clear-cut answer) or open-ended (allowing freedom in the answer). Here is an example of each type, based on the **Thomas, Chess and Birch** study of **temperament:**

- closed question Does your baby like cereal? Yes or No?
- open-ended question What does your baby do which makes you think he doesn't like cereal?

Closed questions give answers which are easy to interpret and to work with – we say they are easy to quantify. For example, when researchers have analysed the answers they might be able to show that 20 per cent of the respondents said their children liked cereal. However, this is rather a crude piece of information – what if a baby likes *some* cereal but not others? How would you answer? One option is to provide questions which let people answer on a range. If we asked 'Does your baby like cereal?', we could allow people to answer 'Not at all/Not very much/Some cereal/Very much'. This gives us more detailed information which is still easy to quantify. (Scoring in Fig. 5.2)

The open-ended question may gain a lot of information, but it would be difficult to compare to other people's answers. This is why the open-ended question is less useful when you are trying to quantify information but is useful for clinical interviews.

- **advantages** are that a survey using a questionnaire is a way of getting information from a lot of people fairly cheaply and quickly, unless you use face-to-face surveys, which are expensive
- **disadvantages** are that you have to rely on people returning the questionnaires, so your sample may be biased (for example, the people who return them may be those who have more time so you may get very few working people or single parents responding); people may not understand your questions, may lie, or may become bored, so your information is inaccurate even before you start to work on it

CORRELATIONAL STUDY

Sometimes psychologists want to find out what behaviours go together, for example to see whether the amount of television watched is related to the amount of aggression shown. Both the variables (television watching, aggressive actions) may *already* be occurring but the psychologist wants to see if they are *related*. They would do this through a correlational study. A correlational study looks at two things (variables) to see if they may be related. We may find that as one variable increases, so does the other. This is a positive correlation. If one variable *decreases* as the *other* decreases, this is *also* a positive correlation. Let us look at a positive correlation through a non-psychological example for a change. This is shown in Fig. 5.3 below.

Alternatively, we may find that as one variable increases, the other *decreases*. This is a negative correlation – for example, the bigger the knickers, the slower the speed.

Fig. 5.3 The fatter the lady, the bigger the knickers (positive correlation)

But a correlational study can only show a relationship between two things, we cannot assume that one thing *causes* the other. In our example we have established a relationship between big knickers and slow speed. We cannot assume that big knickers cause slow speed.

- **advantages** are that a correlational study helps us to find out more about things we cannot control directly; it may form the basis for a follow-up study
- **disadvantages** are that we cannot conclude that one thing causes another, only that the two are related

EXPERIMENT

This is where psychologists start meddling! The experiment has been widely used in psychology, because it enables the psychologist to control what happens and therefore to test cause and *effect.* In an experiment the researcher tries to keep all the variables the same, except one. (A variable is anything that can change and you can see some examples in the next paragraph.) The one variable which the researcher does *not* keep the same is called the independent variable (the IV). The IV is what the experimenter manipulates in order to see what effect it has. An example might help here.

Psychological experiments start with a question, so a researcher might ask: 'Is there a difference between conformity in males and in females?' The researcher is manipulating the *sex* of the subjects – the IV in this experiment is the sex of the subjects. The researcher tries to control as many other variables as possible, so the male and female subjects will be from similar backgrounds, of similar age range and all will undergo the same experiences in the experiment. If the results show a difference in conformity between the male and the female subjects, then this researcher can conclude that the difference is due to the *sex* of the subjects. In other words their sex *causes* this effect. The results are called the dependent variable (see Chapter 6).

There are different kinds of experiment. When the researcher is able to control most of the variables such as where the experiment takes place, who takes part, what they do and when, then this is called a laboratory experiment (with high control). However, if the study takes place in a 'real life' setting (on the street, in a hospital) the researcher is less able to control variables such as the type of people who take part or when the study happens. Natural experiments and field experiments are examples of studies where the researcher has limited control.

For example, imagine you wanted to see whether a programme to reduce **prejudice** in the workplace was successful. You would compare an organisation which was starting such a programme with another similar organisation which was not. However, you would not be able to control who takes part, how committed the management is, how the programme is operated, how prejudiced all the subjects are to begin with. Any of these factors might affect your results. This would be a natural experiment. In contrast, in a field experiment you might have a little more control over who takes part, what happens and when, for example the **Moriarty** beach study in Chapter 18.

- **advantages** of laboratory experiments are that we can be more confident that what we manipulate causes the difference, thus we are able to test *cause* and *effect;* this is less true with natural experiments so researchers have to be more cautious in interpreting their results; we are able to see how people behave *naturally* as a result of the manipulation

- **disadvantages** are that laboratory experiments are very artificial so people may behave differently; because these experiments are so artificial, subjects may guess what it is the researcher is looking for (they pick up the demand characteristics); people, particularly children, do not always follow the instructions exactly; in natural experiments, the researcher cannot be sure that the results are due to the manipulation, but it is a real life situation

PSYCHOMETRIC TESTS

Psychometric tests are tests which have been devised to measure characteristics such as intelligence, personality or attitude. They are usually pencil and paper tests which enable psychologists to compare an individual with people in general. They are used in employment, education and business, perhaps to identify needs in management training or eligibility for a particular school or ability for a job.

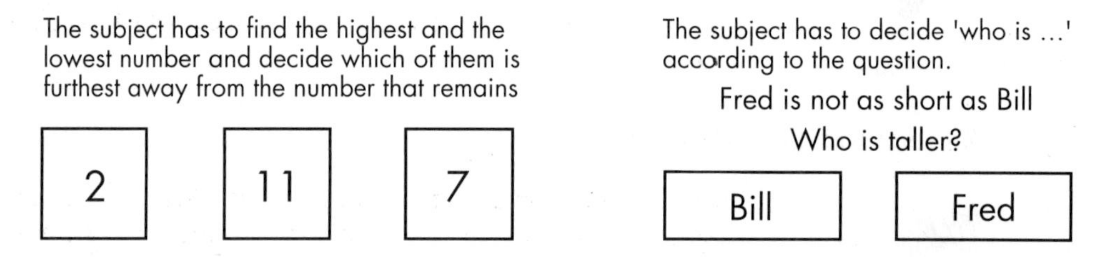

Fig. 5.4 These are two samples from the recruitment tests used by the British Army

Psychometric tests are used only after considerable research to make sure they are:

- standardised – psychometric tests are given to a large number of people to work out the norm for a particular characteristic or ability. For example, an IQ of 100 is the norm; it is the most common score. Those who score 120 are above the norm, and those who score 95 are below the norm. The process by which the norm is established in the first place is called standardisation
- valid – this means they test what they are *supposed* to test. However, this is problematic, because they are testing abstract 'things'. Intelligence, personality or attitude are not things you can see and *measure.* We might think we know what they mean, but that does not say we can measure them objectively. It has been said that intelligence tests do not test intelligence, they only test the ability to *do* intelligence tests
- reliable – this means that every time someone does the test their results are very similar

Psychologists try to meet these criteria, although this was not the case earlier this century. Early tests often showed the bias of the psychologist. As you can see from Chapter 13 Fig. 13.2, the test given to immigrants to America in the early 1920s was biased towards an understanding of middle class American culture. The immigrants were asked to indicate what was missing from each picture. Many were from poor, rural backgrounds. Was it likely that they were familiar with light bulbs, pistols, tennis and record players?

- **advantages** are that psychometric tests are cheap to run; they are quick; they can give useful information about an individual

- **disadvantages** are that they are expensive to buy; they may be used by people who do not understand the information they provide; they require sophisticated marking and interpretation; they may not measure what they are supposed to; they may be biased; they make people think abstract abilities such as personality or intelligence *are* easily measured

As you can see from the studies described in this book, psychologists often use more than one method in their research. For example, in the **Schaffer and Emerson** study (see Chapter 8) interviews with parents may have produced some biased information. This was balanced with observation of the adult-child interactions which gives a more objective view. By using two or more methods, researchers can reduce bias and gain more complete information.

Types of study

Psychologists often make comparisons. There are three types of study which enable them to do that.

LONGITUDINAL STUDY

The longitudinal study looks at the same people over a period of time. Researchers can then follow the *same* individuals through different ages or experiences, and monitor how they change. This type of study may last 12 months or 20 years, depending on what is being studied.

- **advantages** are that you can identify changes which are common to most people; you can compare the long term effects of an experience (for example children who experienced 'Operation Head Start' compared with those who did not); you can identify characteristics which persist and those which tend to disappear; there are no subject variables; it is useful for research in developmental psychology
- **disadvantages** are that you need a fairly large number of subjects and of researchers, as some will drop out over the years; you need long term funding which may be hard to find; it is difficult to change the study once it is under way; your findings may be out of date by the end of the study; social change at a stage in the study may affect the variable you are measuring (for example a major change in educational practice may affect measures of cognitive and social development)

CROSS-SECTIONAL STUDY

A cross-sectional study compares group of subjects who differ in some way. They may differ by social class or by age, for example. We can do this type of study if we want to compare *development* of a particular feature such as moral judgements. But we do not have to wait 12 years for the child to grow up, we can do it all at once by comparing perhaps 6, 8, 10, 12, 14 and 16 year olds. This would enable us to come to some conclusions now, when it is more relevant than in 10 years time. However, because we have *different* subjects in each age group, we have to compensate for subject variables. We do this by having a large sample, perhaps 20 to 40 in each age group.

- **advantages** are that you can get immediate results; it is cheaper to run and takes less time than a longitudinal study; you do not lose subjects

- **disadvantages** are that there are subject variables between groups; social changes may create differences between groups (the 10 year olds may have experienced major educational change which the 14 year olds have not); you cannot gain information on individual development

CROSS-CULTURAL STUDIES

A cross-cultural study enables psychologists to compare people from different cultures. This is one way of discovering the importance of nature or nurture on an individual. For example, it appears that children throughout the world develop their language abilities in much the same order. This suggests that the order in which we acquire language is innate (nature). However, the gestures which people use to show meaning vary widely. They may be approved of in one culture, but offensive in another. This suggests that gestures are learned (nurture), and are a result of the individual's environment.

Early cross-cultural studies tended to be ethnocentric. This means that researchers viewed other cultures through their *own* cultural lens. Thus there was a tendency to find that others lacked abilities which were evident in the researcher's culture. Imagine a researcher coming from a culture in which wearing two hats indicated great power. What would they make of the man in Fig. 5.5?

Fig 5.5 A powerful man?

Although ethnocentrism is still a difficulty, researchers are more aware of such a bias, and now researchers from different cultures frequently co-operate on joint projects. This helps to reduce another problem, which is that to gain a full understanding of someone's behaviour requires an understanding of the culture in which they live.

- **advantages** are that results can provide evidence for the nature or nurture debate by identifying characteristics which seem to be universal, and those which differ from culture to culture; they can highlight the differences between cultures and make us ask if we are right in our own assumptions about what is good or bad, changeable or unchangeable, normal or abnormal
- **disadvantages** are that cross-cultural studies can be expensive and time-consuming; it can be difficult to be sure that you are looking at, or doing, exactly the same thing in each culture; even if you are, you may be *understood* differently in each culture; they can be used to suggest that *our* culture is superior.

Further Reading

Coolican H (1995) *Introduction to Research Methods and Statistics in Psychology*, London, Hodder & Stoughton

EXERCISES

1 From this book, find one example of each of the following. In each case, say why you think the psychologist chose this particular way of studying people:

i) case study
ii) observation study
iii) observational method
iv) survey
v) correlational study
vi) experiment
vii) psychometric test
viii) longitudinal study
ix) cross-sectional study
x) cross-cultural study

2 Using the words from the list above fill in the blanks:

a) A .... is a way of assessing a particular ability.
b) A .... is a way of discovering whether two variables are related.
c) One way of comparing the influence of heredity with that of the environment is to do a ....
d) An .... enables the researcher to test cause and effect.
e) A disadvantage of a .... is that you cannot generalise from your findings.
f) A .... enables us to compare groups over a short period of time.
g) The .... can provide a lot of information fairly cheaply.

h) The .... is a good way of seeing how people behave naturally in an experiment.
i) An advantage of the .... is that there are no subject variables.
j) An .... allows the researcher to find out how people behave in everyday life.

3 Do an observational study at a 'STOP' sign. Observe each private car which comes up to the sign, note whether it stops, almost stops, slows down considerably, or barely slows down at all. Note the driver's sex and estimated age, and whether there were passengers. Do this study as a group, perhaps with two to four observers. To start with, each of you should note all of the above information. After a few cars, compare notes. How much did you miss, how much did you disagree on? Now devise the study so that you work as a group observing each car.

How could you use the information you gain?
How could you present this information visually?
What were some of the problems you came up against?

Chapter 6

Carrying Out and Reporting Practical Research

WHEN PSYCHOLOGISTS WANT TO FIND OUT MORE ABOUT A TOPIC, THEY WILL READ WHAT OTHER PSYCHOLOGISTS HAVE DONE. THEY MAY DECIDE THAT NOBODY HAS LOOKED AT EXACTLY WHAT INTERESTS THEM, OR THEY MAY FIND THAT SOMEONE HAS, BUT THAT THERE WERE FLAWS IN THE STUDY WHICH AFFECTED THE RESULTS. THEY WOULD THEN PLAN THEIR OWN RESEARCH.

IN THIS CHAPTER WE ARE GOING TO IMAGINE THAT WE ARE THE PSYCHOLOGISTS. THE CHAPTER TELLS YOU HOW WE WOULD PLAN OUR RESEARCH AND EACH OF THE STEPS WE SHOULD GO THROUGH. WE LOOK AT HOW TO DECIDE WHAT METHOD TO USE, HOW TO CHOOSE OUR SUBJECTS, WHAT FACTORS MIGHT GIVE US DISTORTED RESULTS AND HOW TO CONTROL THEM. WE LOOK AT HOW TO COLLECT DATA FROM OUR RESEARCH, THEN HOW TO PRESENT IT AND DRAW CONCLUSIONS FROM IT. AT VARIOUS POINTS THERE IS REFERENCE TO HOW WE WOULD WRITE UP OUR WORK IN A PRACTICAL REPORT AND THE CHAPTER ENDS WITH A CHECKLIST OF THE MAIN FEATURES OF A PRACTICAL REPORT.

Aim of the research

You must decide what it is you are trying to find out. For example, if you wanted to observe the sharing behaviour of children in a playgroup, then you could write:

> **Aim** The aim of this study is to observe the sharing behaviour of three and four-year-old children in a playgroup.

Or, if you thought that young people were more likely to stereotype than old people, you could write:

> **Aim** The aim of this study is to see whether young people stereotype more than old people.

You can see there is a difference between the two examples I have used here. In the first, we have no expectations of what will happen in the playgroup. But in the second example, we expect young people to stereotype more. In other words, we can make a *prediction* of what we think will happen. Your research will be testing that prediction.

SUMMARY

The aim of the study says what the purpose is.

WRITING A HYPOTHESIS

If you are testing a prediction in your research, you must write a hypothesis before you start. The hypothesis is a *prediction* of what you expect the results to show. In this stereotyping experiment we might write:

Experimental Hypothesis Young people will stereotype more than old people.

In a correlational study our hypothesis is called the research hypothesis. **Murstein**'s results (see Chapter 9) showed a positive correlation between the attractiveness scores of partners. In other words, the most attractive woman was partnered by one of the most attractive men. Also, the least attractive man was partnered by one of the least attractive women. If we were going to run a similar study, we might write:

Aim The aim of this study is to see whether partners are similar in attractiveness when rated by other people.

Research Hypothesis There will be a positive correlation between the attractiveness of partners when rated by others.

SUMMARY

The hypothesis is a prediction of what you expect to happen.

INDEPENDENT AND DEPENDENT VARIABLES

We have already come across experiments. This is the method of research in which the psychologist tries to control all of the variables except one - the independent variable. Let's look at this in more detail.

In the stereotyping study we are devising, the researcher is interested in whether there is a difference in stereotyping between:

1 young people and 2 old people

So what the researcher is manipulating is the age of the subjects. The thing which the researcher manipulates is called the independent variable (IV). So the independent variable in this experiment is the age of the subjects.

Perhaps the researcher devises a questionnaire to assess stereotyping. What else will be necessary? The experimenter will make sure that subjects are very similar in every respect except age. They will then see what the stereotyping scores are for each group. If there *is* a difference in scores between the young and old, the researcher will conclude that because everything else was the same for all subjects, then the difference is due to *age*. So the results *depend* on what was manipulated. This is why what is measured (the results) is called the dependent variable (DV).

If you are doing an experiment, then when you write it up you must say what the IV and the DV are after you have given the experimental hypothesis. This is how they might look for our stereotyping experiment:

The IV in this experiment is the age of the subjects.
The DV in this experiment is the amount of stereotyping each subject shows.

If you look back to the experimental hypothesis on stereotyping, you will see that the IV and the DV are included in the hypothesis.

SUMMARY

- The independent variable is what the experimenter manipulates.
- The dependent variable is what the experimenter measures.

Design of study

If you are carrying out an experiment, you will probably be comparing two groups of subjects. Subjects are the people you are studying. There are three ways of assigning our subjects to the two groups and they are called independent measures, repeated measures and matched subjects designs. So what exactly are these designs?

INDEPENDENT MEASURES DESIGN

With an independent measures design of study, you have different subjects (or participants) in each group. Some experiments automatically have an independent measures design. If you are going to compare males with females, adopted children with fostered children, five-years-olds with eight-year-olds, one-parent families with two-parent families, and so on you *have* to use an independent measures design of study because it is not possible for a subject to be eligible for both groups. In these examples the *difference* between your subject groups is the feature you are manipulating – in other words it is the independent variable (IV).

If you chose to do an independent measures design with the same *kind* of subjects, you would divide your sample in half to make two groups. Imagine you were studying **impression formation** and several of your subjects were very aware of how people form impressions because they had just been for interviews. If they were all in the same group, this could influence your results. This is a potential problem in the independent measures design so we try to *reduce* this type of subject variable as much as possible. How?

We can make sure that on all the important variables subjects are equally split between the two groups – we can have the same number of males and females in each group for example. Once we have decided how many males will be in each group, we must randomly allocate all the male subjects to the two groups. For example we will give each a number and put the numbers in a box. The numbers are then put into alternate groups as they are taken from the box.

Another way to reduce subject variables in this design is to have a fairly large sample size. This, combined with the allocation of subjects described above, enables us to reduce the subject variables.

REPEATED MEASURES DESIGN

In a repeated measures design of study you have the *same* subjects in each group. You take the *same* subjects through the two conditions of the study. One of the advantages in this design is that because you have the same subjects, then factors like intelligence, motivation, understanding and language will be the same for each condition (because your subjects are the same). So you do not have the problems of reducing subject variables which you have in the independent measures design. Nor do you need to have so many subjects.

But there *is* a problem. Imagine you are studying the effect of reinforcement on a learning task. In the control condition the subjects would not be reinforced, but in the experimental condition they would be. You can see that subjects may do better the second time they do the task because they have done something very similar already. This is known as the practice effect. So a better result in the second condition may be due to the subject's experience of the task, not to the reinforcement.

There is a way to get around this. You split your sample in half, one half does the experimental condition first, then the control condition. The other half of the subjects do the *control* condition first, then the *experimental* condition. This is called counterbalancing. By using counterbalancing, any improvement in your subjects' skills will be equally split between the two groups, and so the improved results cancel each other out.

MATCHED SUBJECTS DESIGN

In a matched subjects design of study there are *different* subjects in each group but they are matched in pairs on the basis of similarity in age, intelligence, skills, background, and of course the same sex. So each subject has a 'twin' in the other group. You need only a few subjects with this design of study, but it is expensive and time-consuming because of the work needed to match the subjects before you can start the study. It is therefore rarely used.

If you are doing an experiment for your practical, you will need to decide which one of these three designs of study to use. You will also need to write it in your report under the **Method** section and say why you used it. Let us return to our stereotyping study, and see how this might look:

> **Design** An independent measures design of study was used because younger subjects were in one group and older subjects in the other.

And here is a reminder of the differences between the three types of design:

SUMMARY

- The independent measures design of study has *different* subjects in each group.
- The repeated measures design of study has the *same* subjects in each group.
- The matched subjects design of study has *different* subjects in each group but they are matched with one of the pair in each group.

Sampling

Whatever type of study you choose, you need to select the people you will be studying. As we have seen, these are called the subjects, although more recently researchers are calling subjects participants. This reflects a changing attitude in psychology – we see people as helping in our research, not as things on which to experiment. Choosing your participants is called sampling, and your sample is the participants in your study.

If you wanted to investigate co-operation in primary school children, then your sample should include children of both sexes, from 7 to 11 years old, from different areas (rural, inner-city), from different backgrounds (class, culture, race). A sample like this would be representative of children in primary schools. You could therefore conclude that whatever you found would probably be true for primary school children in *general,* that is, you are able to generalise your results. If you ran your study in one school, when all the 9 to 11 year olds were out at a sports day, then you could not claim your sample was representative of primary school children. You would have a biased sample.

In real life it is impossible to get a *truly* representative and non-biased sample. In fact a lot of the research on adults has used subjects who are psychology students. Nevertheless, researchers should try to get as representative a sample as possible. You might think that researchers always have a lot of subjects, but you can see from some of the studies reported in this book that often the sample is no more than 40 subjects

We will look at three methods of sampling in detail: these are random sampling quota sampling and opportunity sampling

RANDOM SAMPLING

Be warned, random sampling is not what you think it is! Random means that every *possible* subject (known as the target population) has an equal chance of being selected. For example, if you wanted 30 subjects from a primary school of 120 children (the target population) you could random sample by putting the name of every one of the 120 children on a slip of paper, and placing it in a box. The first 30 slips taken out of the box would become your sample. You could give each child a number instead of using its name.

It is rarely possible for researchers to use random sampling – think about some of the studies you have read about in this book. Studies using undergraduates, or people who answered an advertisement or people sitting on a beach are *not* using random sampling. However, where it is possible it should be done.

QUOTA SAMPLING

If you have ever been stopped by someone on the street doing market research, they are probably using quota sampling. This means selecting a sample which is in proportion, in the relevant characteristics, to the population as a whole. What on earth does this mean? For example, if the market research company wants to know the *age* of the readers of various magazines, *age* is a 'relevant characteristic'. They may find that 20 per cent of the population is between 16 and 25 years old, 30 per cent is 26 to 45 years old, and 30 per cent is 46 years plus. The researcher's sample has to contain the same percentage of each age group. The researcher may have to find 10 people in the age range 16 to 25 years old, 15 between 26 to 45 years old and 15 who are 46 years old or more. You can see that these numbers reflect the population as a whole.

However, the researcher is not using random sampling because once the researcher has filled her quota (for example once she has found 10 people between 16 and 25 years old) she does not need to find any more people. This also explains why you may be ignored by market researchers holding clipboards! So, quota sampling involves identifying the relevant characteristics of your population, finding what proportion each represents, and establishing quotas in the same proportions. Your sample is made up of the first people you can find who fall into one of these categories. Your sample is not complete until you have the required number of participants in each category.

OPPORTUNITY SAMPLING

Opportunity sampling means exactly what it says. You take whoever you can as your subject. If for example you wanted to study gender differences in teenagers, you might use the first males and females you could get hold of, as long as they fitted within the age range, and, of course, agreed to take part. It is not a good way to obtain your sample because there may be a bias; for example you may only ask people to take part who look approachable and co-operative. Opportunity sampling is frequently used by students for their coursework so you need to remember the possibility of bias when drawing conclusions from your results.

Opportunity sampling is also used in field experiments. For example in **Piliavin**'s subway experiment (see Chapter 18) the researchers had no control over who was sitting in the carriage where the 'emergency' took place. But anyone who was there automatically became a participant in the experiment; so this is an example of opportunity sampling.

When you are designing your practical, you will need to think about how to obtain your subjects, and what factors you need to take into account – their age, sex, background and so on. When you write it up, you should say how you selected your sample, and mention any of these factors which you think might be relevant to the study.

Let us see how you might describe your subjects for the stereotyping experiment in the **Method** section of your report:

> **Subjects** were opportunity sampled from a youth group and an old age pensioners' group at an inner-city community centre. There were two males and two females aged between 15 and 18 years old, and two males and two females aged between 61 and 78 years old. They were all literate and had English as a first language.

SUMMARY

- A random sample is one in which each member of the target population has an equal chance of being selected.
- Quota sampling is selecting a sample which is in proportion, in the relevant characteristics, to the population as a whole.
- Opportunity sampling is taking whoever you can as your subject.

Controlling the variables

We have already come across some variables which could affect our results. Subject variables are the ways in which individuals (and therefore our subjects) differ – in mood, occupation, sex, intelligence, memory, distractability and many more. We have seen that we can design our research to try to control these variables, but there are other variables we need to control as well.

Confounding variables are anything which may distort the results of the study. If some subjects do a task when there are noisy roadworks outside the window, but others do it with low noise, this changing noise may affect your results: it would be a confounding variable. So the *physical* environment should be the same for every participant. We also need to make sure that we treat every subject in the same way – that they do exactly the same tasks, with the same materials, in exactly the same order. Each of them must also receive standardised instructions. This means that we say exactly the same thing to each one. *All* of the details that tell the reader which variables you controlled, and how, *must* be included in your report.

SUMMARY

- Subject variables are differences between subjects which may affect your results.
- Confounding variables are anything that may distort the results.

Collecting data

The purpose of any research is to find out more information. We call the information that is obtained the raw data. When we plan our study one of the things we need to think about is what form the data will be in. For example, if we are asking children questions in a study of moral development, then the data we are interested in is their answers to our questions.

However, if we think back to our stereotyping study, we need to decide how we are going to 'measure' stereotyping in our subjects. A psychologist might decide to give them a questionnaire related to stereotyping, and the score each subject got on each question would be the raw data.

On the other hand we could observe their behaviour. This is what **Schaffer and Emerson** did in their study of attachment. If we decide to do this, then we have to decide in advance what *measures* we will use. For example we might record the number of times the mother speaks to the child, has eye contact, touches the child, how long all of these incidents last, and so on. So the psychologist decides these measures in advance, and quite often tests them by practising an observation, just to see if the measures are good enough. Once the researcher is satisfied, then an observation schedule can be devised which the observers will fill in as they observe. Part of a simple observational schedule appears on page 30 under the **observational method**.

You can see that the raw data from this type of study will be much more complicated than some of the others I have mentioned. But your raw data needs to be in a form that you will be able to use when you work out your results. Ideally, the data from each subject should be in a form which makes it fairly easy to compare with all the other subjects. So the way you collect the data should be standardised. This will make the next stage much easier.

SUMMARY

- Check that your study produces data which reflects what you want to find out and that it is in a form which you can use to work out your results.

Presenting data

All the data which you gather in research should appear in the **Results** section of your report. If you have a lot of detailed raw data this goes in an Appendix at the end of the report, but the summary or the key data goes in **Results.**

Imagine you receive completed questionnaires on stereotyping from four young people and four old people. You would give the scores for *each* subject on *each* question in an Appendix. You would give the *total scores* for each subject in the **Results** section of your report. This would enable the reader to see easily whether young people had higher stereotyping scores than old people. The best way of displaying this data would be in a table. This is how it might look:

Subject	Age	Sex	Score
S1	Y	F	23
S2	Y	F	21
S3	Y	M	27
S4	Y	M	17
S5	O	F	20
S6	O	F	19
S7	O	M	22
S8	O	M	17

Table 6.1 Table showing stereotyping scores by subject

Looking at this table it seems as though the younger subjects do have higher scores. One easy way of comparing the two groups' scores is to work out the mean score for each group. Mean is another word for 'average'.
To work out the mean we add up all the scores in the group. Then we take that total and divide it by the *number* of scores we have added up:

Total score for young subjects = 88; divide by 4 = mean of 22

Total score for old subjects = 78; divide by 4 = mean of 19.5

When we compare the mean for each group it appears that the younger subjects *do* have higher scores because the mean is higher at 22. But let us look at the data from our subjects in another way.

If we work out the range of scores we can see how much they vary. To work out the range we use the highest score and take the lowest score away from it:

Young subjects: the highest score minus the lowest is 27 – 17 = range of 10

Old subjects: the highest score minus the lowest is 22 – 17 = range of 5

We can see the range of scores is much larger in the young group. This shows that the stereotyping scores of young subjects varied much more than those of the old subjects. It is important to check the range of scores, because if they differ a lot, as they do here, then it could be because just one or two subjects have *very* unusual scores. This happens in our example because S3's score is very high. In fact, if we took the S3 score out of the calculations for the young group, their mean score would be almost identical to the old group's mean score. It would be 20 compared to 19.5.

Why is this important? It is important because one subject's score is distorting the results. It *appears* from the mean that the young subjects have higher stereotyping scores, but our calculation of the range has highlighted this distortion of the scores. We might think that our experimental hypothesis could be supported if we looked only at the mean score. By calculating the range we see that we cannot be so confident. We will look more at this in the next section.

If you calculate means and ranges, put these *calculations* in an Appendix and put the mean and range figures in the main **Results** section. Finally, here is an example of how you might display these calculations in your report.

Group	Mean	Range
Young	22	10
Old	19.5	5

Table 6.2 Table showing means and ranges of group scores

However, it is not always possible to do this type of calculation with your data. If you did a study of **conservation,** then your data would be the children's answers. You cannot calculate the mean, so can you do anything with such data? Possibly – let us imagine you devise a study comparing 10 males and 10 females, which produces either Yes or No answers. Once you have presented the first Table showing the answers for each subject, you could calculate the *total* answers and show them like this:

Group	Yes	No
Male	7	3
Female	5	5

Table 6.3 Table showing total answers by group
It can be seen from the Table that more males answered Yes than No, but the same number of females answered Yes as No.

It is good practice to put a brief written comment under each of your tables or summaries like the example given in Table 6.3.

There are some types of research which may be difficult to present in tables, or to quantify, for example, an observational study. In this case your observation schedule might be the basis for presentation of your data. You need to think about the best way of showing your reader what you found.

Once we have presented a summary of our data, and shown the relevant calculations, we need to see if we can present the data in any other way which will make it clear to the reader. There are four ways which are useful: the bar chart, the graph, the pie chart and the scattergram. Let us look at each one.

BAR CHART

The bar chart is used to compare amounts and we could draw a bar chart for our stereotyping scores which were shown in Table 6.1:

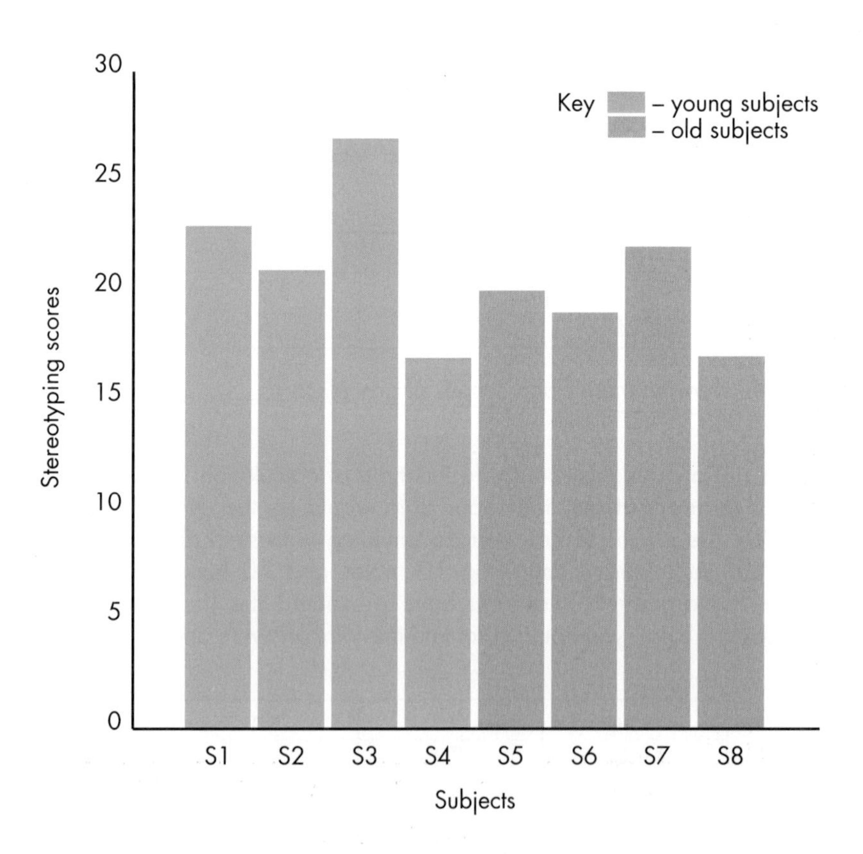

Fig. 6.1 Bar chart showing stereotyping scores by subject
It can be seen from this bar chart that apart from S3's score, all the others are fairly similar.

GRAPH

The graph is used when you want to show how something changes. Say you had collected data on the number of friends children had at various ages, the table below shows the mean for each age.

Age	0	2	4	6	8	10	12	14
Mean of friends	0	1	4	5	7	6	9	10

Table 6.4 Table showing age and mean number of friends

You could then show this data in a graph. A graph is a good way to show how something changes over time. We put the information which is regular, or consistent, along the bottom axis (in this case it would be the ages of the children) and the data which varies more along the upright axis. A graph of the data in Table 6.4 would look something like this:

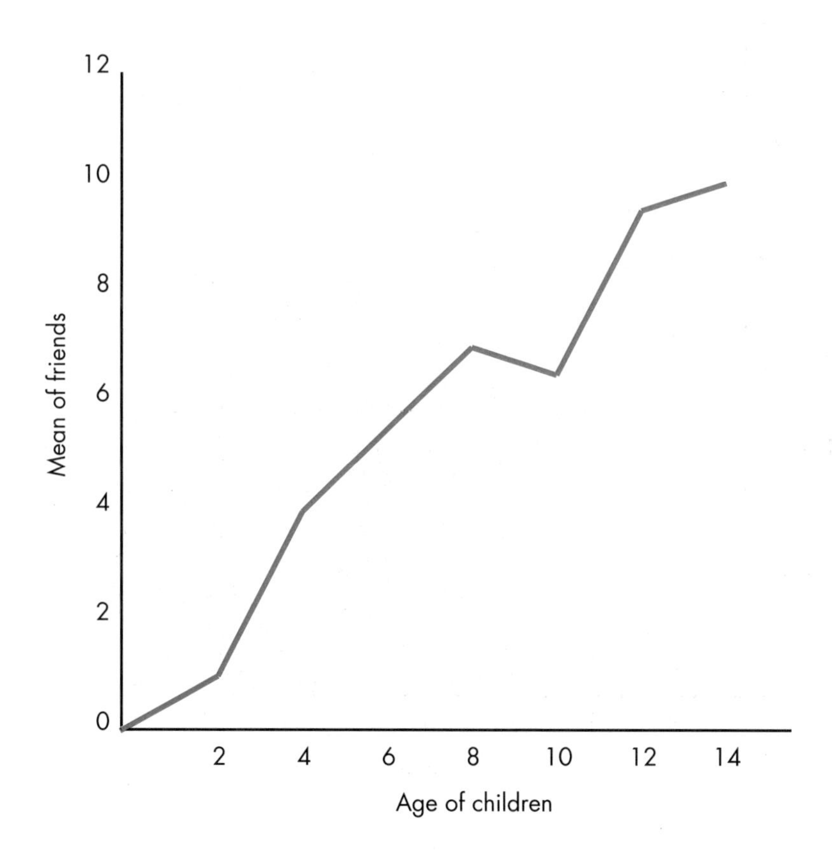

Fig. 6.2 Graph showing mean number of friends of children aged 0 to 14 years old
The graph shows that as children get older the number of their friends increases.

PIE CHART

The pie chart is used when you want to show proportions of something. You can use it only when you know what the total is, and the data you have represents *all* the parts of that total. For example, you might do a study on **temperament** by giving questionnaires to the parents of 10 three-year-olds. From the answers you could identify which children fall into one of the three types of temperament. In your report you would put this information into a table. Then you could draw a pie chart in which the 'pie' represents *all* 10 children, and it is cut into segments which correspond to the number of children in each category of temperament. You need to make sure that the size of each segment corresponds fairly accurately to the proportion of the total, and that you write in *how many* are in each segment and *what categories* they are from. This is what it might look like:

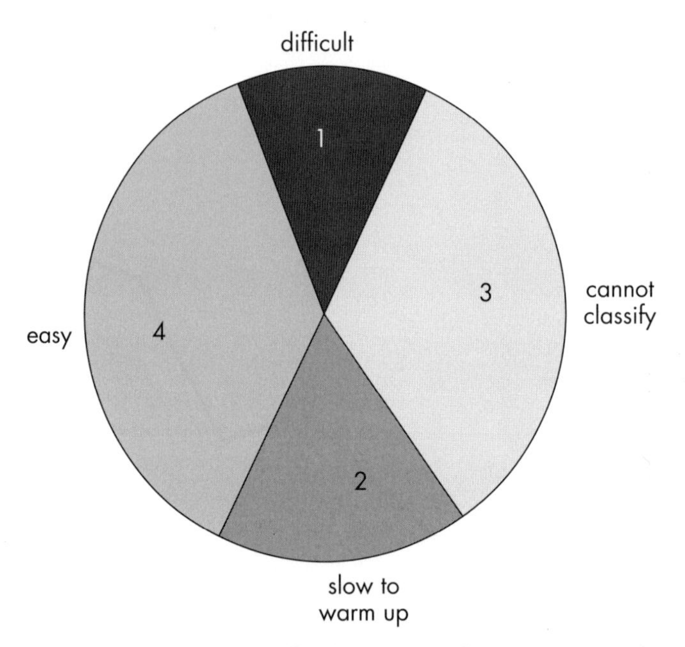

Fig. 6.3 Pie chart showing proportion of children in each temperamental category

SCATTERGRAM

The scattergram is used *only* if you are doing a correlational study. Do you remember that a correlational study tries to discover if there is a relationship between two things? We have come across **Murstein**'s correlational study of the attractiveness of male and female partners. Let's imagine you were to replicate the study and asked subjects to rank male and female partners in order from 1 to 8,with 8 being the most attractive. Table 6.5 shows what the data might look like.

If we were to draw a scattergram of these results it would look like Fig. 6.4.

Pair number	Male score	Female score
1	7	4
2	3	2
3	8	7
4	5	6
5	1	3
6	4	5
7	2	1
8	6	8

Table 6.5 Table showing attractiveness ranking for each subject pair

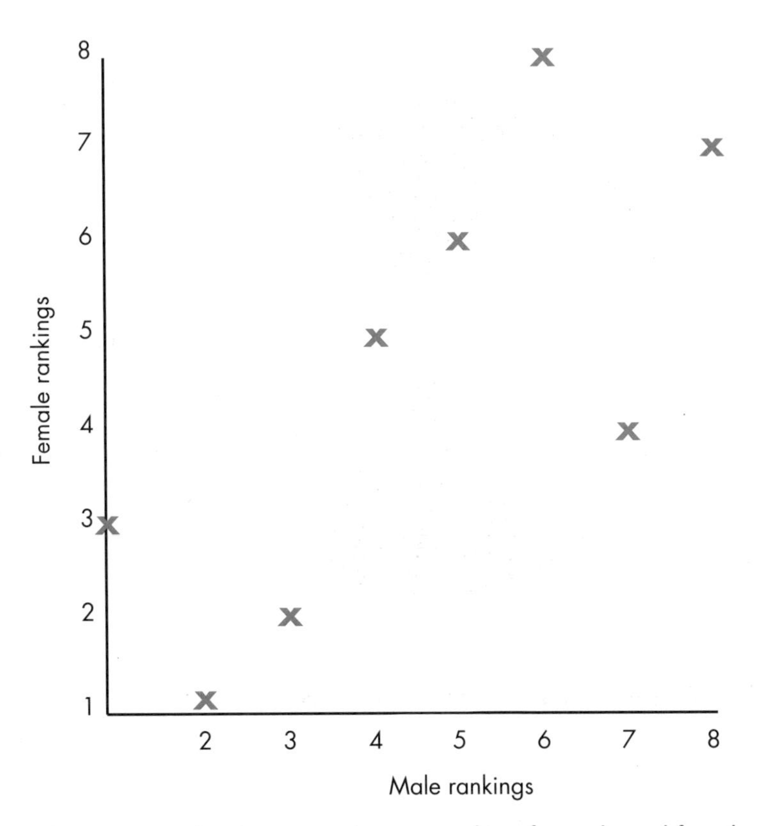

Fig. 6.4 Scattergram showing attractiveness ranking for male and female pairs
It can be seen from this scattergram that there is a positive correlation between rankings of male and female partners.

What would a negative correlation look like on a scattergram? Let us return to the example in Chapter 5 – the large lady on a bike. Our negative correlation was the bigger the knickers, the slower the speed. Ignoring the ethics of asking people what size their knickers are, our results might look something like Fig. 6.5.

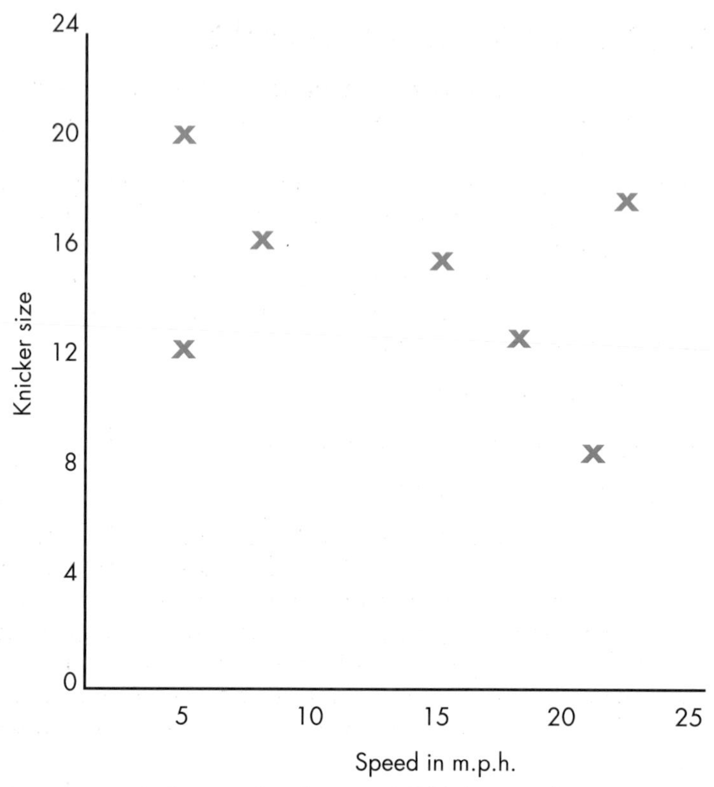

Fig. 6.5 Scattergram showing knicker size and bike speed
It can be seen from the scattergram that there is a slight negative correlation between knicker size and bike speed.

Here is a checklist of what you should include in your **Results.**

SUMMARY

- All the data you obtain should be presented in your report under the section headed Results. It should be correctly headed and labelled and clearly presented, with written comments if appropriate.
- Raw data goes in an Appendix if there is a lot of detail or in the Results section if it is short or simple.
- Summary data, totals, and so on go in Results, in the form of a table if possible.
- Means and ranges should be calculated next, if appropriate, and shown clearly.
- Use any of the following if they are appropriate and if they enable the data to be understood more easily:
  Bar charts for comparing amounts
  Graphs for data which shows change
  Pie charts for proportions of a whole
  Scattergrams for results of a correlational study

Drawing conclusions from the data

Once we have looked at the data, and done appropriate calculations, we should be able to relate it to the **Aims** or to the **Hypothesis** in our study. This is what 'drawing conclusions from the data' means.

If the aim of our study had been to observe the pro-social play of four-year-old children then our conclusions would be a summary of our findings, with comments about any patterns or trends which we had observed.

If we had a hypothesis as well, then our findings must be related to it. Let us assume we had an experimental hypothesis which predicted a *difference* between two groups of scores. If that is what we found then we could say:

The experimental hypothesis was supported.

On the other hand, if we get the same results for each group, we would say:

The experimental hypothesis was not supported.

However, it is not usually so simple. Remember the stereotyping data? Once we had calculated the mean and range, we noted that, apart from one subject's scores, the scores for subjects in *both* groups were very similar. What could we conclude from this? We cannot say with confidence that young people *do* stereotype more than old people. Because of this very small sample (eight subjects) we do not know if our S3 is very unusual, or if we could expect to find that high score quite frequently amongst young people. If we had a larger sample size – perhaps 40 subjects – then we would see how unusual such a score is.

As it is, we cannot say with confidence that there *is* a clear difference between the young and old group scores. If we were studying psychology at a higher level then we would do a statistical calculation which would help us decide how important this difference is. But for our purposes now we have to conclude from the stereotyping scores that young people do not stereotype more than old people, because the difference between the two groups is small. The experimental hypothesis was not supported.

In a correlational study if your scores fall along a fairly straight imaginary line through the crosses on your scattergram *and* go in the direction you predict, then you could conclude that your research hypothesis has been supported. However, if your scores do *not* go in a fairly straight line, as in Fig. 6.5, then you would have to say that your research hypothesis was not supported. Remember though that you *cannot* conclude that one of your variables *causes* the other in a correlational study. If in doubt, check the big knickers and the slow speed in Chapter 5.

Once you have drawn conclusions from your data you need to relate those findings to what other psychologists have found in the same area. Are they similar; are they what you would expect? If they are not, do you know any other psychological explanation for your findings? You should link your findings into other psychological research.

You should also evaluate your own study. Even though you may feel confident that you can draw conclusions from your data, ask yourself:

- What did the subjects say?
- How did they respond to your instructions?
- If you were observing, how accurately do you think your notes reflect what happened?
- If you studied children, do you think they guessed the answers they gave?

- If you gave a questionnaire, do you think your subjects understood the questions?
- Did your subjects know what you were trying to find out?

Once you have finished your study, you may think that there were problems like these. You should mention them in your report, because this is how psychologists learn from each other.

Practical report checklist

This checklist tells you what should be included in the report of your practical exercise.

Report checklist

INTRODUCTION

Aim	Say what you want to do and why, relate it to other work and theory which is set clearly within the syllabus. Say what you want to find out.
Hypothesis	*if appropriate.*
IV and DV	*if appropriate.*

METHOD

Type of design	you used and why, what measures *if appropriate.*
Sample	describe your subjects, how many there are and how you selected them.
Materials	describe any equipment, questionnaires, observation schedules, toys, etc. which you used. Attach copies or sketches if they provide more detail.
Procedure	say where the study took place, how you controlled variables and exactly what you did and said (standardised instructions). Say how you recorded data and debriefed subjects.

RESULTS

Raw data	goes in this section if its simple, details go in an Appendix.
Descriptive statistics	that is, give the mean and range *if appropriate.*
Presentation	of data in the *appropriate* form – tables, words, histogram, scattergram, etc.

DISCUSSION

Relate	your results to your aim, say whether or not the hypothesis is supported *if appropriate*, say whether or not the results are what you expected, and why.
Interpret	your findings by linking them with relevant parts of psychological theory.
Evaluate	your study – what went wrong, what could be improved, do any of the faults explain unexpected findings?

You need not include *everything* on this list, it depends on the type of study you do. If it says 'where appropriate' in the checklist, this means items may *not* be relevant (for example there will not be an IV or DV in a correlational study). To find out whether that item is appropriate for your exercise, look back in this chapter, or ask your teacher.

Your report should have a title, numbered pages and an index, and appendices *if appropriate*. The details provided in this report should enable someone else to copy your study – so you must provide *all* relevant information clearly and in the correct order. Where possible, use the correct terms as they have been explained in this chapter, such as variables, standardised instructions, opportunity sampling, mean, bar chart, and so on.

Further Reading

Coolican H (1995) *Introduction to Research Methods and Statistics in Psychology*, London, Hodder & Stoughton

EXERCISES

1 Display the following data in a table, calculate the means and ranges for four-year-olds and eight-year-olds and display this data in a table. Label all work correctly.
Scores for four-year-olds: S1 - 23, S2 - 30, S3 - 26, S4 - 24, S5 - 27
Scores for eight-year-olds: S6 - 28, S7 - 30, S8 - 37, S9 - 31, S10 - 34
2 Would it be appropriate to draw a pie chart of the stereotyping data in Table 6.1? Explain your answer.
3 Would it be appropriate to draw a graph of the Yes/No data in Table 6.3? Explain your answer.
4 Would it be appropriate to draw a bar chart of the friendship data in Table 6.4? Explain your answer.

Chapter 7
Ethics in Psychological Research

ETHICS ARE THE DESIRABLE STANDARDS OF BEHAVIOUR WE USE TOWARDS OTHERS. IF WE BEHAVE ETHICALLY, THEN WE TREAT OTHERS WITH RESPECT AND CONCERN FOR THEIR WELL-BEING. WE DO NOT TAKE ADVANTAGE OF THEIR TRUST OR THEIR LACK OF KNOWLEDGE. ETHICS APPLY TO HUMAN BEINGS AND ANIMALS.

Why are ethics important?

Much of psychological research involves human beings and some of it involves animals. Often they know less about what is happening to them than the psychologist does. Therefore we *must not* take advantage of their situation.

In order to help us behave in the right way, ethical guidelines have been established by the British Psychological Society. We must always work within these guidelines in any studies we carry out with others. The most important points are given here:

DISTRESS

You must ensure that those taking part in research will not be caused any distress. This means, for example, that you must not embarrass, upset, frighten or harm participants. Participants should be protected from risk. For example if your study involved frightening subjects, this could cause a heart attack. Subjects should feel as good about themselves when they finish your study as when they started.

CONSENT

Participants (or those responsible for them if they are children) must consent to take part in studies. This means that you must ask participants if they will take part. This may not be possible in a natural experiment or some kinds of observational study. To study participants without consent would be ethically acceptable so long as what happens to the participants could just as likely happen to them in everyday life. For example, if research involves observing people in a bus queue, those people may be observed by *anyone* when they are in the queue.

DECEPTION

Participants must be deceived as little as possible, and any deception must not cause distress. You must give participants some idea of what your study involves and what to expect. If you deceive them, then they will have agreed to take part without knowing fully what to expect. In this case you must ask for their consent at the debriefing stage.

DEBRIEFING

Participants must be debriefed at the end of the study. This means that you must give participants a general idea of what you were doing. If serious deception has been involved, then thorough debriefing is essential and the researcher must answer any general questions and ensure that participants are reassured.

COMPETENCE

Psychologists must be competent to carry out their research. For example, people might think you are competent to help them with their problems because you are studying psychology. You must be very cautious if they ask your advice.

WITHDRAWAL

Participants must be allowed to withdraw from a study whenever they wish. They must be reminded of their right to withdraw if it is a long study or if they appear to be distressed.

CONFIDENTIALITY

Information about the identity of participants and any information gained from them is confidential. For example, you must never give the names of participants, or any information which would make them identifiable unless the participants agree.

ANIMALS

Where animals are to be confined, constrained, harmed or stressed in any way, researchers must think whether the knowledge they would gain makes the way the animals are treated justifiable. Researchers should find other ways of researching if possible, must use as few animals as they can and must meet their needs for food and space. Procedures must conform to special guidelines and many can only be done by those holding a Home Office licence.

CONDUCT

You must always behave honestly – you must not use other people's wording and claim it is yours, you must not invent data and you must not copy other people's work.

It is sometimes difficult to plan research within these guidelines. It is difficult to run a study without *some* degree of deception, for example. Nevertheless, some psychologists have devised clever ways of running studies which do not break these guidelines.

Others have not. You can see that some of the research reported in this book breaks these ethical guidelines, possibly because the research took place before the guidelines became so strict. Research in the early part of this century tended to treat participants as passive and sometimes gave little thought to their rights.

However, in the last 30 years there has been increasing concern that psychologists behave ethically. We must behave as responsible human beings, and also, if we behave unethically it discredits psychology and the work of other psychologists. People may refuse to help with future research if they have been offended by unethical experiments.

You must be sure that your practical exercise, and the way you answer your examination questions, show that you understand and respect these guidelines.

Further Reading

Association for the Teaching of Psychology (1992) *Ethics in Psychological Research*. (This is provided as Appendix A in the Syllabus Support Material book which is produced by the Southern Examining Group for GCSE Psychology)

Coolican H (1995) *Introduction to Research Methods and Statistics in Psychology*, London, Hodder & Stoughton

EXERCISES

Find three studies in this book which break these ethical guidelines.
Explain why they do so.

SOCIAL AND ANTI-SOCIAL RELATIONSHIPS

SECTION C

Introduction

In the first half of this section we are going to look at how the individual develops relationships with other people. We start by examining the infant's first relationships and why they are important, then we move on to how the child's friendships develop. We consider why other people are important to us, what effect they have on our behaviour and why we prefer some people more than others. All these topics are covered in Chapters 8 and 9.

The second half of this section is about relationships with others which are unpleasant or unfair – anti-social relationships. We look in particular at how prejudice and aggression affect our behaviour towards others, as well as considering how such behaviour can be reduced. These topics are covered in Chapters 10 and 11.

Chapter 8

Making Attachments to Others

IN THIS CHAPTER WE ARE GOING TO LOOK AT HOW CHILDREN DEVELOP AN EMOTIONAL BOND WITH OTHERS. WE ARE INTERESTED IN THE DIFFERENT KINDS OF BONDS, WHY THEY ARE IMPORTANT AND WHAT HAPPENS IF THEY ARE BROKEN, OR DO NOT EVEN FORM IN THE FIRST PLACE.

What is an attachment and how does it develop?

An **attachment** is a close emotional bond felt by one person towards another. A good early attachment seems to be important for a child's long term development.

The interaction between an infant and its carer is an important influence on the development of attachment. Soon after birth the infant can cry, make eye contact, can grasp and be soothed. These are all types of attachment behaviour. Other types of attachment behaviour develop during the first two or three months – smiling, reaching and arm waving, for example. These behaviours invite carers to respond to the baby. The carers learn how to respond to the baby, how to attract its attention, make it smile or soothe it. This is the basis of the attachment process – the interaction between the two people.

For the first three months, most babies respond equally to any carer, but then they start to change. They begin to respond more to the people who are familiar to them. So a baby may wave its arms or smile when it sees its father's face, but there will be little reaction from the baby when it sees a stranger. The baby continues to respond to those it interacts with most until about six or seven months old. It then begins to show a special preference for one or two people.

How do we know when an attachment has developed?

We know that the baby has an attachment to someone when it shows two particular behaviours. For example, when its mother leaves the room, the baby may cry. This is called **separation distress**. It shows that the baby feels insecure when this special person is out of sight. Another sign that the baby has developed an attachment is if a stranger comes close and the baby moves away from the stranger and towards its father. This is called **stranger fear**. It shows that the baby is fearful of strangers and gains security from this special person.

We know the baby has formed an attachment when it shows **separation distress** and **stranger fear**. The attachment is to the person it looks to for security, comfort and protection and has usually developed by 12-months-old.

How do attachments vary?

Research has shown that attachments can be **weak or strong, insecure or secure**. The '**strength** of the attachment' means how strong the attachment behaviours are – for example how often the child goes to its attached person, how tightly it clings. The '**security** of the attachment' means how confident the child is that its special person will provide what it needs.

Fig. 8.1 If this baby's attachment is secure she will soon venture further from her mother

The security of attachment was tested by **Mary Ainsworth** in her '**strange situation**' studies. In these studies, the child played alone in a room whilst mother, father or stranger came and went. The observers recorded the child's play activities and its responses to each person. These children (who were the subjects in the study) were about 12-months-old. Ainsworth and her colleagues concluded that they could see three types of attachment:

1. **securely attached** children were happy when mother was present, were distressed by her absence and went to her quickly when she returned. The stranger provided little comfort. They found that 70 per cent of the children could be classed as securely attached
2. **anxious avoidant** children were those who avoided the mother and were indifferent to her presence or absence. Greatest distress was shown when these children were alone, but the stranger could comfort them just as well as the mother. This group contained 15 per cent of all the subjects

3 **anxious resistant** children were those who seemed unsure of the mother. They played less than the others, and seemed more anxious about the mother's presence They showed distress in her absence, and would go to her quickly when she returned, but then struggle to get away. These children also resisted strangers

Ainsworth said that these last two types of children were insecurely attached to their mothers. This means that the attachment appears to be weak or that they do not feel secure in their attachment.

Why do attachments vary like this?

Psychologists have proposed a number of reasons why attachments vary like this. Here are some of them.

QUALITY OF INTERACTION

It seems that the **attachment** depends on how sensitively the carer responds to the baby's signals. For example, a carer who can tell the difference between a baby's cry for food and a cry of pain will be able to respond accurately to the baby's needs. This is called 'sensitive responsiveness' by **Rudolph Schaffer and Peggy Emerson**. Details of their study appear later in this chapter.

TEMPERAMENT

Some babies dislike new experiences; they may cry a lot and be very hard to comfort. These are characteristics of the 'difficult' temperament (see Chapter 12). This behaviour is similar to Ainsworth's 'anxious resistant' behaviour. Children with a 'difficult' temperament may have problems developing their **attachments.** Their carers may find it hard to be loving and caring because it is difficult to understand these children's needs, and carers may feel they are not caring very well. In this case the attachment may be weak or insecure because *neither* partner is able to build the attachment easily.

CHARACTERISTICS OF CARERS

The carer's characteristics are important for the development of a secure **attachment.** **Alan Sroufe** says mothers are 'psychologically unavailable' when they avoid or reject their babies. Their lack of interaction with their infants may lead to Ainsworth's 'anxious avoidant' attachment. In contrast, some research shows that when mothers are rejecting, their babies may become more clingy.

CONSISTENCY OF CARE

Consistency means that the carer should be seen often by the baby, and should behave in the same way all the time. So if a carer is moody and withdrawn sometimes and then very responsive and entertaining, the type of care is not consistent. This may make it more difficult for the baby to develop a secure **attachment.** One study found that some one year olds who were securely attached became anxiously attached by 18 months old when their mothers were very highly stressed.

AMOUNT OF STIMULATION

Schaffer and Emerson also found that stronger attachments were related to greater amounts of stimulation from the carer. Stimulation includes using a lot of different tones of voice, changing facial expressions often, and touching and playing with the baby.

Fig 8.2 This baby's attention is captured by his mother's facial expression

Why are attachments important?

Psychologists have studied topics such as how well children play with others, how they solve problems and how aggressive they are. They found that children with secure **attachments** have fewer difficulties as they go through childhood than those with insecure attachments. Attachments seem to be very important for three main reasons:

S

C

- they help the child to develop **sociability** – to learn how to get on with others
- they help the child develop **emotionally** – to be confident and develop self-esteem
- they help the child's **cognitive development** – how to talk, think and understand the world

You will see how attachment is related to these abilities later in this section of the book, for example in Chapters 9 and 13.

One of the people who felt very strongly that a good early **attachment** was essential for a child to develop properly was **John Bowlby**. He was working from the 1940s up until the 1980s and his ideas were very influential. We will look at what Bowlby said, and why. Then we will look at the criticisms of his ideas.

John Bowlby's ideas

Bowlby's own research involved two groups containing 44 juveniles in each. One group were juvenile thieves; the other consisted of juveniles who were emotionally disturbed but had no known criminal involvement. He investigated the early years of all these subjects using the case study method. This involved talking to others who knew the young people, and looking at their past records from school, or doctors, for example.

He found that more than half of the juvenile thieves had been separated from their mothers for longer than six months during their first five years. In the other group only two had had such a separation. He also found that several of the young thieves showed 'affectionless psychopathy' (they were not able to care about or feel affection for others). Bowlby concluded that the reason for the anti-social behaviour in the first group was due to separation from their mothers.

An example of a study which was a basis for Bowlby's ideas was that carried out by **Rene Spitz and Katherine Wolf**. They observed babies being brought up by their mothers in a prison. At the age of six to eight months old (when **attachment** first occurs) the babies were separated from their mothers for three months and cared for by others. Spitz and Wolf noted that the babies cried more and failed to gain weight. However, when they were re-united with their mothers they returned to normal.

Bowlby's ideas were based on these types of findings, and also on the findings of researchers who had studied animal behaviour. It appeared that, for example, monkeys were born with an instinct to stay close to their mothers. The mother monkeys also appeared to have an instinct to care for their young. This led Bowlby to propose the following two theories.

Theory of monotropy

This means having a single attachment. **Bowlby** said that both the infant and the mother had an instinct – a biological need – to bond together. If the mother was not available then a 'permanent mother substitute' would do. But what is essential is that this relationship is not like any other attachment the child has. The one with the mother is *the essential relationship* if the child is to develop properly. Bowlby said this instinct was at its strongest during the first year or so of the baby's life. If this special attachment had not formed by three years of age, which he said was the sensitive period, then it was probably too late for it to form.

I

I

Maternal deprivation theory

Bowlby said that if a child did not develop a strong unbroken attachment with its mother during this sensitive period, or if the attachment was broken, then the child would develop long term social and emotional problems, possibly even affectionless psycopathy.

S

So, Bowlby was arguing that mother and infant had a biological need to develop an attachment; nobody else could fill this special need. If the child did not have a strong unbroken attachment to its mother during its early years there would be serious long term problems in its development.

WERE BOWLBY'S CONCLUSIONS RIGHT?

There has been a lot of criticism of Bowlby's ideas. It now seems that **maternal deprivation** may be more complicated than he thought. To begin with we can look again at his own study and the Spitz and Wolf study. There are criticisms of the methods they used, which may have led them to the wrong conclusions.

Bowlby's sample was biased. To look at the long term effects of **maternal deprivation** *all* his subjects should have been selected because of separation from their mothers. He could then have looked at how they developed. Many of them may not have become juvenile thieves. But, because one of his groups consisted of juvenile thieves, it *appeared* that a large proportion of maternally deprived children became juvenile thieves.

Another criticism is that **Bowlby**'s research was retrospective. This means he was looking backwards in time to what had happened to these youngsters in their early years. It is unlikely that he had complete records of what happened in the past. It is also very difficult for subjects to remember accurately what happened to them. So although retrospective work is necessary it is not always reliable. This is one of the weaknesses of the case study method.

As for the **Spitz and Wolf** study, the babies clearly suffered after separation from their mothers. But there were *other* changes in the babies' lives as well. Although their new carers were young mothers, they did not know these babies. They would not feel the same emotional commitment to them, and would not be able to understand the babies' efforts to communicate. The babies would feel they were in different environments because the familiar patterns of care and comfort were changed. So it could have been *these* changes that distressed the babies, not only separation from their mothers.

Criticisms such as these make the basis for **Bowlby**'s conclusions appear rather weak. But his ideas encouraged psychologists to look at this topic in more detail and a lot of their research challenges his claims. What conclusions have other psychologists come to?

Theory of monotropy – a single early attachment?

Rudi Schaffer and Peggy Emerson studied the way infants formed **attachments.** You can see in the box opposite what they did.

So the Schaffer and Emerson study contradicts **Bowlby**'s claims for a single attachment to the mother in several ways. It also shows the importance of the father, yet Bowlby said the father had no direct emotional importance to the child.

Although we refer to the 'carer' of the child in this chapter, in reality a lot of the early research looked *only* at the mother-child relationship. The **Schaffer and Emerson** study was one of the first to show the importance of the *father*. Since then several studies have looked at the *father-child* relationship. **Ross Parke** found that fathers touched, cuddled and talked to their newborn infants just as much as the mothers did. However, as the babies get older fathers show different patterns of interaction than mothers. Their play is more vigorous and unpredictable and they use less 'baby talk'. **Michael Lamb** found that from seven to eight-months-old babies showed strong **attachments** to both parents, but still preferred the mother when they were frightened.

Schaffer and Emerson (1964)

Aim of study	The aim of the study was to look at the way first attachments were formed.
Type of study	This was a longitudinal study which took place over 12 months.
Method	The method used was naturalistic observation and interview.
Sample	The subjects were 60 Glasgow infants.
Procedure	The babies were visited monthly and observed when they were with others. Schaffer and Emerson decided that a baby had become attached to a carer when it showed 'separation upset' after the carer left.
Results	The results of the observations showed that the first attachment appeared at about seven months old. However, many of the babies had more than one attachment by 10-months-old. They were attached to mother, father, grandparents, brothers, sisters and neighbours. The mother was the main attached figure only for about half of the children at 18-months-old. Of the rest, most were attached to their father. The researchers also found that attachments were most likely to form with those who responded accurately to the baby's signals. If the main carer ignored the baby's signals, then there was often greater attachment to someone the baby saw less, but who responded to it more.
Conclusions	Schaffer and Emerson concluded that babies could develop several attachments at the same time, and that where there was a main attachment, it was not always to its mother. They also concluded that the strength of the attachment was due to the amount of 'sensitive responsiveness' the carer showed, not to how much time the carer spent with the baby.

Another challenge to Bowlby's idea that **attachments** could not form after three years of age comes from studies of children who spent their early years in institutions. For example, **Barbara Tizard, Judith Rees and Jill Hodges** followed the development of children who had been in residential nurseries (that is, in institutionalised care) from only a few months old until they were three years old. Some were then adopted, some returned to their mothers, some remained in the nurseries. They were also compared with a control group, who had spent all their lives in their own families. In this longitudinal study the children were assessed at two, four and eight years old. At two-years-old none of the institutionalised children had formed an **attachment,** but by eight years old those who were adopted had formed good **attachments.** Also their social and intellectual development was better than that of children returned to their own families.

S

Fig. 8.3 How important do you think this father will be to his baby?

The study by Tizard, Rees and Hodges shows that **attachments** *can* form after three years of age. It also shows that the best place for children is *not* always with their own families – **Bowlby** said even a bad family was better than an institution.

Maternal deprivation – what exactly is it?

Michael Rutter said **Bowlby**'s term 'maternal deprivation' was too general. It covered a range of different circumstances, each of which needed to be examined. Rutter said we needed to distinguish between:

- **maternal privation**, which occurs when there is a *lack* of an attachment to the mother (or permanent mother figure). This might be because a child is brought up in a residential nursery with many different carers, or because a mother largely ignores the child
- **maternal deprivation**, which occurs when a child is *separated* from the mother. This may be due to the child going into hospital, the mother going away to look

after her parents, or the father having custody after a divorce, or even the death of the mother. In these situations an attachment will have formed, but is then broken to some degree

Let us look at Rutter's criticisms in more detail.

MATERNAL PRIVATION

Maternal privation means not having formed an attachment. Children who have been maternally privated often show poorer social and intellectual development than children who have an attachment. Psychologists have pointed out that this may be because these children do not only lack an attachment to their mother, they also lack the social and intellectual *stimulation* that occurs through such an attachment. This was particularly true for children in institutional care.

For example, a study by **Harold Skeels** and his colleagues in 1939 showed that this poorer development is not due to lack of a mother. He tested the IQ of 25 children in an orphanage who were between one and two years old. (A person's IQ is their score on an intelligence test, and an IQ of 100 for a child indicates a normal score for their age.) Half of the children, with an average IQ of 64, were then sent to a school for mentally retarded girls.

Here they were looked after by individual girls, and had a lot more toys and attention. This social and mental stimulation increased their average IQ to 92 within two years. In contrast, the children who stayed in the orphanage had initially shown an average IQ of 86, but two years later this had dropped to 60. When Skeels followed all these subjects through to adulthood in 1966, he found most of this latter group had stayed in institutions. However, all of the other group had normal lives – marrying, having children and had been self-supporting.

Clearly, it is the interaction and stimulation of the carer which helps normal social and intellectual development. It is the lack of *stimulation* which leads to poorer development, not lack of an *attachment to the mother* as **Bowlby** claimed. The **Skeels** study is an example of the effect of the environment on an individual's development.

MATERNAL DEPRIVATION AND SEPARATION

Rutter suggested that we look at the child's experiences as a whole, for example the length of separation and the family circumstances, not just the relationship with the mother. He said that Bowlby did not differentiate between the **short term** and **long term** effects of separation, and most of Bowlby's ideas were based on long term separation.

Short term effects after **separation** are similar in many young children who are separated from an attached figure. These effects are shown vividly in **James and Joyce Robertson**'s film of John, who stayed in a residential nursery at 17 months of age when his mother had a second baby. He showed the typical three stages:

1. **distress** – the child cries, protests and shows physical agitation
2. **despair** – the child is miserable and listless
3. **detachment** – the child seems to have accepted the situation and shows little interest when reunited with the attached figure. He may be active in separating himself from the attached figure – struggling to be put down if cuddled for example

John was separated from his mother, left in a strange place, with strange people and objects, and a strange routine. It is likely that this strangeness was *also* the reason for his great distress, not just the separation from his mother. With the opportunity to form a new attachment and familiar things around the child, its distress is greatly reduced. For example, children show less distress if they are admitted to hospital with a brother or sister.

Rutter proposed from other research that this distress was most marked in children between six months and four years old. Even then, not all children showed it. He pointed out that if children had experienced *happy* separations, then they were usually less distressed by *unhappy* separations, such as a stay in hospital.

Bowlby argued that it is the loss of maternal care which is crucial to the child. However the research we have just examined suggests that the **short term** effects of separation are as much the result of unfamiliarity, the child's age and its ability to cope with separations as to do with the loss of *maternal* care.

Rutter studied the **long term** effects of early separation from mothers of 9 to 12 year old boys from London and the Isle of Wight. He looked particularly at anti-social behaviour and found there was *more* in boys from families where the parents' marriage was rated as 'very poor' or where parent-child relationships were cold or neglectful. There was no difference in anti-social behaviour between boys who had separated from *one* parent and those who had separated from *both* parents.

Results showed that when a parent died, a child was only slightly more likely to become delinquent than a child from an 'intact' home. In contrast, a child who became separated because a discordant home broke up was *twice* as likely to become delinquent. Rutter suggested that this difference may be due to the *distortion* of the relationships (for example, arguing, lack of affection, stress) in the discordant home. It cannot be due to the *disruption* of the bond (as **Bowlby** claimed), because where the disruption was final (in death) there was only a slight increase in delinquency.

Boys separated because of illness or housing problems did not become maladjusted. But where there were a lot of arguments and unhappiness in families, boys were more likely to show anti-social behaviour. From these results, Rutter concluded that long term problems are related to *family discord* not specifically to separation from the mother.

It could be that discord in the home means there is a failure to form attachments and it is this which may lead to 'affectionless psychopathy', according to **Rutter**'s research. Note that he said that it is the *lack of attachments*, not specifically an attachment to mother, which may be the cause. However Rutter pointed out that *why* and *how* family discord is related to anti-social behaviour has yet to be fully investigated. He suggested that it may be related to:

- the child's temperament
- parenting (or child-rearing) styles
- social learning factors

HOW IMPORTANT ARE THE EARLY YEARS?

Bowlby claimed that unless the maternal attachment was formed within the first three years, there would be long term problems. However, we have already seen some evidence which contradicts this. The longitudinal study by Tizard, Rees and Hodges shows adopted children can overcome early problems, and so did Skeels study of children at the school for mentally retarded girls.

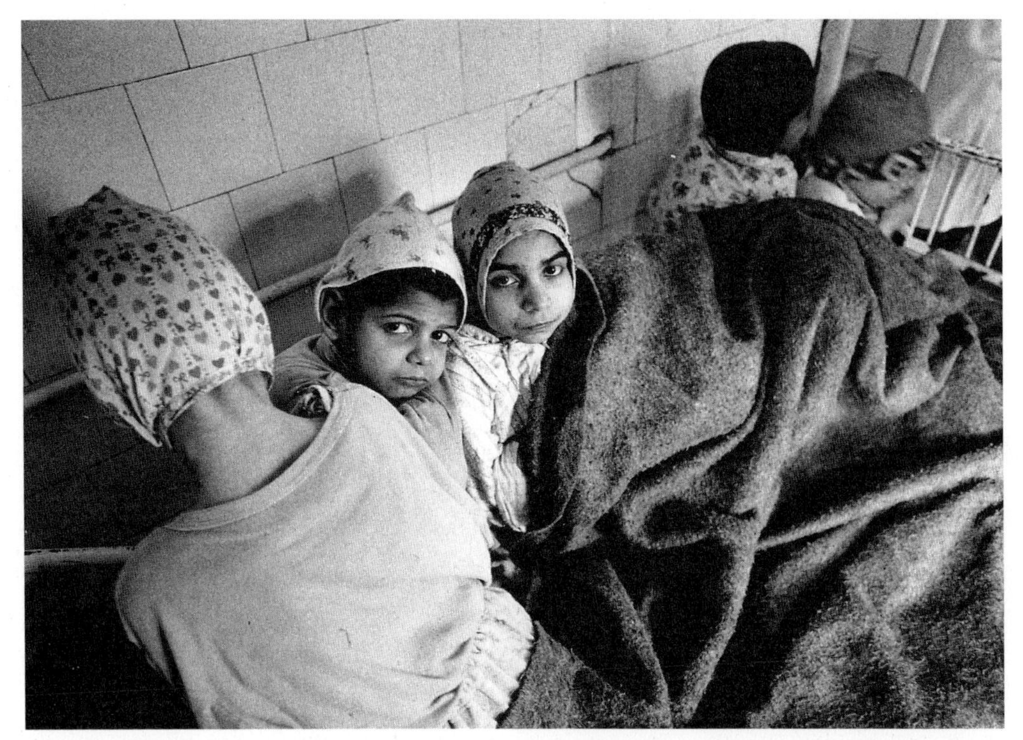

Fig. 8.4 Bowlby would say these Romanian orphans have experienced permanent damage, but the Clarkes would say the damage could be repaired. After reading this chapter, what would you say?

Two psychologists – **Ann and Alan Clarke** – have challenged the idea that the early years are so crucial. They stress the *flexibility* of human development, and point out that early learning can be forgotten, or overlaid by new experiences. This means that the individual's *whole* development is what matters, not particularly the early years. Indeed they propose that there is no sensitive period because the developing human is sensitive to different experiences at different times. This also means that early problems can be reversed. They refer to many studies to substantiate their claims.

In summary then, Bowlby's early claims about the key role of the mother have been widely challenged. It appears that several people can 'mother' a child and that problems which seem to be associated with 'maternal deprivation' may be due to other causes. So we must also consider the atmosphere at home, how strange the child's new environment is, whether there has been *any* chance to form an attachment, and how much stimulation and attention the child receives. As well as this, we must be aware that early problems can be overcome with the right kind of care.

What is the effect of divorce on children?

One example of separation and its consequences is when parents divorce or separate. As the incidence of divorce increases, so has research on its effects on children. However, this is a difficult topic for psychologists to study. The main problems are with methodology and with ethics. Some of the difficulties are described below.

WHAT IS THE BEST METHOD FOR STUDYING DIVORCE?

To look at the effect on children, you need to study them at various stages in the divorce process. You need to decide what type of study to do.

One type of study would be a longitudinal one In this you would follow particular children as they experienced each stage of divorce. You would need to know what the children are like before the divorce process started – are they outgoing, moody, quiet, slow to learn, happy at school, naughty and so on? Once you know this, you can see how these characteristics change, or new ones appear as the divorce proceeds.

Another type of study is a cross-sectional study, in which you would look at a sample of children whose parents were at various *stages* of divorce. However you would need a very large sample because the children at each stage would need to be similar in age, family background, intelligence, sex and so on. Another drawback to a cross-sectional study is that it does not reveal what your subjects were like *before* the divorce. So their behaviour during the divorce may be as a result of the divorce, or part of their normal behaviour – you cannot be sure which.

Whichever type of study you chose, you would need to find parents who were going to divorce, or who were already in the process of it. How would you do this? One method could be to advertise, but this would give you a biased sample. For example the parents who responded might be mostly those going through a relatively painless divorce. Your sample would therefore consist only of children experiencing minor upset. To have a good sample you would also need children whose parents' divorce is painful. Some of the ethical problems of all this are shown opposite.

WHAT FACTORS AFFECT THE CHILD'S RESPONSE TO DIVORCE?

Despite these difficulties, psychologists have been able to study divorce. From a longitudinal study of 60 divorcing families carried out by **J. Wallerstein and J. Kelly** two important points seem to emerge. Divorce is often disruptive whatever the child's age – some children show signs of disturbance more than five years later. However, children differ widely in their responses, and there are ways in which the disruptive effects can be reduced. What are some of the main findings?

Emotional responses

Mavis Hetherington identified two phases in the child's response to divorce. First is the **crisis phase,** when the emotional and behavioural responses may be quite marked. During this phase children typically feel angry, guilty, afraid or depressed. This period includes the reorganisation and change in family balance after divorce. It is followed by the **adjustment phase**, when the child shows they are adapting to the new situation.

Age

Wallerstein and Kelly found that children aged three to five years old show the most severe immediate symptoms. Younger children seem to show fewer long term effects. However, older children show more sadness or anger and these symptoms may persist for up to 10 years according to a follow-up study.

Ethical problems in studying divorce

- **confidentiality** – how do you find parents who are divorcing – through marriage guidance clinics? lawyers? social workers? The work of these people is confidential
- **not causing distress** – once you have your subjects, how do you gain your information? You might observe parents and children, interview them as well as their friends, family, teachers. This is going to interfere in what is already a distressing experience. Psychologists must ensure that people taking part in their research are not caused any additional distress. How are researchers to gain information without adding to the distress? One way is to use researchers who are also trained as counsellors. This means they may be able to minimise the distress and even help their subjects
- **withdrawing from a study** – once you have made contact with your families, are you sure you will have enough of them? Subjects withdraw from research studies because they move away, become ill or their circumstances change in some way. With research on divorce there is another possible reason for withdrawal. Psychologists must remind their subjects that they can withdraw from a study at any time. Divorce is a distressing experience for all involved. It is therefore quite likely that a parent may decide that the involvement in the research study is adding to the problems and so withdraw. This means that a child who has been studied may leave before the research is complete

Sex

Mavis Hetherington found that boys appear to show conduct disorders and suffer more than girls in the short term. There is some more recent evidence however that girls may show the effects later, in their adolescence. Why might boys suffer more? It could be because the mother usually has custody and therefore the father will be absent. According to **Freud**'s theory, the boy needs a father present in order to identify with him in the phallic stage and so develop as a man. The boy will therefore show problems if the father is absent. This absence is also the explanation for problems according to social learning theory. This says that the boy needs a strong, nurturing male on whom to model his behaviour. Without this model, the boy may have problems in his development. These explanations are contradicted by research which found that boys show more conduct disorders than girls even in *unbroken* discordant homes – here the father is present.

I

L

However, other ideas have been proposed. Girls may have better 'coping mechanisms' in times of stress. Another possibility is that boys may be treated differently from girls in times of conflict in the home.

Attachment

The security of the **attachment** may change during the divorce. Both parents will be experiencing stress – they may be withdrawn, angry, depressed, having financial or housing problems. Their behaviour towards the child may change and this in turn may affect the attachment with the child (remember that *consistency* is a factor in attachment).

For these reasons a secure attachment may become insecure. Similarly, there will be separation from the parent who does not have custody: this will have an impact on the attachment to that parent. Mavis Hetherington found that a strong attachment to the custody parent seemed to make conduct disorders less likely.

Lessons can be learned from other work on **attachment.** When separation takes place, the effects will be reduced if the child has frequent contact with the non-custodial parent. Equally, if there are few other changes in the child's life – the same school, home, contact with grandparents and so on – then separation will be less disruptive.

Fig. 8.5 If there is a major change in this baby's life, these grandparents will provide some stability

Temperament

I

Children with a 'difficult' **temperament** are the most likely to develop psychiatric disorders. **Michael Rutter** found such children were twice as likely to be the target for potential criticism. Research has shown that where there is marked discord in the home, the child with an 'easy' temperament seems to experience less conflict.

Home environment

If the home environment is very stressful prior to the divorce, then there appear to be greater problems for children. This may be less to do with the divorce than with the disruption in the home – remember **Michael Rutter**'s findings? It was conflict in the home which was related to anti-social behaviour, not separation from the mother. This point is supported by **Mavis Hetherington**'s study. Hetherington and her colleagues found that children who stayed in intact homes where there was discord showed more disturbance than children two years after their parents divorced. They found that as family relationships improved the disorders in the children became fewer.

Social support

There is considerable evidence that social support can ease the difficulties associated with divorce. **Hetherington** and her colleagues looked at how much help and emotional support came from family and friends. It seemed that parents found it easier to keep a stable and happy home life for their children when they had this support, rather than coping with problems alone. A stable and happy home environment reduces the upset for the child.

S

In summary then, there is a lot of evidence to show that children find divorce stressful. They differ in their responses according to their age, sex, temperament and other variables. However, there are ways in which the harmful effects can be reduced – by minimising conflict between the parents, maintaining attachments as much as possible and making few change in the child's environment.

Further reading

Bee H (1992) *The Developing Child* (6th ed), New York, Harper Collins
Rutter M (1981) *Maternal Deprivation Reassessed,* Harmondsworth, Penguin

EXERCISES

1 Describe Harold Skeels' study in your own words, giving the aim, procedure, results and conclusions.
2 List three of Bowlby's ideas and write a sentence describing each of them.
3 Describe one study which supports Bowlby's ideas and say why it does.
4 Describe one study which contradicts Bowlby's ideas and say why it does.
5 Give two ways in which a three-year-old boy might be affected by his parents' divorce. Give two different ways in which a 10-year-old girl might be affected.
6 Imagine you were going to design a study based on Wallerstein and Kelly's findings about age differences and divorce. You are going to compare the symptoms of four year olds and 10 year olds immediately after their parents' divorce. Write an experimental hypothesis for your study.

Chapter 9

Widening Social Relationships

IN THIS CHAPTER WE ARE GOING TO LOOK AT OUR RELATIONSHIPS WITH OTHER PEOPLE – THE DEVELOPMENT OF FRIENDSHIPS BETWEEN CHILDREN, WHY PEOPLE ARE ATTRACTED TO EACH OTHER, AND HOW OTHER PEOPLE MAY AFFECT OUR BEHAVIOUR.

How do children develop relationships with their peers?

S

If we follow children's play patterns we can see how their relationships with their peers develop. Research has shown that the way in which children play together goes through several stages. What are they?

TYPE OF PLAY

Solitary play

This means that even when other children are around, the child plays alone. Although children do this throughout childhood, it most often occurs in babies. If you put two 10 month olds together, they are not very interested in each other. This could be because of the child's **egocentrism** (see page 182) at that age. However, babies clearly enjoy playing with older children and adults. It could be that these 'playmates' know how to interact with the baby in a way it understands, whereas another baby does not.

Parallel play

By the second year, the child shows more interest in others of its age. Two year olds may play side by side, occasionally watching the other, or offering a toy – this is called parallel play.

Co-operative play

By three years of age, most children will play with others, and the amount of interaction has increased. By four years old, children will play complex games together, where there will be several 'players' and the success of the game depends on each one's contribution. So a game of hospitals needs a patient, nurse and doctor for example.

FACTORS AFFECTING EARLY RELATIONSHIPS

At this age children are learning to depend on others and to co-operate – important qualities in the development of friendships. Research suggests that some factors are related to a child's ability to make good relationships.

One factor is the amount of opportunity the child has to play with others. Research has shown that parents who encourage other children to come to play and provide games involving co-operation also have more popular children. The value of a pre-school group has also been shown. This is one of the points made by **Lawrence Harper and Karen Huie** in their observational study of three and four year olds in a pre-school playgroup. They also discussed some other interesting results.

S

Harper and Huie (1985)

Sample Subjects were between 24 to 35 children aged three to five years enrolled in a University pre-school playgroup. The majority were from white middle-class families and all had English as a first language.

Results Results showed that the children's social play was affected by sex, age, familiarity with others and previous experience in playgroups. They found that newcomers to the group spent more time with adults, but social interactions between peers increased as newcomers became acquainted. It took between 5 and 12 weeks for newcomers to become accepted. They also found children of *all* ages showed parallel play and solitary play. They noted that interaction between peers was different from interaction with an adult.

Conclusions Harper and Huie proposed that parallel play took place at all ages because this was the way a newcomer or younger member became accepted as part of a group. This enabled them to learn how to play with the group, but was also something over which they had no control – often they were just 'tagging along' because they were frequently ignored by the group. The researchers also found that solitary play was *different* to social play and should not be seen as simply 'non-social' play.

What other factors seem to be important in children's relationships? Evidence from **attachment** studies shows that securely attached children tend to have better relationships with their peers in the early years. The child who is supportive, friendly and positive is more popular than the child who is aggressive or punitive.

S

By about four years old children appear to behave differently with *some* of the children they play with. We might say these are clear beginnings of friendship.

How do patterns of friendship change as children develop?

S

When could you say a friendship has developed? When people *consistently prefer* to spend time with each other rather than with others, then that is evidence of friendship. This *preference* can be seen in children as young as four years old. How do friendships develop from this point? Research suggests that there are three phases which can be loosely divided as – up to six years old, 7 to 13 years old and 14 or older. Let us look at how friendships differ in each of these phases.

FRIENDSHIP UP TO SIX YEARS OLD

S

Children in this first phase show friendship towards those they spend more time with. This may be because the children live next door to each other or see each other frequently at playgroup. Perhaps they both share the same play interests – dressing up games for example – and so spend more time together than with others. Even at three years old, the majority of children spend more time with others of the same sex.

They treat their friends differently, they show more positive and less negative behaviour to friends than non-friends, and try to respond to friends' needs. They may share sweets or toys.

FRIENDSHIPS BETWEEN SEVEN AND THIRTEEN YEARS OLD

S

By about seven years old, children's friendship patterns start to change. Whether this is because of their own development, or because at this age they enter a new social world – school – it is difficult to determine. Age and school are two variables which it is hard to separate if we want to determine the cause of changing friendship patterns.

One major change is that children's friends are now largely of the same sex. There is also a difference between boys' friendships and girls' friendships.

- **girls** tend to form smaller groups – perhaps two or three – and their relationships are more intimate, with more sharing of secrets and worries
- **boys** tend to form larger groups, and relationships with others in the group are usually looser

This division between boys and girls is one which children show very clearly in the school playground. Not only do they group themselves by sex, but there is a strong sense of group identity – each group having a territory and an activity which others are not supposed to disrupt. When this does happen, there is chasing, teasing and so on, but the children usually re-form to their single-sex activity.

When asked about friendship, children may say friends should help each other out. This usually means material help such as taking computer games to play at a friend's house or helping a friend to tidy her room so they can both go swimming. They say this is the kind of thing friends do.

Fig. 9.1 This child doesn't seem to be part of a group. Can you think of any reasons why?

FRIENDSHIPS FROM 14 YEARS OLD ONWARDS

From 14 years old onwards, a youngster's peer group becomes one of the most important influences on his or her behaviour and development. Research suggests that small group friendships move gradually to become part of a larger mixed-sex group, and gradually from this evolve boy-girl (heterosexual) relationships. Nevertheless, earlier same-sex friendship groupings may survive through this change, and emerge intact and more intimate. This may be because evidence shows that people understand friends can not provide *all* needs, and in order to survive friendships need to be flexible.

Friends now tend to give psychological as well as material support. For example, this might mean not laughing at someone, or giving them advice.

Robert Selman gave children a 'friendship' problem and asked what they would do. From their answers he proposed that there are levels of friendship.

Level 0 – friendship is based on whoever is closest, so it is unlikely to last
Level 1 – one-way assistance, if there is a problem you make it up by giving something to the other child
Level 2 – two-way co-operation. The child can understand different levels of intimacy (typical of pre-adolescents)
Level 3 – the relationship becomes more intimate and there is mutual sharing. It is alright if there are differences between you: this can deepen the friendship. Solutions to problems may need to be sensitively handled
Level 4 – the child realises that sometimes friendships cannot be changed to accommodate every individual. Sometimes a friendship has to end because an individual can only be expected to change – to accommodate others – to a certain degree.

Selman did not give ages – he said the stage of friendship depends on the child's experiences and how well the child is able to reflect on them.

C

To summarise then, some of the characteristics of friendships which we have looked at for different ages are closely related to **Piaget**'s **cognitive developmental** theory. To begin with the child's understanding is focused on visible, external features. Gradually it becomes able to understand more abstract and complex characteristics. At the same time it becomes able to understand another's point of view. In addition we have seen that the sex of friends and the size of the friendship group varies depending on the child's sex and age.

What attracts one person to another?

Psychologists who have studied the reasons why we may be attracted to others have suggested several important factors. Let us look at each of them in turn.

SIMILARITY

S

Similarity between two people is one reason why they become friends. Research has shown that people say they prefer others who are from similar backgrounds, are of similar ages, and with similar attitudes, similar beliefs, similar interests and so on. **Steven Duck** found that we are attracted to those who share our ideas and attitudes. He said this is because we have similar personal construct systems (see Chapter 19) – we see the world in the same way. Seeing the world in the same way makes it easier and more pleasurable to interact and this could be the reason for the initial attraction. It could also be that being with people who share our attitudes and values gives us social support for our own beliefs.

Theodore Newcomb followed the development of friendships between male students at the University of Michigan. First the students were given tests and questionnaires to complete. From the results of these some students were given rooms with others who were *similar* to them. Other students were given rooms with those who were *dissimilar*. Newcomb found that those who were similar liked each other better, and became better friends, than the dissimilar students.

In one series of studies **Donn Byrne** gave subjects questionnaires which affected their attitude to others. It appeared these others had similar attitudes to the subjects. Byrne then found that the more *similar* the subject thought the other was, the *more* the subject liked them. This has been found across age and educational groups and across cultures. It has important implications for reducing prejudice and aggression.

Not only do friendships tend to form between those who are similar, but it appears to be a major factor in more intimate relationships. Research has shown that partners who stayed together tended to be more similar in age, intelligence and physical attractiveness than partners who were dissimilar.

FAMILIARITY

S

Several studies have shown that we prefer someone who is familiar. This may be because we get to know them, or because we are physically close to them. **Newcomb** carried out another study at the University of Michigan one year later. In this he assigned roommates together in the basis of their *differences*. He found that they were still more likely to become friends, despite being different. This suggests that **familiarity** is more powerful than **similarity** as a predictor of friendships.

Robert Zajonc wanted to see if there was a correlation between a familiar face and a subject's liking of the face. He showed his subjects a lot of photographs of unknown faces. Subjects saw some of the photographs several times, so the faces became familiar. Subjects were then asked how much they thought they liked each of the people shown in the photographs. The results showed that the faces they liked most were the ones they had seen most, so there was a positive correlation between the number of times the photograph had been seen and the rating for liking.

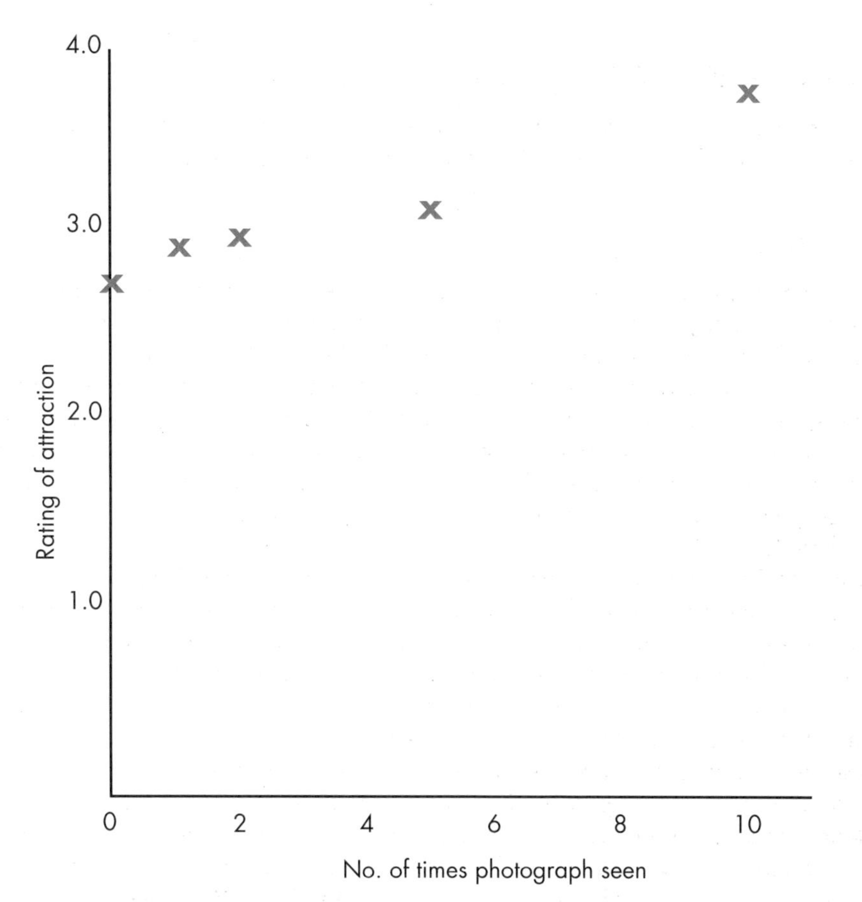

Fig. 9.2 Scattergram showing ratings of attraction and number of times photograph seen (from R. Zajonc 1968)

From this **Zajonc** concluded that people were liked more when they were familiar. Why should this be so? It could be that we feel more secure with something familiar. However, it is not so simple. It appears that dislike can also be increased by familiarity. One study had subjects wait in a laboratory with a female confederate. With some subjects she was pleasant, and others unpleasant, but she then sat down close to them. Results showed that subjects meeting the unpleasant confederate disliked her even more when she sat close. However those meeting the pleasant confederate liked her more when she sat close. So it seems that proximity can strengthen one's feelings.

PHYSICAL ATTRACTIVENESS

Physical attractiveness appears to be a crucial factor in the first stages of a relationship. One study involved a 'computer dance' for students. Students completed a personality assessment so they could be matched with a partner by computer. In fact partners were randomly selected. Each student was also rated by independent judges on their attractiveness. Afterwards students were asked what they thought of their partners. The researchers found that the most important reason for whether one person liked another was **physical attractiveness.** This was also the main reason why couples had continued to see each other after the dance. Personality and similarity did not come into it!

One reason why physical attractiveness may be so important is because of the **'halo effect'** (see Chapter 19). This means that we judge people who have a particular quality to have other, similar qualities. We think someone who is physically attractive is likely to have other attractive features – they will be pleasant, warm, intelligent and so on. These features make them desirable friends. However, research also shows that they are not necessarily thought to be more trustworthy or honest. In contrast **Alice Eagly** and her colleagues found that the more *additional* information a person has, the less physical attraction matters. Although this seems to conflict with the computer dance findings, the Eagly study was carried out 25 years later – perhaps people make less biased judgements now.

Another reason for the influence of physical attractiveness could be the **primacy** effect (see Chapter 19). This is when the *first* thing we notice has the strongest impact on our impression of the other person. We are likely to notice physical aspects before we notice personality aspects.

EXCHANGE THEORY

Attraction to someone else may be due to the fact that we see some benefits in a relationship with this person. This may seem a rather calculating way of viewing relationships, but some psychologists have proposed that we look at our relationships in terms of *rewards and costs*. They say we weigh up the rewards ('he is really good-looking'; 'she makes me laugh') and the costs ('I'll have to go out of my way to see her'; 'he talks about himself a lot') of entering a relationship. When the rewards are greater than the costs, then we are more likely to enter a relationship than when the costs are more than the rewards. This is called **exchange theory** and was devised by **J. Thibaut and H. Kelley**.

You can see how the ideas in exchange theory can be related to similarity and familiarity. For example, the *rewards* of a friendship with someone who is like you means you can do the things you like with someone else. If you were not similar, then you could spend a lot of time doing things you don't like – the costs would be too high for this relationship to get going!

Research also suggests that we prefer people who are competent but also sometimes those who are *incompetent*. How can we explain this? According to exchange theory ideas, we are attracted to those who are competent because they may be able to help us, or we can bask in their glory. However, if people are very competent this makes us feel inferior. So the costs outweigh the rewards of getting to know such people. Equally, when someone who is normally competent *fails*, this increases our liking for them. Social exchange theory might say that this is because it makes us feel *superior*.

Psychologists who have studied physical attraction have suggested that these principles of *rewards and costs* also apply in what is called the **matching hypothesis**. This hypothesis predicts that when we look for partners, we will estimate our own attractiveness and look for someone equally, or slightly more attractive than ourselves. We don't waste our time searching for a dream! If we did, the costs (time, disappointment, rejection) would be greater than the rewards (the chance of finding a dream).

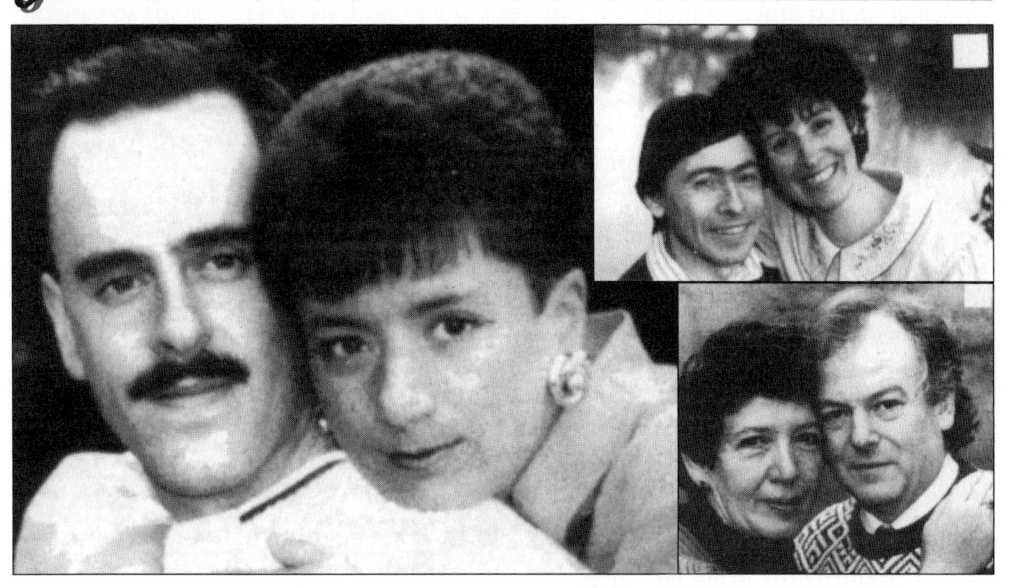

Fig. 9.3 Why do you think Dateline chose these photographs?

Similarly we are not attracted to someone much less attractive than ourselves, because although the costs may be fewer, the rewards are very small too. To check the matching hypothesis, look at the photographs in the 'Marriages' section of your local newspaper!

So similarity, familiarity and physical attractiveness influence who we are attracted to. Exchange theory suggests how we evaluate such features, and also whether or not relationships will develop.

How do other people affect our behaviour?

You may be surprised at how much other people can affect your behaviour. Do you feel different when you are part of a large group of people? If you have to do some work in class, does it matter whether you work alone or in groups of six? Although you may not be aware of it, a lot of the things we do, or don't do, are influenced by other people. We are going to look at four ways in which other people affect our behaviour – social loafing, social facilitation, social conformity and deindividuation.

SOCIAL LOAFING OR 'LET THE OTHERS TAKE THE STRAIN'

S

When people are working together in a group, each individual tends to reduce his or her own effort. This is true whether people are clapping or pulling in a tug of war. This is known as **social loafing** – putting less effort into something when others are doing it as well. So our behaviour is affected, even though no-one tries purposely to change it. **Bibb Latané** and his colleagues have done several studies which show this effect. For example subjects were asked to clap as loud as they could, sometimes alone, or with one other or in a group of four or six. Subjects wore headsets and blindfolds so they did not know what the others were doing, and the researchers monitored the amount of noise the subjects made. They found that the larger the group, the less effort the individual made. They concluded that people were making less effort because others were doing the same thing.

Why? **Latané** and his colleagues proposed that people feel they can hide in the group. In a later study, when subjects were told that their clapping would be monitored individually, there was no **social loafing**, seemingly because subjects knew their contribution could be evaluated. Another explanation relates to what we know about others in the group. Where other group members said they were going to work as hard as they could, then there was no social loafing effect, but when subjects thought others were going to loaf, so did they. Research which looked at social loafing in a more demanding situation found that it does not occur when the activity has consequences for the *subject*. When the task was thought to be of benefit to the subject's own college there was no social loafing, but there *was* loafing when it would only benefit a college far away.

SOCIAL FACILITATION OR 'STOP WATCHING ME!'

S

Social facilitation is the term used for the way that the presence of another person can affect how well we do something.

If you have ever done something alongside someone else, and started to do it faster (Swimming? Unloading a shopping trolley? Filling up your car?) this is called the **coaction effect**. It occurs when two or more people are doing similar tasks side by side. Although they are not competing against each other, they *behave* as though they are.

Research on the coaction effect in the 1930s also led to the finding that an *audience* also made people work quicker than when they were alone. This **audience effect** worked in two different ways though. If subjects were doing *easy* tasks they performed them faster when there was an audience. However when the task was *difficult* then subjects performed worse. How can this be explained?

It was 30 years before **Robert Zajonc** proposed that the **mere presence** of others is enough to affect our performance on a task. They have this effect because they cause *arousal*. When we experience this arousal it energises our behaviour. If we are doing something easy, we do it better, but if the task is complicated, then our arousal makes it harder for us.

Nickolas Cottrell on the other hand proposed that the presence of others makes us concerned about what they will think of us. He called this **evaluation apprehension**. If we are confident about our ability, then the awareness of being watched makes us do the task well. If we are not confident, then, whilst trying to do the task, we are constantly worrying about what those others will think if, or when, we make mistakes. This is particularly true if these others are experts.

Fig. 9.4 According to the coaction effect, these typists working in 1929 were performing better than if they had been working alone

One criticism of many of these studies was that they *already* contained an *evaluation* aspect because subjects knew they were taking part in an experiment. In an attempt to remove such evaluation, **Bernard Schmitt** and his colleagues had their subjects take part in an experiment without realising it. Subjects thought they were taking part in a 'sensory deprivation' study. This means subjects are unable to see, hear and so on. Before taking part, they were asked to enter various pieces of information about themselves on a computer. They entered their name and, later down the list, had to enter it again *backwards*. Each letter had to be interspersed with decreasing numbers. The computer automatically recorded how long each of these tasks took. Have you guessed that this bit is actually the *experiment*, and one of these was the easy task and the other the difficult one?

Schmitt put his subjects into one of three conditions. In one condition subjects entered the information with someone watching just behind them (evaluation apprehension). In another they were left alone to enter the information and were told to ring a bell when they had finished. In the third condition there was another person in the room who was facing away from them and who wore a blindfold and earphones (mere presence). Subjects were told that this other person was already part way through the 'sensory deprivation' experiment. Schmitt's results are shown in the table below.

Nature of task	Subject alone	Mere presence	Evaluation apprehension
Easy	15	10	7
Difficult	53	73	63

Table 9.1 Completion time in seconds (from B. Schmitt et al. 1985)

Schmitt concluded that performance on a well-learned task is improved by the mere presence of others, and even more when others can evaluate performance. In contrast, performance on a difficult task decreases in the presence of others.

SOCIAL CONFORMITY OR 'I DON'T WANT TO LOOK A FOOL'

S

Social conformity means following the actions or opinions of others rather than your own. An early study of social conformity was carried out by **Muzafer Sherif**. He was newly arrived in the USA in the 1930s, and was interested in how people conformed to the social norms he saw in this unfamiliar culture.

Sherif devised a study using the **autokinetic effect**. This effect occurs if you shine a dot of light in a darkened room – it *appears* to move, although in fact it is still. In one condition Sherif had some subjects see this light, and then they told him how far they thought it moved. After several trials he had them sit in small groups, see the light, and then each one told him how far they thought it had moved. In the second condition subjects saw the light when part of a group and *then* saw it as individuals. The results showed that in the first condition personal estimates moved towards the group norm. In the second condition a group norm became established and this shaped subjects' personal estimates in the second part of the experiment.

S

From these results **Sherif** concluded that this showed how much individuals will change their own judgements in order to conform to a group norm. However, **Solomon Asch** and others have said that because of the *uncertainty* that subjects felt, they were looking to others to gain *their* opinion. The study was of conformity to a group norm in conditions of uncertainty. More interestingly, said Asch, how likely is it that an individual would go *against* the group norm when there is no uncertainty?

So **Asch** did a long series of studies of **conformity** in groups of six to nine people. There was one subject, but all the rest were confederates. This means that they were *pretending* to be subjects, but were in fact told to give wrong answers on certain trials. Asch presented the group with lines of different lengths, and they had to judge which one was the same length as the test line.

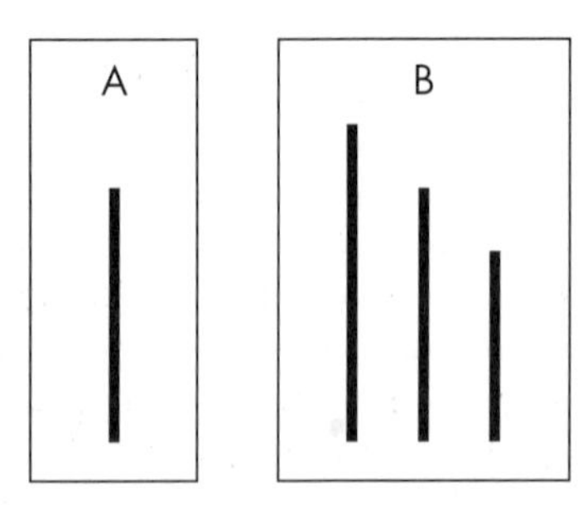

Fig. 9.5 An example of the test line and the comparison lines in the Asch experiment

On some occasions the confederates would all give a wrong answer, and Asch was interested to hear what the subject would do. Would he conform to the rest of the group, and give an answer which was clearly wrong, or would he say what he really thought?

In control trials there were virtually no mistakes in judging the correct line when subjects were tested alone. But when in a group, **Asch** found that 25 per cent of his subjects conformed to the rest of the group on *most* of the occasions when the group was wrong. But overall, 75 per cent of his subjects conformed to the 'wrong' answer at least *once*. These results clearly show the effect of **conformity.**

When asked afterwards, conforming subjects had said things like 'I didn't want to spoil the experiment', 'I didn't want to let the others down'. In further experiments **Asch** arranged for the lines to be more similar or for one of the confederates to give a right answer. In these cases there was much less conforming. However, if this confederate only gave the right answer on early trials, but later gave wrong answers along with the rest of the group, the *subject* then reverted to giving wrong answers too. In other words subjects again conformed with the group norm.

Fig. 9.6 The subject – Number 6 – gives his estimate after each of the five men before him, then justifies his answer (from S. Asch 1958)

One of the criticisms of **Asch**'s study was the artificial nature of the experiment. For example, none of the confederates protested when the subject gave a different answer to theirs. The study was repeated by another psychologist, but in this case there was only *one* confederate. Everyone else was a subject so of course they all gave the right answers. However, on some trials the confederate gave a *wrong* answer. As soon as this happened, the rest of the group reacted to the wrong answer, saying 'You must be joking', 'Can you see properly?' and so on. This was a natural response to what they were hearing, and this shows how *artificial* Asch's group was. The criticism is that this artificiality would have strengthened the sense of an 'experiment' and encouraged the subject to support it. In other words, the demand characteristics might have been apparent to subjects.

It was acknowledged that subjects were more likely to conform when face-to-face with others. **Richard Crutchfield** devised a series of experiments in which subjects sat in booths, with a row of lights in front of them. Crutchfield manipulated the lights to give the impression that they represented how *others* who were being asked the same question had responded. He asked many different questions – some of them easy to answer correctly, for example 'the life expectancy of American males is only about 25 years – true or false?' Others were more complicated. Nevertheless he also found on average about one third conformity, and this was much less when subjects were questioned individually. **Crutchfield** also found a wide difference in conformity between his subjects – some were very conforming, and others very independent. These differences are not apparent when we look at 'average' scores.

What can we conclude from these studies of conformity? One suggestion is that subjects conform to the views of others when they are uncertain; the other is that they conform when they want to be part of the group. Let us compare these two explanations.

Normative influence

Normative influence occurs when people want to gain the approval or acceptance of others in the group. To do this, they conform to the group's view, or the group **norms**. However, they may *say* one thing but *believe* another. This is **compliance** – when you change what you *say* or *do* to conform to group norms, but you do *not* change your views. Some of Crutchfield's studies and most of Asch's studies would be examples of **normative** influence.

S

Informational influence

Informational influence occurs when individuals are uncertain and so look to others for their views. We do this often: it is an important way of finding out about the world. If the views we obtain are convincing enough, then we will adopt those views. This means we will express them and *also* believe them. This is sometimes called **internalisation**. Sherif's study is an example of **informational** influence, as are the studies by Asch and by Crutchfield when the information is ambiguous.

DEINDIVIDUATION OR 'HERE WE GO, HERE WE GO, HERE WE GO...'

S

Individuals are **deindividuated** when they become less aware of themselves and have less control over their own behaviour. How does deindividuation come about? **E. Diener** has proposed that four factors lead to reduced self-awareness. This in turn leads to changes which may affect behaviour. If we put all this in a diagram it might be clearer (see Fig. 9.7).

As you can see, some of the causes result from being part of a crowd. The effect of *one* of these factors – anonymity – was tested by **Philip Zimbardo**. He had female subjects, in groups of four, give 'electric shocks' to his confederates. In one condition the women wore identical coats and hoods so they were anonymous. In the other condition, the women wore their own clothes, had name tags identifying them and spoke to each other using their own names. Zimbardo found the anonymous women gave twice as many shocks as the 'individuated' ones.

However, the experiment was criticised because the 'anonymous' women looked like members of the Ku Klux Klan. Other researchers repeated the experiment but added

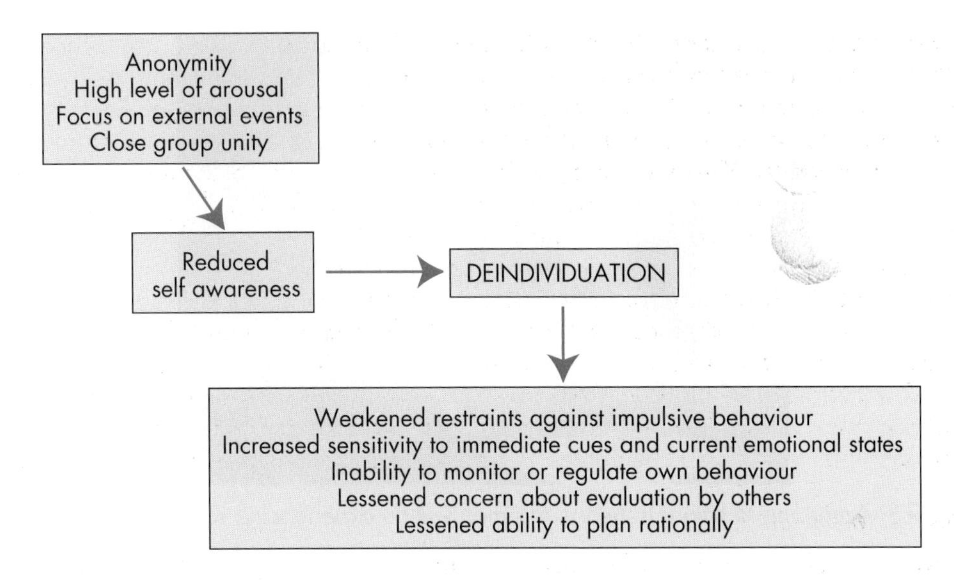

Fig. 9.7 The causes and results of deindividuation (from E. Diener 1979)

another group who wore nurses' uniforms. The results were that the 'nurses' gave *fewer* shocks than the individuals, and the 'Ku Klux Klan' (a group associated with violence) only slightly more. This suggests that anonymity is not a major factor in deindividuation, and also that **roles** have a powerful effect on behaviour.

So **deindividuation** has been proposed as an explanation for the aggressive or destructive behaviour of individuals when part of a crowd – reduced self-awareness leads to deindividuation and then anti-social acts. An alternative is that people in groups follow **group norms**, and are therefore more likely to do what others do. The way *others* in the group behave reinforces their own actions. According to this view, group behaviour reinforces whatever the group norms are – if they are aggressive then aggression will increase, if they are peaceful, then peaceful behaviour will be maintained.

Putting the theories together

One theory which incorporates several of these findings about the way others influence our behaviour is **Social Impact** theory. It was proposed by **Bibb Latané**, who said that other people influenced us for a variety of reasons – how important they are to us (social facilitation) or how many there are of them (social loafing). He used a light bulb to explain this. The effect others have on us is like the effect a light bulb has in lighting an object. Here is Latané's explanation:

- The more *bulbs* there are, the greater the light. So the more 'others' there are, the more impact on our behaviour they have. However, just as shining *two* light bulbs on an object will illuminate it much better than one, so two others will have much more influence than one. *However*, if you have 20 bulbs shining, the addition of one more makes little difference to the amount of light, so the addition of one more person makes little difference if there are already 20. We saw this in Asch's conformity studies and Latané's social loafing work.

Fig. 9.8 According to Latané's theory, this man will be experiencing some social impact

- The *closer* the bulbs are, the greater the light. This means that the closer in time or space that 'others' are, the more likely they are to affect our behaviour. For example, in deindividuation the others are close: this is one thing which gives us a sense of group or crowd. Therefore our behaviour is more likely to conform to the crowd norms. The presence of someone right next to us when we are doing a complicated task will have greater influence than if they were at the other side of the room.
- The *brighter* the bulbs are, the greater the light. This refers to how *important* the 'others' are to us. If we want their approval (as in normative influence) or if they are particularly able to evaluate our performance (as experts are in studies of social facilitation), then the more impact they will have on our behaviour.

Social impact theory shows the influence which others have on our behaviour. However, it does not tell us *how* this influence works. Psychologists have found this a difficult question to answer, as we have seen in the debate about social facilitation.

Further Reading

Bee H (1992) *The Developing Child* (6th ed), New York, Harper Collins
Deaux K, Dane F and Wrightsman L (1993) *Social Psychology in the 90s* (6th ed), Pacific Grove, Brooks/Cole

EXERCISES

1. Why did Harper and Huie use an observational study?
2. What research method did Selman use? Explain your answer.
3. Why was a control trial used in the Asch experiment?
4. Show the scores on the scattergram of Zajonc's results in the form of a table.
5. In Schmitt's study, why did he draw these conclusions?
6. Imagine three girls – 3, 9 and 15 years old. Give two characteristics of each of their friendships.
7. Describe the results and conclusions of two studies which show that other people influence our behaviour.

Chapter 10
Prejudice

IN THIS CHAPTER WE ARE GOING TO LOOK AT WHY AND HOW PEOPLE DEVELOP NEGATIVE ATTITUDES TO OTHERS, OFTEN WITHOUT KNOWING THEM. THIS NEGATIVE ATTITUDE IS CALLED PREJUDICE AND WE WILL ALSO CONSIDER HOW PREJUDICE AFFECTS OUR BEHAVIOUR AS WELL AS WHETHER IT IS POSSIBLE TO REDUCE PREJUDICE.

What is prejudice and why is it important?

Prejudice is an extreme attitude for or against a group or an individual because he or she is a member of that group. However, in psychology it has largely been taken to mean an attitude *against* a group. Prejudice is what we think we *know* of someone and how we *feel* about them too.

Prejudice is important because our behaviour is often influenced by our attitudes. So if we have a hostile attitude to others, we are likely to treat them badly. This is **discriminating** against them – which is unjust and sometimes illegal. We will start by examining where stereotypes and prejudice come from. There are several explanations and we will look at them under three headings: psychodynamic, cognitive-informational, and social learning.

Psychodynamic explanations of prejudice

Psychodynamic ideas focus on the emotional and motivational reasons for prejudice. We will look at two explanations – one is that it is a due to **personality type** and the other that it is due to **scapegoating**.

THE AUTHORITARIAN PERSONALITY

The notion that **prejudice** can be due to a personality type was proposed by **T. Adorno** in 1950. He was researching to find an explanation for the behaviour of Nazi soldiers in World War II. He and his colleagues proposed that a child brought up with excessive discipline could become very obedient to those in authority, and would tend to view things in rigid terms of right or wrong. They called this the **authoritarian personality**. However this harsh discipline would create aggression which could not

I

be directed at the parents. In the authoritarian personality, because those with more power are feared, this hostility is aimed at others who are seen as weaker. These are usually members of groups who have lower social status.

Research has suggested that there is a relationship between the authoritarian personality and prejudice. However, this does not explain why large groups of people are prejudiced nor does it explain *which* weaker groups we might be prejudiced against. The second psychodynamic explanation does.

SCAPEGOATING

I

The process of blaming others for your own problems is called **scapegoating**. It is based on the idea that there are *always* frustrations in living, and these can build up in some people. Circumstances such as unemployment or poor housing may add to these frustrations. **Gordon Allport** proposed that this frustration leads to hostile feelings which have to be released. You can see the relationship between this and the **frustration-aggression hypothesis** (see Chapter 11 on Aggression). Often this hostility and aggression cannot be directed at the causes, because they are many and complicated. Instead it is displaced on to those who are less powerful. So the **defence mechanism** of **displacement** is used as an outlet for frustration.

There is evidence that those who feel most threatened during an economic recession show an increase in prejudice against particular groups. In the 1930s Adolf Hitler blamed Germany's economic problems on the Jews – they became the **scapegoats**. He was actively encouraging scapegoating as a way of turning people against the Jews.

Cognitive-information explanations of stereotyping and prejudice

These explanations relate to the way in which people process information. As we shall see, people tend to *distort* information in order to process it. Two ways in which people process information about others are by **categorising** and by **stereotyping**.

CATEGORISATION

C

Research has shown that when we put things into groups (for example lines or shapes or attitudes), we exaggerate the differences *between* the groups and exaggerate the similarities *within* them. This is **categorisation** and is one of the *basic* cognitive tendencies. **Henri Tajfel** pointed out that we also categorise people, but in a particular way. We divide them into two basic groups – the in-group (of which we are a member) and the out-group – the rest. Here again, we exaggerate the differences between the in-group and the out-group. We also think that *within* each group, the members are more alike than they really are. Tajfel called this **social categorisation** and proposed that just the *knowledge* of another group is enough to create this in-group/out-group effect.

Why is this important? **Tajfel** showed that not only do we categorise people but we *favour* the in-group over the out-group. In a series of experiments, Tajfel and his colleagues assigned subjects to groups by the toss of a coin, so it was clear to them that their membership of a particular group was *only* due to the toss of a coin. Results showed that when the subjects were asked to allocate points, they largely favoured members of their own group.

This preference for in-group members has been produced in many other experiments, and results show that we think members of the out-group are less attractive, less intelligent, less able and so on. When our group fails it is due to bad luck, when the other group fails it is because they are not very good. In other words we are **prejudiced** towards them because we have a *negative* attitude. This research also shows that we *treat* members of our in-group better than the out-group, in other words we **discriminate** against the out-group.

Tajfel says our self-esteem is closely related to the groups we belong to – our psychology class, football team, neighbourhood and so on. By increasing the status of *our* group, our self-esteem is increased. The *more* we need to raise our self-esteem, the more we are likely to put down the out-group. Our attitude to them will be more negative – in other words we will be more prejudiced.

STEREOTYPING

How do we identify these 'other groups'. We do it by **stereotyping**. A stereotype is a **schema** (a mental framework) for an identifiable group of people. We might assume that, for example, old people are forgetful, hard of hearing and talk about the past a lot. This is our stereotype for old people and it contains information about their appearance, characteristics and behaviour. When we see an old person, our stereotype is automatically triggered. The point is, we might be wrong!

Fig.10.1 Does this information fit your stereotype of an old person?

In this example of a stereotype *age* is the trigger, but the identifying feature might be sex, race, physical disablement, religion, sexual orientation, body size and so on.

C

We know that the stereotype is a **schema**, but let's check what a schema is and does. It is a mental framework which we have about something or someone, and it is based on experience. The schema is a way of organising information, and we use it to filter *new* information we come across. The point about the schema is that it *directs* our attention to information which fits in to our schema: we notice what we expect to notice. We also 'remember' things which we did not see, but which are part of our schema. How does this relate to stereotyping?

A **stereotype** is a schema for a group of people – such as women, Italians, judges, social workers, travellers, gays. When we see a member of a group for which we have a stereotype, we assume they have the traits we associate with that stereotype. This is an example of bias – we do not see people as they *are*, but through a 'lens' which changes what we see. The 'lens' is the stereotype.

In one investigation of stereotyping, subjects watched a video of two people having a discussion. Subjects had to classify the behaviour they saw, which included one person pushing the other. The psychologists manipulated the race of the actors – either two white people, two black people, or black and white. Subjects who saw the black actor doing the shoving rated his behaviour as more violent compared with subjects who saw the white actor doing the shoving. These results show that subjects interpreted the behaviour they saw on the basis of the actor's *race*. They also show how stereotyping filters out information we receive.

If our stereotype has a negative feature (for example that a group is aggressive or is lazy) then we will look for negative information about them, and tend to ignore the positive. This stereotype may lead us to have negative *feelings* about them too (we feel unease, fear, resentment, dislike). In other words, we are **prejudiced**.

Stereotyping reflects our need to be consistent. It is our effort to process the maximum amount of information with minimal cognitive effort. One reason we discount non-confirming evidence is because we are reluctant to make the necessary effort – we are 'cognitive misers'. This has important implications for how we can change **stereotypes**.

C

To summarise then, cognitive-informational explanations highlight the human tendency to categorise and to stereotype. Both processes encourage the creation and maintenance of negative attitudes to others which may in turn be linked with negative feelings. This is the cognitive-informational basis of prejudice.

We have established how we process information about others, but where does this information come from? How do we learn what the key features of a group are supposed to be? It comes from experience – either direct experience with a member of another group, or more often, through what we hear or see around us. Now we need to turn to social learning explanations of stereotyping and prejudice.

Social learning explanations of stereotyping and prejudice

L

The **social learning** explanation says that prejudice is learned, as other attitudes are. Social learning theory says children learn by observing models, in particular those who are seen as nurturing, powerful and similar. So parents, older family members, teachers, friends, sports and music personalities, TV characters and so on will have considerable influence on a child's attitude to others.

Alfred Davey and his colleagues looked at **prejudice** and **discrimination** in England. They were interested in children's views of themselves, the ethnic group to which they belonged, and other ethnic groups. They gave 7 to 11 year old children (of either white, Asian or West Indian parentage) various tests. Results showed that half of the West Indian and Asian children wanted to be white, suggesting they were aware that whites got better treatment. This preference did not seem to be related to where they lived, or what the ethnic mix of their school was.

Davey also surveyed parents of these children to assess *their* attitudes. Some details from this part of the research are given below.

Davey *et al.* (1983)

Aim of study The aim was to determine parents' attitudes and behaviours towards their childrens' experience of various ethnic groups.

Method A survey was used employing face-to-face interviews.

Sample The sample comprised parents of the children taking part in the study – 256 of the children were of white, 128 of West Indian and 128 of Asian parentage.

Materials The survey comprised open-ended questions. Initial questions were of a general nature relating to the child's school and friends, later questions related to attitudes to other ethnic groups. A sample of the questions is shown below:

6 What do you think of your child's school?
11 Are there any children you don't like your child to play with? Why is that?
18 Some people think it's a good thing that children of different races should be in the same school. What do you think?
25 Suppose you heard your child call a white/black child (opposite colour to parent) names, what would you say to him/her?

Procedure Interviewers were from the same ethnic group and spoke the same language as those being interviewed. Questions were linked by informal comments, so that the interview was more like a natural conversation. All parents received standardised instructions. 'I'm ...(researcher's name). I'm connected with the study that ...(child's name) took part in at school, about children growing up and their ideas. Do you mind if I take notes? You do understand that this is completely confidential. We're not using anyone's names. We just want to compare the ideas of parents in London and Yorkshire about children growing up.'

Davey classified those who showed strong in-group favouritism and out-group hostility as being ethnocentric. Someone who is ethnocentric views the world through his or her own ethnic perspective, all other groups are assessed as inferior to one's own. Davey and his colleagues found that there was no strong link between the intergroup attitudes expressed by children and those expressed by their parents. However there *was* a strong link between parents who were *very* ethnocentric and their children's high ethnocentrism. Equally, parents who were *very* low in ethnocentrism tended to have children who were low also. Many parents felt the school had an important role in educating children about *other* religions and cultures. The results show a correlation between strongly held attitudes and behaviour in parent and in child. Social learning theory would explain the correlation by saying the child has learned this through modelling the parent's behaviour.

L

The child's natural tendency to categorise is strengthened by the categorising it sees and hears around it. A child may observe models who say – 'typical woman'; 'they're all the same, these trade unions'; 'I blame the single mothers'. Such models *emphasise* a group label and provide information about the *content* of a **stereotype**.

According to social learning theory, the individual's development occurs through exposure to a wide variety of models and those models will be more or less important to the child at various times in that child's development. However, once a **stereotype** is established, it will *filter out* inconsistent information. Therefore the information from later models may have little impact and the stereotype will be unlikely to change. This has important implications when we look at trying to reduce prejudice.

Not only do children learn the content of stereotypes from models but models provide information about how they *feel* towards others. This is one way in which children learn **prejudice**. Research suggests that at a fairly young age children will make prejudiced statements about others, although their behaviour shows no discrimination.

Social learning theorists propose that initially children will observe and model the behaviour of others, but gradually, through being selective about *where* they imitate behaviour, and how they are reinforced, they come to **internalise** what they see and hear. So the stereotypes and prejudice become internalised.

An example of how stereotypes and prejudice can be created and changed by modelling also highlights the influence of the **media**. During World War II, American government propaganda shaped American attitudes to Japanese and Germans as negative, and towards Russians (who were allies) as positive – hardworking and so on. After the war as the Americans and the Russians became enemies, the propaganda changed and the Russians were portrayed in a negative way – as cruel for example. Research showed that the propaganda worked because American attitudes towards Russians became much more negative.

S

We could put this another way – the American social norm towards Russians changed. It became acceptable, even proof of being a good American, to put the Russians down. Several psychologists have proposed that social norms are far more important in prejudice and discrimination than individual causes. For example, an American researcher studied black and white coal miners in West Virginia in the early 1950s. He found that there was complete integration below the ground (at work) and almost complete segregation above ground (at play). Surely if one group is prejudiced against another, then behaviour should be consistent? The fact that it varied like this suggests that one set of social norms operated below ground – perhaps because all the miners shared a common experience. The social norms operating *above* ground were those of the wider society in which these men lived.

L

What is important for us here is that children *learn* social norms through observational learning and through gaining approval for speaking and acting in accordance with social norms. They learn that different norms apply in different situations. This approval may come from adults and from other children. Thus the norms are perpetuated. In the next section we will look at a study by **Muzafer Sherif** which investigated the creation and effect of group norms.

So, we have looked at several explanations for prejudice, some of which say prejudice is due to the individual's own emotional needs and others which suggest it is more to do with the lazy or thoughtless way in which we view our world or the degree to which we are influenced by others.

Fig. 10.2 Do Bernie Grant and Dianne Abbott fit your stereotype of an MP?

What is the difference between prejudice and discrimination?

Prejudice is the negative attitude we hold towards someone because they belong to a particular group and **discrimination** is the way we *behave* towards someone. When we discriminate against a group, we treat the members of one group less well than our own group. Discriminatory behaviour can include keeping a distance, ignoring, preferring others, using an unfriendly tone of voice, harassing, speaking badly of, or towards, others, attacking and even killing. We may discriminate against someone because we are prejudiced against them. However, the link may not be quite as direct as it seems. Let us see why.

One study which suggests a weak link between prejudice (attitude) and discrimination (behaviour) was carried out in the USA by LaPiere in the early 1930s. **LaPiere** toured the USA with a Chinese couple, visiting 250 hotels, restaurants and similar places. Despite **prejudice** against the Chinese at this time, they were only turned away from one establishment. At the end of the trip each of the establishments was sent a questionnaire asking, amongst other things, whether it would accept Chinese customers. Over 90 per cent of the returned questionnaires said they would not. Psychologists suggest that an attitude is more likely to determine behaviour when:

- we feel strongly about it – for example if we are very prejudiced
- it relates directly to us – for example if it is necessary for our self-esteem
- it is easily accessible – it will be if we stereotype frequently
- situational pressures allow us to express it – for example if the social norms or the roles we are playing allow us to express our attitude

S

Thomas Pettigrew has suggested that different **social norms** exist in different settings, as we saw with the miners in West Virginia. He found that when *behaviour* was forced to change – because of anti-discrimination laws – then people's *attitudes* changed. He found that after a new anti-discrimination law 60 per cent of people became more positive, that is, the **group norms** changed. So prejudice and discrimination are reflected in social norms, and they change as social norms change.

An explanation for the reason why *behaviour* may change *attitudes* comes from **Daryl Bem's self-perception theory**. He says that it is difficult for us to know what we think or feel, so we look at our own *behaviour* to find out what we *really* think. According to this view then, our behaviour will tell us whether or not we are prejudiced.

So the link between **prejudice** and **discrimination** is not direct. We may be prejudiced, but not feel able to show it. On the other hand, we may not be very prejudiced, but will appear to be when in a group which is prejudiced. Alternatively, we may not know what we think until we behave in a particular way.

How can prejudice and discrimination be reduced?

Psychologists have studied many ways of reducing **prejudice.** Success depends on the *cause* of prejudice and discrimination in the first place. For example, it has been argued that those with the **authoritarian personality** are unlikely to change their attitudes because these are necessary to maintain each individual's self-esteem. However, this only applies to a few people, and psychologists have found techniques with others which have had some success. These include increasing contact between members of groups, co-operation, challenging stereotypes, changing social norms and changing the self-fulfilling prophecy. Let us look at them in some detail.

INCREASING CONTACT

C

This means increasing the opportunity for **contact** between the prejudiced and those who experience prejudice. More contact should give people more information about others, and thus break down **stereotypes** and reduce generalisations about members of the out-group. However research has shown that it is not simply enough to bring people together. One study arranged for very prejudiced whites to work with blacks on a series of joint tasks. Results showed that six months later 40 per cent of the participants were much less prejudiced, 40 per cent had not changed their attitudes and 20 per cent had become more prejudiced.

A major area of research has been in schools in the United States, where some schools were segregated. In the 1960s the attempts to desegregate them, and therefore have black and white students together, were not as successful as was hoped. A possible explanation comes from a series of studies by **Muzafer Sherif** and his associates. In what is known as the **Robbers' Cave** experiment, the researchers changed the relations between two groups. What happened as a result of changing intergroup relations? (See page 100.)

Sherif concluded that where groups are in *conflict,* prejudice and discrimination are more likely to result. In contrast, where there is *co-operation* between groups, there is less likely to be **prejudice** and **discrimination.** Research in other real life settings, such as industry, have produced similar results. One reason for the failure to reduce prejudice and discrimination by mixing black and white students could be the classroom environment. This is a competitive environment, and so the differences between groups will be exaggerated and relationships will tend to be hostile. How can we get around this problem?

S

CO-OPERATION

In the **Robbers' Cave** study prejudice and discrimination were almost eliminated when the boys worked on joint tasks which were important to them. **E. Aronson** and his colleagues used this idea of **co-operation** when they were called in by a desegregated Texas school to devise some ways of reducing prejudice between whites and blacks. They developed the **jigsaw technique**. This requires small groups of racially mixed students, each of which has to work on a *part* of a lesson. In order for the whole class to cover *all* the material, the individuals in the groups have to work together first, and then they have to communicate their group work to the rest of the class.

When **Aronson** evaluated the strategy he found increased co-operation, self-esteem and academic performance. He also noted more positive perceptions of those of the other racial group. Although **prejudice** and **discrimination** were reduced in the classroom, these new perceptions were *not* necessarily applied to members of the racial group as a whole. It appears then that these students saw each other as *exceptions* to the **stereotypes,** but the stereotypes themselves did not change very much. Other research supports these findings, that although co-operation strategies *can* reduce prejudice, the individual may not generalise these new attitudes to others when they are in a *different* setting. This may be because social norms are different in the other setting.

S

There is another reason why co-operation may not work. Research suggests that if a mixed group *fails* in their task, then the blame may fall on the victims of prejudice within the group. Thus the task must be fairly easy to accomplish, or at least be difficult to label as a 'failure', so that the group experience success.

So what do co-operation strategies tell us? In principle they *can work*. One explanation why the **Robbers' Cave** study appeared to be so successful was because the *differences* between the boys was artificially created. They were all basically very similar. Real life is different – there are *physical* differences between people which make them easy to categorise; there may be social norms *supporting* prejudice; there may be differences in social status between groups. These factors also need to be tackled.

Sherif *et al.* (1961)

Aim of study The aim of the study was to show changes in behaviour as a result of changes in intergroup relationships.

Type of study This was a longitudinal study taking place over three weeks

Method This was a field experiment using observational methods

Study design This was a matched subjects design of study.

Sample The sample was 22 middle-class white boys, aged 12 years. They were attending a summer camp. They were not known to each other and all were psychologically well-adjusted from stable homes. The participants were matched in pairs as closely as possible for physical and psychological characteristics. One of each pair was assigned to each group.

Procedure There were four stages in the experiment. Once the boys were assigned to a group, normal summer camp activities took place. Camp counsellors were in fact trained researchers, who observed the boys' behaviour throughout the study. After several days, the second stage started when a series of intergroup contests was announced by the counsellors. The group winning the series would get a silver cup, and each boy would get a penknife. The third stage began when the contests ended. The fourth stage started with the introduction of jobs which required *all* the boys to co-operate.

Results Observers found that in the first stage both groups quickly established their own cultures. They named themselves the 'Rattlers' and the 'Eagles' and developed group norms. There was a little in-group favouritism at the expense of the out-group. But hostility quickly arose in the second stage, with competition. Groups derided and attacked each other. Each group became more united, and the more aggressive boys became leaders. When the contests were over, there was still a lot of prejudice and discrimination towards the others. It was not until the fourth stage that this changed. When the boys *had* to co-operate, for example to pull a truck back to camp in order to get there in time for lunch, the intergroup hostility disappeared.

Conclusions Sherif and his colleagues concluded that:

1 groups develop group norms
2 conflict between groups leads to prejudice and discrimination towards the out-group and increases unity of the in-group
3 co-operation between groups reduces prejudice and discrimination

CHALLENGING STEREOTYPES

C

If parents and educators *discourage* the formation of **stereotypes** then the 'lens' through which we gain information will be weaker. **Sandra Bem** has shown the effect a stereotype can have in her work on gender schemas (see Chapter 14). She points out that parents have an important role in *counteracting* stereotypes and in pointing out to children when stereotypes are being portrayed in the media. This kind of influence could make a child's thinking more *flexible* and less stereotypical.

If **stereotypes** are challenged, then they should start to break down. However, we have already seen how resistant stereotypes are. Research suggests that challenging information should be *strong* in order to change a stereotype.

S

For example, it was thought that individuals must be of equal status in their job, education or social background in order to change stereotypes. But research suggests that when members of two groups are in contact, it is invariably the *higher status* members who dominate – they tend to initiate things, be listened to by others, and their views are more likely to be followed. Therefore, to have members of equal status is still not enough to 'tip the balance'. It is necessary to have *higher status* members of the out-group (for example people with better jobs or better skills) in order to change stereotypes.

L

Albert Bandura noted the impact of the **mass media** on attitudes and behaviour. By mass media we mean television, radio, films, videos, books, comics, computer games and so on. Models are presented through the media – in advertisements, as programme presenters, film or pop stars, sports people, characters in books or cartoons. These are all potential models, so what they do and say can have a considerable influence on **prejudice** and **discrimination.** If models are presented in **stereotypical** ways, the stereotypes are reinforced. If they are presented *non-stereotypically*, then there is more chance that the viewer or reader will change their stereotype (Fig. 10.3).

If you remember that prejudice and discrimination are associated with *negative* feelings and behaviour, then another way in which the media can be influential is to present *positive* images. This might mean showing black people who have achieved success or physically disabled people who are active.

CHANGING SOCIAL NORMS

S

Social norms can be affected *officially* – by making laws, and *unofficially* – by changing what is considered acceptable or appropriate behaviour. We saw from **Thomas Pettigrew**'s study that people's attitude became more positive as a result of anti-discrimination laws. If the law makes it illegal to discriminate, then people's behaviour will change. According to **self-perception theory**, this will lead to an attitude change as well. However, Pettigrew's research also shows that *forcing* people to change will actually *strengthen* some people's prejudice and discrimination.

A study carried out by **Teun van Dijk** in Holland and America looked at how racism is communicated between whites. Racism is prejudice based on race. He produced evidence to show that, although the social norm may be not to *show* racism, within various subgroups (such as the family, in the workplace, amongst neighbours) racist talk and behaviour was acceptable. van Dijk's point is that challenging racism at the *official* level is only part of the solution. Racism, or indeed any form of prejudice and discrimination, needs to be tackled at the *unofficial* level as well.

Northern Ireland's Protestants are commonly seen as stubborn, negative and puritanical. A four-part series examines this stereotype and tries to discover the forces and influences that help to determine how Protestants react and think.

Fig. 10.3 Does this description suggest the radio programme will try to break down or reinforce this stereotype?

S

At the unofficial level this means the *individual* refusing to conform to social norms if they permit prejudice or discrimination. It also means challenging *others* when they conform to these norms.

CHANGING THE SELF-FULFILLING PROPHECY

The **self-fulfilling prophecy** can have a profound effect on an individual's behaviour (see Chapter 15). When we have particular expectations of someone, we treat them in a particular way. The way they respond to this may fulfil our initial expectations, and so prove we are right.

C. Word and colleagues devised a study which showed this very vividly. White college students played the role of interviewers of either black or white 'applicants'. These applicants were confederates of the experimenters. The behaviour of the interviewers was observed and was found to be less friendly towards black 'applicants'. The white interviewers also sat further away and their interviews were shorter. In a second stage, *white* confederates were trained to do interviews using the *same* discriminatory behaviour as the previous subjects. Once trained, they 'interviewed' *white* applicants. Judges watched videos of the white applicants' behaviour to rate them on ability and performance. The researchers found that those with the lowest ratings were the applicants who had received the discriminatory treatment. They concluded that poor performance was due to discriminatory treatment, not to any genuine lack of ability.

What can this tell us about reducing **prejudice** and **discrimination?** On the one hand it highlights behaviours which we may not be aware of. It may be illegal openly to discriminate, but you can still show discrimination by, for example, non-verbal behaviour.

It also highlights the behaviour of those who experience discrimination. One way of stopping this **self-fulfilling prophecy** from coming true is *not* to respond as expected. For example, the Black Power, feminist and gay rights movements have all worked to increase the assertiveness and self-confidence of their members. This helps them to avoid falling in to the self-fulfilling prophecy trap. It also forces discriminators to change their expectations and perhaps their behaviour.

Finally then, prejudice is complex and if it serves to support the individual's sense of self-esteem or sense of belonging to a group, then to change the attitude means to threaten the individual – no wonder attitudes can be hard to change! Nevertheless, where prejudice is more to do with cognitive laziness, not really noticing people as indi-

Fig. 10.4 When members of minority groups increase their self-confidence they are more able to challenge stereotypical expectations

viduals and conforming to opinions and behaviours we see about us, then prejudice and discrimination *can* change. The responsibility of those in positions of influence to behave in non-discriminatory ways is also of crucial importance both for changing attitudes and as models for others.

Further Reading

Deaux K, Dane F and Wrightsman L (1993) *Social Psychology in the 90s* (6th ed), Pacific Grove, Brooks/Cole

EXERCISES

1. What are the weaknesses of using questionnaires in research? Relate your answer to the LaPiere study.
2. Why were the participants in Sherif's study matched?
3. Define stereotyping, prejudice and discrimination.
4. Choose any two explanations for the origins of prejudice and describe two ways in which they differ.
5. If someone in a group shows prejudice, how could you change their attitude?
6. Describe how having a social role (such as teacher, parent, neighbour) might prevent someone from expressing prejudice.

Chapter 11

Aggression

IN THIS CHAPTER WE ARE GOING TO LOOK AT AGGRESSION – WHAT IT IS AND WHERE IT COMES FROM. THEN WE CONSIDER THE WAY THAT PARENTS MIGHT AFFECT A CHILD'S LEVELS OF AGGRESSION AND FINALLY HOW AGGRESSION CAN BE REDUCED.

What is aggression?

Although there is no agreed definition, **aggression** is generally considered to be behaviour which harms, or intends to harm, another. Psychologists have distinguished between **hostile** aggression (intending to harm someone) and **instrumental** aggression (harming someone for a reason, such as because they are attacking you) as well as between **physical** aggression and **verbal** aggression.

We will look at several theories which attempt to explain where aggression comes from. You will see that some stress the idea that aggression is innate, and others that it is learned. In other words aggression is another topic in the nature or nurture debate.

Ethological explanations for aggression

Ethology is the study of animals in their natural environment and ethologists are interested in how animal behaviours increase their chances of survival and the reproduction of their species. According to the ethological explanation, **aggression** protects a species. Not only does it enable members of a species to kill other species for food, but it ensures their own survival. For example, female animals are aggressive when protecting their young, young males will fight to gain a mate. They will also fight to gain and protect territory, which ensures that others disperse to find new food supplies which they, in turn, will then fight to protect.

Konrad Lorenz, a well-known ethologist, said animals did not kill their own species. He said their fighting contains *appeasement rituals*. This means that when one of the pair behaves in a particular way, the other stops fighting. For example, if you watch two cats fighting, one may stop and turn his head to the side, exposing his neck. Lorenz said this particular behaviour is ritualised in cats and *inhibits* the aggression of the other cat. Although it would be easy for the other cat to attack, in fact he stops. In this way, there is a clear winner, but the species is not reduced in number.

I

What has this got to do with human aggression? **Lorenz** claimed that **aggression** fulfilled similar purposes for humans, and that we have instinctive appeasement rituals to stop the other aggressing, for example smiling, kneeling or bowing the head. Lorenz pointed out that with the development of weapons of destruction (cannons, machine guns, bombs) which *separate* human aggressors, these appeasement rituals cannot come into effect to stop aggression.

Fig. 11.1 Lorenz said that weapons like these prevent our instinctive appeasement rituals from overriding our aggression

I

Ethologists see **aggression** as an instinct: therefore we can never get rid of it: all we can do is try to control it. They argue that it builds up, and if not released (through sport for example), could lead to an *explosion* of aggression.

This explanation has been criticised however. More recent ethological research has shown that animals *do* kill members of their own species, sometimes even the infants. Another criticism is that you cannot generalise directly from non-human to human behaviour. We are much more complex. Factors such as language or social norms will affect *how* an instinct is expressed. Research on reducing aggression through watching or taking part in competitive sports shows that this actually *increases* aggression. So perhaps the **ethological** explanation has limited use.

S

Psychodynamic explanations for aggression

There are two ways in which **psychodynamic** ideas explain aggression – it is part of the **death instinct** or due to **frustration**.

THE DEATH INSTINCT

Shocked by all the killing in World War I, **Freud** worked to find a psychoanalytic explanation for this aggression. He proposed that aggression is part of our **death instinct**, which he called **thanatos**. He said each of us has this **instinct** for *self-destruction*.

I

However, it conflicts with the *life instinct* (the **libido**). In order to manage these conflicting instincts we direct the self-destructive one outwards, towards others. In Freud's view then, we aggress against others in order to preserve ourselves.

As we can never be rid of **aggression, Freud** proposed the best way to manage it was through competitive sports or observing something aggressive. He said this would help us release the build up of aggression. Research shows that this does not happen; in fact these techniques tend to *increase* aggression.

FRUSTRATION-AGGRESSION HYPOTHESIS

A later adaptation of Freud's ideas was proposed by **Dollard** and his associates. They said aggression was *not* an instinct, but it was produced by **frustration**. This became known as the **frustration-aggression hypothesis**. They claimed that people are motivated to reach goals, but if they are blocked, then frustration occurs. For example if a task is too difficult, or someone stops us from doing something, then we will become frustrated and aggress. In this hypothesis, frustration *always* leads to aggression.

However, some studies showed that aggression is only raised slightly when subjects are frustrated, and later the hypothesis was changed to say that frustration *may* cause aggression. Individuals might not aggress for example because they might think it wrong. We can put this in **psychoanalytic** terms, (see page 122 for an explanation), by saying the **id** (which is frustrated because it cannot get what it wants) is controlled by the **superego** (it is wrong to be aggressive).

The notion of frustration has been taken up by **Leonard Berkowitz** who says that frustration does not cause aggression directly but *does* arouse **anger**. The anger in turn creates a *readiness* to act aggressively. What happens next is due to the individual's learning. In other words, if there are 'cues' in the environment – a gun for example – this makes the individual more likely to be aggressive. We will look at some of Berkowitz' research in more detail below.

L

Another 'cue' could be seeing someone who has been the victim of **aggression** before. Seeing the victim could make the individual more likely to be aggressive. This is related to **scapegoating** which we covered in Chapter 10. We saw there how particular groups (such as Jews or blacks) become the targets of aggression when people are frustrated.

Learning theory explanations for aggression

From the learning theory viewpoint, aggression is not an innate drive. It is learned in the social setting. There are three explanations within learning theory – that aggression is learned through classical conditioning, operant conditioning and through observational learning.

CLASSICAL CONDITIONING

Do you remember what happens in classical conditioning? After two stimuli have been paired together several times, the response which *one* of them triggers automatically can be created by the *other* stimulus. **Berkowitz** proposed that people learn to associate particular stimuli (such as guns, or Jews or watching a boxing match) with *anger* or ways of *releasing* anger. When the individual is frustrated this creates a readiness to

L

act aggressively. Seeing this 'anger' stimulus actually *directs* and *increases* **aggression.** Berkowitz found that subjects who were made angry showed higher levels of aggression when there was an 'aggressive' cue around, such as a weapon, rather than a badminton racket.

Several studies have confirmed this 'weapons effect' but others have *not* found it. One explanation could be that the presence of weapons intensifies the anger, but this will *only* be expressed in a way which the individual feels is appropriate at that time. The **Berkowitz** study gave subjects the opportunity to be aggressive while they were taking part in the experiment. Their behaviour could have been affected by the demand characteristics of the experiment. However similar studies carried out as a natural experiment show that the less worried the individual is about being judged, the more he or she tends to show the weapons effect.

OPERANT CONDITIONING

According to operant conditioning principles behaviour is likely to be repeated if it is reinforced. On the other hand, if it is punished it is likely to weaken. So how does aggressive behaviour start? Look at the little girl in the picture below.

Fig 11.2 What will happen if this little girl's aggression is successful?

If she manages to get the toy off the little boy, then she is rewarded – she has got what she wanted. Next time she wants something off another child she will grab it. She is receiving positive reinforcement for her aggression and so is likely to repeat it.

This is just what **Gerald Patterson** found in his observational study of young children – those who got what they wanted through aggression were more likely to be aggressive again. On the other hand, what if this little boy fights back and is able to hang on to his toy? Patterson found that if this happened, the boy would be more likely to fight back *next* time. This is an example of negative reinforcement – if a behaviour (fighting back) stops an unpleasant experience (being attacked) it is more likely to be repeated.

There are many other reinforcements for **aggressive** behaviour, whether in children or adults: approval from others, increased status, increased self-esteem, attention from parents and so on. **Robert Sears** and his colleagues found that boys were sometimes *rewarded* for aggressive behaviour by their parents. Parents saw it as appropriate behaviour for boys (what we call **sex-typed** behaviour) and therefore approved of it.

Punishment is aimed at *weakening* behaviour, making it less likely to happen. Results from the **Sears** study showed that girls were punished more often than boys for **aggressive** behaviour, whether it was directed at other children or at their parents. Some psychologists argue that this is why girls show *less* aggression than boys, because they are punished for it and boys are reinforced for it.

L

However, research on the effects of punishment show that it is not very effective. It has been argued that punishment *increases* the individual's frustration, and this has to find an outlet which is often in the form of **aggression!** Those doing the punishing are modelling aggression, so the child can also find new ways to be aggressive by copying that behaviour. Small children can be seen 'punishing' their teddies or dolls in exactly the same way as their parents have punished them. Research suggests that to be effective in weakening behaviour, punishment must be related to a good relationship between child and punisher. We will look at why this might be so when we examine the role of parents later in this chapter.

SOCIAL LEARNING

Social learning explanations for aggression propose that it comes from observing others and seeing the *outcome* of the behaviour of others. **Albert Bandura** did many experiments early in the 1960s which examined the influence of a model on aggressive behaviour. We will look first at some of his ideas and then examine the **media** as a provider of aggressive models.

L

In Bandura's early experiments an adult modelled **aggressive** behaviour towards a large inflatable doll – called a Bobo doll. The children then had the opportunity to play with the doll while the model was nearby. Fig. 11.3 shows what **Bandura** and his colleagues saw.

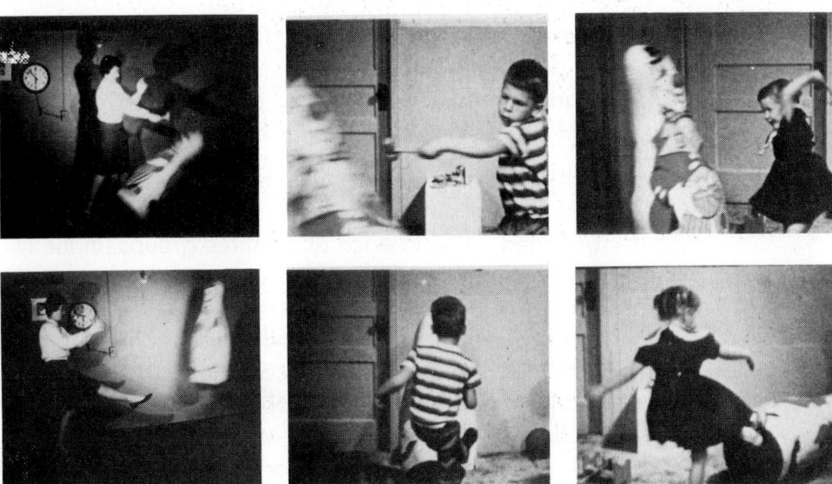

Fig. 11.3 Here you can see the aggressive behaviour of the female model, and the subsequent behaviour of a boy and girl who watched a model (from A. Bandura et al. 1961)

However, Bandura and his colleagues also wanted to see what would happen if the model was not present during the play stage. This is what they did.

Bandura, Ross and Ross (1961)

Aim of study	The aim of the study was to see whether children imitated a model's behaviour when that model was absent, and to see whether children imitated the behaviour of the same sex model more than the opposite sex model.
Experimental hypothesis I	Subjects exposed to aggressive models will show significantly more aggressive behaviour, and those exposed to non-aggressive models will show significantly less aggressive behaviour, than the control group.
Experimental hypothesis II	Subjects will show significantly more imitation of the same sex model than the opposite sex model.
Independent variables	The IV in this study were the behaviour of the model (aggressive or non-aggressive) and the sex of the model (male or female).
Dependent variable	The DV in this study was the aggressive behaviours shown by the children.
Design of study	This was an experimental design of three groups of subjects – one experimental group saw an aggressive model, another saw a non-aggressive model and a third was the control group.
Subjects	Subjects were 36 boys and 36 girls from three to five and a half years old who were attending a University nursery school.
Materials	Materials were a large inflatable doll (Bobo doll), a mallet and peg board, dart guns, and various 'non-aggressive' toys such as a tea set, crayons, trucks and plastic farm animals.
Procedure	Subjects were rated for level of aggression and grouped in threes for similar levels. They were then randomly assigned – one to each of the three groups. In the two experimental conditions subjects were divided into sub-groups of boys and girls. Each subject was taken individually to play in a room with toys. In the aggressive condition, an adult in the room started to punch the Bobo doll and hit it with the mallet (physical aggression) and spoke aggressively ('hit him', 'kick him'). In the non-aggressive condition the adult assembled toys and ignored the Bobo doll. The control group did not got through this stage. Each subject

was then taken to another room containing a similar range of toys and left to play whilst its behaviour was observed.

Results

Sex of subject	Aggressive F model	Aggressive M model
Female	19	9
Male	17	38

Table 11.1 Table showing mean scores of imitative aggression (from A. Bandura et al. 1961)

Conclusions **Bandura, Ross and Ross** concluded that children exposed to aggressive models did show significantly more aggressive behaviour than control subjects. However there was no significant difference in aggression between those seeing non-aggressive models and the control group. Subjects also showed significantly more imitation of the same sex model.

Bandura's research showed how much the child understood and applied the behaviour it observed. Not only did the children imitate the same sex models more, but they knew what appropriate behaviour was for those models. Some of his young subjects commented that 'ladies shouldn't do things like that'.

Bandura says reinforcement is a part of social learning. He found children are more likely to copy a model who is rewarded. This is called **vicarious reinforcement**, because the child receives reinforcement *indirectly*. In addition, he found that children sometimes show behaviours in *particular* situations. This showed they had learned the behaviour but only *performed* it at certain times. Why? Bandura's explanation is that if a situation is rewarding for a child, then the behaviour will be performed. For example, a child might learn that his teacher disapproves when he acts out violent scenes from films he has seen. But his aggressive behaviour wins admiration from his peers, so he does it in the playground instead.

L

Research also shows that some models are more likely to be imitated than others, in particular those who are **powerful, nurturant** or **similar** to the child. This is clearly important when we think about *who* those models are likely to be – their peers, parents, teachers and other adults the child comes into contact with, as well as sports or media personalities and characters in films and television programmes.

L

The **media**'s influence on **aggression** has been widely debated and researched. When we talk of the media we mean videos, films, television and radio programmes, books, magazines, newspapers, comics and computer games. So, what have psychologists discovered?

First, there is a lot of evidence to show that there is a positive correlation between the amount of violent television watched and amount of aggressive behaviour. *However*, we must not fall into the trap of saying this means violent programmes *cause* aggressive behaviour. We only have a correlation – a relationship. An explanation for this finding

Fig. 11.4 This Palestinian boy with a gun in Bethlehem is imitating a powerful model and being rewarded by his peers

could be that aggressive children will show more aggressive behaviours *and* prefer to watch violent television programmes.

Leonard Eron carried out a longitudinal study, and found a positive correlation between a child's viewing violent films at eight years old and levels of aggression at 18 years old. This relationship was true for boys, but not for girls. Other research suggests that watching violent programmes may raise children's aggression over the short term, but it appears that it may have less effect over the long term unless the child is already predisposed towards aggression.

Aggressive models in the **media** show children and adults *new* ways to be aggressive. The number of 'copycat' crimes, based on a film or news report, have been widely noted by police in several countries. Many storylines are based on conflict which is resolved by **aggression**. Often the conflict is between the 'good guys' and the 'bad guys'. So not only does the child see that the best way to resolve conflict is by aggression, but also that it is *acceptable* to use aggression. There is also concern that seeing a lot of violence and aggression makes people *immune* to it – they become more tolerant of it in society and in the way people behave towards each other.

To summarise then, the ethological and psychodynamic explanations for aggression stress that it is innate, whereas learning explanations stress the role of the environment. This means that our experiences with family, friends and school, as well as the media have an impact on aggression.

What effect do child rearing styles have on aggression?

As you might expect from the material we have already covered in this chapter, there is a lot of evidence that the way parents bring up their children is related to the levels of **aggression** the children show. Let us look first at some of this evidence.

Diana Baumrind observed families of pre-school children, noting the parents' behaviour towards their children. She was interested in the amount of *warmth* the parents showed, how clear and consistent the parents' rules were, how *independent* children were expected to be and how much the parents talked to and listened to their children. **Robert Sears** and his colleagues studied how 379 parents in Boston disciplined their five-year-old children and then followed them up six years later to see how much aggression they showed.

Both of these studies proposed that there were three distinctive *parenting styles*. Their findings are combined and summarised here:

PERMISSIVE PARENTS

These parents were warm but were not consistent with rules, they did not discuss or explain things to their children. They used little discipline and tended to have aggressive children, who remained aggressive.

AUTHORITARIAN PARENTS

These parents were not warm, nor did they discuss or explain things, but they expected their children to be independent. They also expected their children to do as they were told, often disciplined them and were quite harsh. Their children were aggressive when young, and became less aggressive but more anxious six years later.

AUTHORITATIVE PARENTS

These parents were warm, explained to their children what was expected of them and why, and made rules clear and consistent. Their discipline was restrained and fair. Their children were less aggressive and remained that way.

Eleanor Maccoby and John Martin have added a fourth type:

NEGLECTING OR REJECTING PARENTS

These parents are indifferent to their children and therefore do not get involved in child-rearing. Research shows that children of parents who could be classed as neglecting tend to show more anti-social behaviour which persists as they grow up. Parents who are rejecting towards their children also have more aggressive children.

So what influence do these four styles of parenting have on children's aggression? One study looked at why certain children were popular. They found co-operation and lack of aggression were important factors. The popular children tended to come from families in which parents typically showed the **authoritative** parenting style – warmth, low in physical punishment, actively discouraging aggression.

The nature of the **attachment** seems to be an important factor in aggression and disobedience. **Susan Londerville and Mary Main** looked at the relationship between the child's attachment to its mother at one year old and its co-operation and obedience at two years of age. They found that less securely attached children were less compliant – they were more often actively disobedient and unco-operative. There was a similar correlation between disobedient children and the mother's style of discipline. With these children, mothers tended to speak more harshly, use commands ('stop that') and use physical intervention more.

L

How does a parent handle punishment? The research suggests that if a parent has a warm and loving relationship with the child, then punishment will be much more effective. What a parent says, and the action he or she takes, will be more powerful in a warm relationship than a rejecting one. **Gerald Patterson** has also advised that punishment should be very mild and take place as early in the sequence of 'wrong' behaviours as possible. If punishment is left until things have got out of hand it is more likely to be excessive, accompanied by hostility, and offers a bad model for the child. This is supported by **Leonard Eron**'s longitudinal study, in which he found that there was less **aggression** in adolescence and adulthood amongst those who seemed more clearly identified with their parents and who reported more guilt after doing something wrong.

L

I

There are several possible explanations for these findings, which relate to some of the theories we have come across. For example, according to social learning theory, **aggressive** parents may act as aggressive models, just as warm and fair parents will also. According to **Freud**, the child who is harshly disciplined will become unable to release his or her death instinct, and this will create anxiety and possibly explosions of aggression. If a parent explains to the child why its behaviour is wrong, then this helps the child understand more about his or her world, it encourages them to take the other person's viewpoint and to think about the *consequences* of their actions. This relates to the child's **cognitive** development and should help them reduce or control their aggression.

C

Although we have focused on the parents' behaviour here, you know that many psychologists propose that the individual's behaviour is a result of their interaction with others. Much of the evidence we have looked at is correlational, so we cannot assume from correlational evidence that parents *cause* particular behaviours. There are many variables, such as the child's **temperament** or the social circumstances. For example, a child with a **difficult** temperament will bring out different responses from a parent than a child with an **easy** temperament. A child who behaves aggressively from a very early age may not respond to reasoned discipline, and a parent may resort to harsher methods. These examples show how the child's behaviour can encourage a particular parenting style. Social factors such as poverty, poor housing or health, lack of social support may also have an impact on the behaviour of *both* parent and child which leads to increased aggression.

I

S

So we can see that **aggression** seems to be the result of several interacting variables, both innate and learned. Evidence for this interaction comes from parenting studies.

Are there ways of reducing aggression?

Fortunately, the answer seems to be *yes*. We will look at some proposals from psychology including positive reinforcement, non-aggressive models, removal of aggressive cues, incompatible responses, cognitive interventions and fostering empathy.

POSITIVE REINFORCEMENT

L

Positive reinforcement of behaviour which is *not* aggressive encourages that type of behaviour and makes aggressive behaviour *less* likely to happen. Equally, aggressive behaviour should *not* be reinforced. We saw examples of this when we looked at parental influences. Sometimes children behave aggressively in order to gain attention from adults. In such cases, the adult who responds with anger and argument will actually be *rewarding* the child by giving attention. Psychologists propose that aggressive behaviour should be calmly stopped, *but* that the child be given lots of attention when it is *not* being aggressive.

NON-AGGRESSIVE MODELS

L

Using the ideas of observational learning, people imitate the behaviour of models. Seeing models who are not **aggressive** should lead to less aggression. This has been shown by many psychologists, including **Robert Baron**, whose subjects thought they were giving electric shocks to a 'victim'. He found that adults who saw a non-aggressive model gave fewer 'shocks' than subjects in a control group who did not see a model.

Importantly, when a subject sees both aggressive and non-aggressive models *at the same time* then the influence of the aggressive model can be erased by the non-aggressive model. This shows the benefit of having non-aggressive models in society, even though aggressive models cannot be eliminated.

REMOVAL OF AGGRESSIVE CUES

According to **Leonard Berkowitz**' research on **aggressive cues** – whether guns or a boxing match – one way of reducing aggression is to remove cues. One of his points was the wide availability of guns in America. However, many such cues also come from what we see in films and on television as well as within our society. According to Berkowitz' proposals, demonstrators are more likely to be aggressive when police are dressed like those in the picture below.

Fig. 11.5 Policing a demonstration

INCOMPATIBLE RESPONSES

Psychologists have proposed that people find it difficult to show two *conflicting* responses at the same time. If one possible response is **aggressive,** then another, such as humour, should lessen aggression. **Robert Baron** set up a field experiment creating frustration by having a confederate car breakdown at traffic lights in front of a male driver. He then arranged for various experimental conditions to occur. In some conditions a woman dressed as a clown crossed the street, in others she was scantily dressed, and in other she was on crutches. In the control conditions either a normally dressed woman crossed, or no-one at all. Hidden observers noted the drivers' reactions to their frustration. They found that in all of the experimental conditions the drivers showed less evidence of aggression. **Baron** concluded that humour, sexual arousal and empathy all reduced aggression.

COGNITIVE INTERVENTIONS

C

This means making people think about what they see and do. In one study, psychologists asked children to write about the ways in which television is not like real life and why it is bad to imitate television violence. A week later the children were videoed reading their essays and taking part in a talk show about the same subjects. The researchers found that not only did it change children's attitudes, but two years later they were still showing lower levels of aggression.

If someone gets served before you in a shop, how do you react? Some people see the behaviour of others as a direct attack and respond **aggressively.** One way of helping them to show less aggression is to encourage them to see *different* causes for the behaviour of others. If they can be encouraged to see the behaviour of others as due to forgetfulness, carelessness, or being in a bad mood, they may be less likely to respond as though the behaviour was a personal attack. These are called 'mitigating circumstances', in other words they are *reasons* for others' behaviour. Research has shown they can be very effective in reducing aggressive responses.

Research which has looked at men's attitudes to rape has shown that when they receive information about the victim's experience, male subjects are able to present arguments against rape and be more sympathetic to rape victims and less tolerant of sexual violence.

FOSTERING EMPATHY

Fostering empathy means encouraging the aggressor to experience the emotions of the victim. The study mentioned above enabled men to identify with the emotions of a rape victim and made them less willing to accept the messages in sexually violent films. One study which encouraged empathy in children had them taking roles. Sometimes they were able to give out sweets, then they would have to play the part of a child who is 'left out' when the sweets go round. Switching to the part of someone who receives bad treatment appeared to make them more sensitive to the emotions of others and lowered aggression levels. Techniques like this one are sometimes used to combat bullying in schools.

To sum up, we can see from some of these proposals that if we reduced the aggression in our environment, then aggression should drop. Helping people to understand their behaviour and reinforcing them when it is not aggressive, should also reduce aggression. However, we have not considered one aspect of aggression here and that is the difference in aggressive behaviour between males and females. This is examined in more detail in Chapter 14.

Further Reading

Bee H (1992) *The Developing Child* (6th ed), New York, Harper Collins
Deaux K, Dane F and Wrightsman L (1993) *Social Psychology in the 90s* (6th ed), Pacific Grove, Brooks/Cole

EXERCISES

1 What are demand characteristics? How might they explain Berkowitz' findings?
2 What measures of aggression could Baron have used in his study of incompatible responses?
3 Draw a bar chart to show the results of the Bandura, Ross and Ross study.
4 Choose any two explanations for aggression and describe two ways in which they differ.
5 Why did Bandura and his colleagues think that children were more likely to imitate the behaviour of the same sex model rather than the opposite sex model?
6 How could you use ideas from learning theory to explain the results which Eron found for girls?
7 Chose one parenting style and say how you think it is related to children's behaviour.

INDIVIDUALITY AND IDENTITY

SECTION D

Introduction

In this section we focus on the development of the individual. Each of the four chapters relates to a particular aspect of individual development – personality, intelligence, gender and the concept of self.

We will be able to compare different theories, by considering how each of them explains development in a different way. We will also have the opportunity to contrast the effect of heredity with that of the environment on individual development.

Chapter 12

The Development of Personality

IN THIS CHAPTER WE ARE GOING TO LOOK AT SOME EXPLANATIONS OF HOW PERSONALITY DEVELOPS. PERSONALITY IS ANOTHER OF THOSE WORDS WHICH WE USE FREELY, YET IS VERY HARD TO DEFINE. PSYCHOLOGISTS HAVE TRIED NEVERTHELESS, AND SOME WORK HAS FOCUSED ON WHETHER THERE ARE PATTERNS OR STYLES IN THE WAY WE BEHAVE. OTHER PSYCHOLOGISTS HAVE TRIED TO EXPLAIN WHERE SUCH PATTERNS ORIGINATE. IT IS THIS, HOW PERSONALITY DEVELOPS, WHICH IS OUR MAIN CONCERN IN THIS CHAPTER.

What is personality and how does it develop?

Personality is the word used to describe a person's characteristics. The characteristics that form the personality are those which they show in many situations, and which seem to be permanent. We tend to see these characteristics as forming a coherent whole. This means that we can say what *type* of person they are, and that we expect they will always be that type of person, so to some degree we can predict the way they will behave in the future. We could define **personality** as the pattern of individual characteristics which are permanent and which combine to make each person unique.

We will look at four explanations for the way in which personality develops in each of us. Some stress inherited factors and others learned factors. The first three we will examine are psychodynamic, radical behaviourist and social learning theories and finally we will examine an explanation which is biologically based – temperament.

Psychodynamic explanations of personality development

Several psychodynamic theories attempt to explain the development of personality. We will examine two: **Freud**'s theory which emphasises the part instincts play, and **Erikson**'s which emphasises the relationship between the child and its social setting.

FREUD'S PSYCHOSEXUAL THEORY

Freud said that our behaviour was driven by instincts. The infant is born with these instincts, which constantly need gratification. One example is hunger. Our personality

develops through the way we manage these instincts. The unconscious was a key element in Freud's ideas because he said that our instincts, motivations and anxieties were largely unconscious, as were the techniques we used to cope with them. Because they were in the unconscious, we were not aware of these instincts, but nevertheless they affected our behaviour and attitudes and thus contributed to our personality.

Three parts of personality

I

At birth the infant is a bundle of unconscious instincts which Freud called the **id.** This id is demanding, selfish and impulsive because it *only* wants gratification – Freud called it the **pleasure** principle. However, as the child develops he or she comes to realise that demands cannot always be met. Children find that they have to wait to get home before they can have lunch, or go to the toilet. They have to share the chocolate biscuits with their friends. They have to share their mother's affection with their siblings. How do they cope with this realisation?

Freud said that a second part of personality develops, which he called the **ego** – the **reality** principle. The child gradually transfers some of the energy from the id to the ego. The ego is the conscious part of personality and the child tries to find more realistic ways to gratify the id's demands. However, the child also becomes aware of what it should do – it learns this chiefly from parents according to Freud. As a result, a third part of personality develops, called the **superego** – the **morality** principle. The superego is *also* an unconscious part of personality and relates to the kind of person we want to be. It is made up of two parts – the **ego ideal** (the kind of person we want to be) and the **conscience** (which stops us from doing things we know to be wrong).

These three parts of personality are present and active by about six years of age, according to Freud. They function throughout our lives as our inner, unconscious needs meet the demands of reality. Imagine you have to revise for a test tomorrow. Your id wants to watch TV and eat a bar of chocolate, your superego knows you must revise. Which part wins? This dilemma creates **anxiety** and how you resolve it depends on your ego.

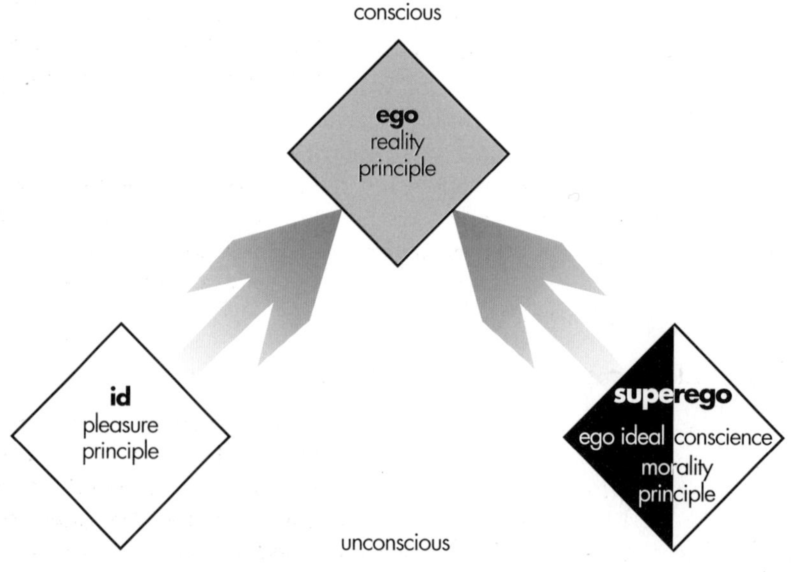

Fig. 12.1 The three parts of personality

Ego defence mechanisms

This pressure on the **ego** leads us to find ways of coping with it. **Freud** identified several strategies which we use unconsciously, and he called them **ego defence mechanisms**. Here is a selection:

- **denial** – this is when we refuse to accept something because it creates to much anxiety; for example a smoker might refuse to acknowledge the risks of smoking
- **identification with the aggressor** – this is when fear of someone else creates so much anxiety that we identify with them – adopt their behaviour and attitudes. We will come across an example of this on the next page
- **sublimation** – this is channelling impulses into acceptable activities, such as playing competitive sports as a channel for aggressive impulses
- **reaction formation** – this is when we behave in the *opposite* way to what we feel. For example we may behave in a very polite and considerate way towards someone against whom we are prejudiced

Psychosexual stages of development

Another developmental aspect of **Freud's** theory concerns the sexual drives, which he called the **libido**. He said that as the child's body matures, different areas of it become particularly sensitive. The libido is focused on each of these areas in turn, and it can be gratified by stimulating the part of the body on which it is focused. If the child does not receive enough stimulation, or too much, then the libido may become **fixated** or stuck at that area. If fixation *does* occur it may have an effect on the child's later personality.

Freud called these various stages of development the five **psychosexual stages**. Let us look at them before we see what personality characteristics he predicted as a result of **fixation** at any stage.

1 Oral stage (birth to one year)

At this stage Freud said that the focus of the libido was around the mouth. The baby gains pleasure from sucking, from putting things in its mouth. However, if it has too much, or too little, stimulation, it may become **orally fixated**. This means that it will continue to look for oral stimulation when the libido has moved on to the next stage.

2 Anal stage (one to three years)

The **libido** moves to the anal area, and the baby gains pleasure and satisfaction from going to the toilet. Freud said that if the child is not allowed to gain enough satisfaction from emptying its bowels, then it may become **anally fixated**. For example, if an adult is always hurrying the child, or if the child always has to 'perform' whenever it sits on a potty, then this may lead to anal fixation.

3 Phallic stage (three to five years)

At this stage the genitals become more sensitive and the libido becomes focused here. Freud said that the child also begins to have unconscious longings for its *opposite* sex parent. This leads to a conflict within the child, because it is frightened that the *same* sex parent will punish it for these feelings. Freud called this the **Oedipus conflict** in boys. The boy is torn between desire for his mother and fear that his father will castrate him. This conflict causes the boy anxiety; what does he do?

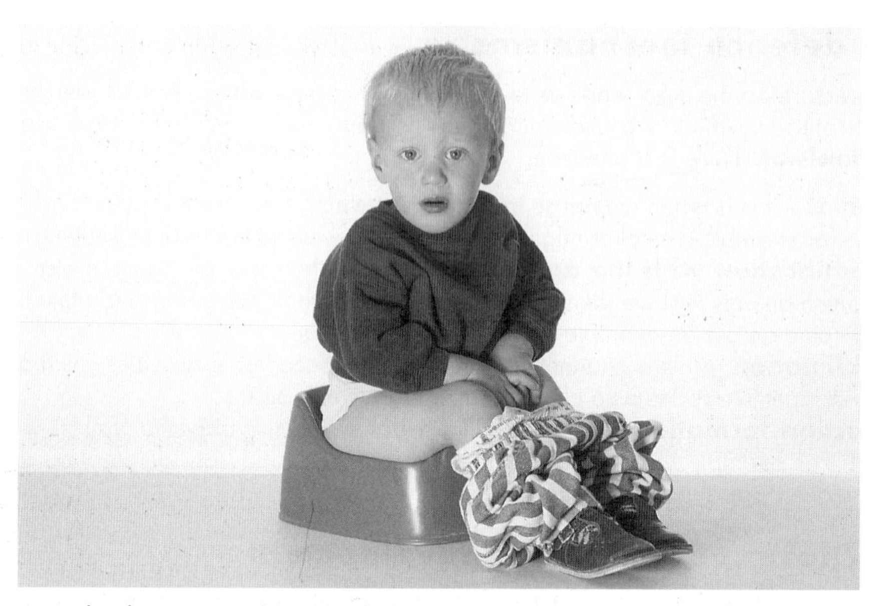

Fig.12.2 What happens to the child during the anal stage could affect its later personality, according to Freud

Freud said he unconsciously adopts a **defence mechanism**, he **identifies with the aggressor**. He tries to become like his father. This makes it less likely his father will harm him, and also makes the boy more powerful and closer to his mother. All of these processes are **unconscious** in the child. Through **identification** with his father the boy takes on the father's values, ideas, behaviours, morals and so on. It is in this way that the child comes to behave as a male, to parent and to develop a moral sense. Freud said this is how the **superego** develops, because the child **internalises** his father's values.

Freud was less clear about how a girl copes with her conflict, known as the **Electra conflict.** He said that because she has no penis she thinks she has already been castrated. She therefore has less to fear from her mother so her identification with her mother is less strong. Nevertheless, this is how she too comes to behave as a female and to develop a moral sense – though Freud felt the girl's moral sense, would be less strong.

4 Latency stage (five to twelve years)

Freud said that during this period the **libido** is diffused throughout the body, and the child continues to identify and interact with others of the same sex.

5 Genital stage (over twelve years old)

As the bodily changes of adolescence take place, the individual becomes more preoccupied with those of the opposite sex. If he or she has successfully accomplished each of the previous psychosexual stages then they should be able to form mature relationships and satisfy the **id**'s needs realistically. However, if there is **fixation** or **unresolved conflict** then this may hinder sexual relationships.

Here are some of the personality traits Freud predicted as a result of fixation.

Stage	Traits
Oral stage	dependent, trusting, gullible, excessive interest in eating, drinking, smoking, argumentative, envious
Anal stage	anal retentive personality – orderly, clean, miserly, obstinate, cruel anal expulsive personality – untidy, generous, impulsive
Phallic stage	vain, reckless, self-centred, ambitious, exploits others
Latency	normally there is no fixation at this stage
Genital stage	fixation here is normal

Table 12.1 Personality traits resulting from fixation

CRITICISMS OF FREUD

There have been several criticisms of **Freud**'s ideas. One is that it is not possible to test his predictions. It is impossible to follow a child's development so closely to see what the outcome is. It is also impossible to test his concepts, such as **ego** and **fixation.**

Because people use defence mechanisms it is not possible to test whether a fixation does lead to a particular personality trait. For example **reaction formation** is coping with anxiety by saying the opposite. Therefore you cannot *really* find out what someone feels. Another criticism is that Freud's theory was based on case studies of his clients, who were middle class Jewish women, living in Vienna, who came to him because of their problems. Not only were his subjects unrepresentative of people (or children) in general, his method of research was the case study, which has several weaknesses.

ERIKSON'S PSYCHOSOCIAL THEORY

Erik Erikson was a psychoanalyst who started to publish his ideas in the 1960s. His ideas concentrated on the **ego** – the conscious part of personality – and how the child and adult develop their sense of *identity*. He proposed that the child has to work through various tasks, and what these tasks are depends partly on the child's maturation and partly on the demands of the society in which he or she lives. Like Freud, Erikson said the task, or problem, has to be successfully resolved at each stage, or there may be problems for the individual later on.

S

Erikson proposed eight stages of development, but we will focus on the first five which take us to adulthood.

1 Trust versus mistrust

The task is to develop trust in others and confidence we can make things happen. This develops from a good secure attachment with another (approximately birth to one year old).

2 Autonomy versus shame/doubt

The task is to develop trust in our own ability to make choices (approximately two to three years old).

3 Initiative versus guilt

Here the task is to achieve goals, this requires planning and being assertive (approximately four to five years old).

4 Industry versus inferiority

The task is to learn the skills and norms of our society (six to 12 years old).

5 Identity versus role confusion

The task is to absorb physical changes, decide on occupational goals and achieve sexual identity (13 to 18 years old).

The way in which the child copes with these tasks will determine what **Erikson** called *ego qualities* such as **trust, intimacy** or **autonomy.** The degree to which we have these qualities, or their opposites such as **mistrust,** will determine the kind of person we are.

Radical behaviourist explanations of personality development

L

The radical behaviourist explanation says that personality develops as a result of operant conditioning. The principles of operant conditioning are that behaviour:

- is *strengthened* by reinforcement
- is *weakened* by punishment
- which is partially reinforced will take longer to become extinguished

This means that a child who is rewarded for a particular behaviour – for sharing sweets or tidying its room – will become a generous and obedient, tidy child. The child who seeks attention and gets it (which is rewarding) by refusing to return a toy or drawing on the wallpaper will become selfish and destructive. A child who is punished for hitting his baby brother should become less aggressive towards him.

L

If any behaviour is partially reinforced then it is likely to last longer than if it is reinforced every time it occurs. In reality, very few behaviours *are* reinforced every time, and so radical behaviourists would say that we can see how a parent is developing a child's personality by partial reinforcement.

L

One of the weaknesses with this explanation is that it only sees the child as having things done to it – personality is little more than an accumulation of reinforced behaviours because it is created by reinforcement and punishment. The radical behaviourist can explain why a child may behave in a different way in different settings, because a teacher may reinforce helpful behaviour and a parent might not. But this is not what we think of as personality, because it should be more consistent than this.

Another weakness with the radical behaviourist explanation is that it relates only to behaviour not to any underlying traits: it ignores the existence of the mind, of intention and of understanding.

Social learning explanations of personality development

L

According to this theory the child's personality develops as a result of several processes. The work of **Albert Bandura**, a leading social learning theorist, is given in detail in Chapter 11, but here we will look at a summary of his ideas, in particular modelling, reinforcement and punishment, and self-efficacy.

MODELLING

Bandura proposed that the child learns by observing others and modelling their behaviour. These others may be parents, siblings, friends, TV characters, teachers and so on. The child is more likely to model itself on those who are **nurturant, powerful** or **similar.** As the child develops, different models will become more or less important. Imagine the different kinds of models a three year old and a fourteen year old might use. Also, as the child matures it is able to notice, remember and reproduce more complex behaviour, so not only will the child *observe* different models, but it will *show* different kinds of behaviour.

L

Some of these models will become more important than others, and then the child will attend less to a specific behaviour and more to the many ways that the model behaves. Eventually the child will **internalise** that model's behaviours so that it will be able to act as the model would act in a situation it has never seen the model in.

REINFORCEMENT AND PUNISHMENT

The child is more likely to model the behaviour of someone who is seen to be reinforced and less likely to copy the behaviour of someone who is punished. This is called **vicarious learning**. However, the idea of reinforcement works in another way as well. The child may copy the behaviour which it has seen reinforced, but what happens next is important. If the child's copied behaviour is *reinforced,* the child is more likely to repeat it.

L

Let's imagine that a little girl sees another girl having fun with a dog in the park. The next time she goes to a park she may run up to a dog so she can play with it. If the dog turns and barks, then the child is unlikely to copy the 'having fun with a dog' behaviour for a while (if at all!) because it was not rewarding.

What if our little girl doesn't go to the park but has a visitor who brings a dog. The child may play with the dog by imitating the behaviours of the child she saw in the park. If this behaviour is rewarding, then the child is likely to use these behaviours on other dogs in other settings.

SELF-EFFICACY

Bandura says that through the process of **internalising** a model's behaviour, learning which settings or circumstances are rewarding for which kinds of behaviour, the child achieves **self-efficacy**. This is related to the child's self-concept, and is when the child is able to predict outcomes of behaviour and to have certain expectations about itself. These expectations and standards form the core of the child's personality.

L

Although this is a much richer explanation than that of the radical behaviourist because it includes the child's *own* interpretation of a model's behaviour, and gives a more convincing explanation of why individuals differ, it still proposes that the child's personality is the result of its observations.

Temperament as an explanation of personality development

WHAT IS TEMPERAMENT?

Temperament is our style of responding to our environment. In Fig. 12.3, the baby on the left could be described as *active* whereas the other baby seems *passive*. This is an example of two different ways in which we respond to our environment.

Fig. 12.3 Different styles of responding?

I

Research on **temperament** suggests that because a particular style of responding appears to persist throughout life, then temperament is innate. However, there is a difficulty in studying temperament because there is no agreement as to how you can *measure* it. Although we have seen it is a 'style of responding', just how you classify the responses, and measure them, has proved very difficult. You will see in the work we will look at in this section that there is a range of classifications which psychologists have taken to be measures of temperament.

I

Some psychologists have tried to find out how much of temperament is due to innate factors by using twin studies or cross-cultural studies. Others have looked at the persistence of temperament by carrying out longitudinal studies. We will look at a study which represent each of these methods.

A LONGITUDINAL STUDY OF TEMPERAMENT

A longitudinal study carried out by **Alexander Thomas, Stella Chess and Herbert Birch** followed the development of a large number of children in the New York area. Let's look at the details.

Thomas, Chess and Birch (1968)

Aim of study The aim of the study was to define temperamental characteristics in children and identify their role in the development of children's behaviour.

Type of study This was a longitudinal study which took place over 12 years.

Method The methods used were interviews, observations and intelligence tests.

Subjects The 136 subjects were from 85 middle-class families in the New York City area of the United States. They were mainly from Jewish families (78 per cent) and one third of them were only children and half were from families with two children.

Procedure Parents were interviewed regularly about the child's routine behaviour and its response to changes in its experiences. They were asked about their attitudes and child-care practices when their child was three years old

Teachers were asked about the child's adaptation to school and its functioning at school once a year. Observations were made once a year of the child in school and its play and problem-solving activities at three and six years old. At these ages the child was also given standard psychological tests.

Different researchers were used for different assessments, to avoid a 'halo' effect. For example the researcher who observed the child in class did not interview the teacher. Interviewer and observer ratings were compared periodically, so as to check for reliability.

Results The researchers devised nine dimensions of temperament and from that categorised their subjects as falling into 1 of three temperamental constellations:

	% of sample in each category
the **easy child**	40%
the **difficult child**	10%
the **slow to warm up child**	15%
children falling into more than one category	35%

Conclusions Thomas, Chess and Birch concluded that they had identified nine dimensions of temperament. They decided that children's scores on each of these dimensions were linked, and therefore that three categories of temperament could be defined. They also concluded that these temperamental traits seemed to persist as the child developed. This suggests that temperament is innate.

What are the characteristics of each of these three types of temperament?

- **the easy child** has regular habits, is adaptable, approaches new experiences positively and is usually fairly happy
- **the difficult child** has irregular habits, is slow or unable to adapt, approaches new situations negatively, is often unhappy and responds very vigorously to things; it is irritable and cries more than children in the other types
- **the slow to warm up child** tends to be passive, it is not happy with new experiences, but is usually happy once it adapts; it is mild in the way it responds, unlike the difficult child

As you can see, **Thomas, Chess and Birch** were able to classify two-thirds of their sample as falling into one of these three types. The remaining one-third showed characteristics related to two or more types. They also proposed that temperament is innate, because these traits persisted as the child developed. Research which examines this in more detail has been carried out with twins.

TWIN STUDIES OF TEMPERAMENT

Arnold Buss and Robert Plomin studied pairs of twins using three dimensions of behaviour:

- **emotionality** – this is how easily a person becomes very upset or very excited. The more emotional a person is, the harder it is for them to calm down
- **activity** – this is how much energy a person puts into their activity. A person with high activity levels will talk rapidly and move about a lot
- **sociability** – this is how much a person wants to be with other people. Someone scoring high on sociability will prefer to spend their time with others rather than alone; they seem to need interaction with other people

Buss and Plomin compared the scores between each pair of twins. They wanted to see, for example, if a child who scored high on **sociability** had a twin who *also* scored high on sociability. If this was the case, then there was a strong correlation between the scores for this pair of twins. If **temperament** is genetic, then the twins which have identical genes (identical twins – MZ) should have a higher correlation of scores than the twins who are fraternal (DZ – who have half of their genes in common).

The researchers worked through the scores for all the children and compared the correlations. They found that there were much higher correlations between scores for identical twins than scores for fraternal twins. From these results **Buss and Plomin** concluded that **temperament** had a genetic basis, that it is innate. Other research has shown that the genetic base may not be as strong as these results suggest. A study in Finland with a sample size of 12,000 pairs of *adult* twins found a *similar* difference in correlation between identical and fraternal twins to the Buss and Plomin study. The Finnish study was looking at two traits – sociability and emotional instability.

Yet again we come across the problems of separating the environmental factors from the genetic ones. Because identical twins are treated in a more similar way than fraternal ones, then this may be another reason for the higher correlation, and it would weaken the case for a genetic argument.

A CROSS-CULTURAL STUDY OF TEMPERAMENT

If we compare children from different cultures and find similarities in their style of responding this would suggest **temperament** is innate. However, if there are *differences* this suggests it is learned as a result of the children's experiences.

I

S

Most of the work we have looked at so far has been done in the USA. However, **Daniel Freedman's** cross-cultural research on temperament shows interesting results. He looked at newborn babies who were Caucasian, Japanese, Navaho or Chinese. He found that the Caucasian babies tended to be the most active and hardest to console; the Japanese were vigorous but fairly easy to console; and that the Chinese and Navaho were relatively placid. Observation of the mothers' behaviour showed that Japanese and Chinese mothers talked *less* to their infants than the Caucasian mothers.

HOW DOES TEMPERAMENT RELATE TO PERSONALITY?

S

We can see in **Freedman**'s study the interaction between the newborn temperament *and* the mother's behaviour. Freedman points out that one reinforces the other and so the behaviours are likely to strengthen over time. He says that this is how cultural differences emerge, because the way the mother responds reflects the culture they live in. This is also true on an individual level: the mother's response may strengthen the child's responses.

Thomas and Chess go further and consider the child's *total* environment. They say that how the child's personality develops will depend on how well its temperament *fits* with its environment. For example, a 'slow to warm up' child will be more comfortable in a slow-paced, easy going home. But the demands of school, with a strict timetable and quick changes of activity, may be very stressful for the child. The way it responds will in turn affect the response of those around it.

Buss and Plomin have proposed that children who show *extremes* of a temperament type, such as children high in emotionality or very 'difficult' children, force their environment to adapt to *them*. For example, **Michael Rutter** found that 'difficult' children are punished more. In contrast, children in the middle range of a temperament type seem to adapt *to* their environment.

So the baby's **temperament** affects how it interacts with its environment and how others respond to it. The nature of this interaction will in turn influence the development of personality. The effect of this interaction is very complex and psychologists have few answers at the moment. Some suggest that the 'difficult' temperament has a strong *direct* effect on the child's personality – it leads to weak attachments, difficulty in forming relationships with others, poor attention in school and so on. But evidence points more to the child with a 'difficult' temperament as being *vulnerable* because it finds many experiences more stressful than the other temperamental types would. Tolerance, patience and support may protect this vulnerability.

Evidence from the New York study suggests that there is a moderately strong correlation between **temperament** characteristics at various ages in the early years. But between early adolescence and early adulthood the correlation becomes stronger. This suggests that the child's early experiences *can* strengthen or weaken its style of responding, but by 12 or 13 years old this style is more established.

The evidence suggests that temperament has important implications for the child's experiences. It relates to its cognitive development, the parent's child rearing style, the effects of reward and punishment, its relationships with others, self-concept, levels of aggression and so on. All of these factors contribute to the child's personality.

We have looked at several explanations for how personality develops. In the table below you can see a summary of their similarities and the differences between them.

	Psychodynamic theories	Radical behaviourist	Social learning theory	Temperament
Biological factors?	instinct	none	none	innate
Environmental factors?	social relationships and tasks	others reinforce or punish	others as models and sources of reinforcement and punishment	how will they 'fit'
Parental role?	identification with same sex parent	reinforcing or punishing behaviour	act as model and reinforcer or punisher	how parent interacts and responds
Nature of personality development?	development in stages	accumulates gradually	develops gradually	basis is apparent in early months
Child's role?	fairly passive	passive	fairly active	active
How important are cognitive factors?	not important	irrelevant	fairly important	not important
How important are the early years?	very	not particularly	not particularly	very

Table 12.2 The similarities and differences between explanations for the development of personality

Further Reading

Bee H (1992) *The Developing Child* (6th ed), New York, Harper Collins

EXERCISES

1 Describe three weaknesses in Freud's theory, using information from this chapter and the information on case studies in Chapter 5.
2 Using radical behaviourist ideas, describe how a child might develop one of the following personality traits – shyness, tolerance, laziness.
3 What does the 'halo' effect mean in the Thomas, Chess and Birch study?
4 Compare the behaviour of the Japanese and Chinese infants in Freedman's study. How might their mothers have 'created' this difference?
5 Choose any two explanations for the development of personality and show one way in which they are similar and one way in which they differ.

Chapter 13
Intelligence

YOU MIGHT THINK THAT YOU KNOW WHAT THIS CHAPTER IS ABOUT, BUT PSYCHOLOGISTS WOULD BE LESS CERTAIN. THIS IS BECAUSE THERE IS STILL NO AGREED ANSWER TO THE QUESTION — WHAT IS INTELLIGENCE? WE COULD SAY PEOPLE THAT ARE INTELLIGENT CAN LEARN A LANGUAGE VERY QUICKLY, CALCULATE COMPLEX SUMS IN THEIR HEADS, DO SEVERAL THINGS AT ONCE, SOLVE PROBLEMS, REMEMBER THE DETAILS OF WHAT THEY READ, PLAY A TUNE THEY HAVE HEARD ONLY ONCE OR THINK QUICKLY. THE ABILITY TO DO THESE THINGS IS WHAT WE CALL BEING INTELLIGENT, BUT IN FACT THESE ARE ONLY EXAMPLES OF INTELLIGENT BEHAVIOUR, A 'WAY' OF DOING THINGS. BUT PSYCHOLOGISTS AND OTHERS HAVE ALSO TREATED INTELLIGENCE AS A 'THING', MEASURING IT, ASKING WHETHER INTELLIGENCE IS A GLOBAL ABILITY OR LOTS OF SEPARATE MENTAL ABILITIES, FOR EXAMPLE, OR USING THE RESULTS OF INTELLIGENCE TESTS TO SHOW THAT SOME PEOPLE ARE INFERIOR TO OTHERS. THIS LACK OF AGREEMENT PRESENTS US WITH A PROBLEM – IF WE CANNOT DEFINE INTELLIGENCE HOW CAN WE MEASURE IT?

WE WILL RETURN TO THESE TOPICS LATER BUT FOR NOW WE ARE GOING TO START BY LOOKING AT ATTEMPTS TO MEASURE INTELLIGENCE. WE WILL THEN GO ON TO CONSIDER RESEARCH WHICH HAS LOOKED AT THE INFLUENCE OF HEREDITY AND OF THE ENVIRONMENT ON INTELLIGENCE. THIS IS AN EXAMPLE OF THE NATURE OR NURTURE DEBATE IN PSYCHOLOGY.

What is IQ and how is it calculated?

IQ means **intelligence quotient** and it is a person's score on an intelligence test. IQ tests have largely been used in the education system, for example to select children for different types of education or to identify problems. Let us look at how intelligence tests started, and how they have developed.

SIMON AND BINET'S TEST – FRANCE

C

At the beginning of this century **Alfred Binet** was employed by the French government to find a way of identifying children who were intellectually slower than their peers. They would go to special schools which could help them, and avoid them slowing down the others. Binet thought that **intelligence** was something which developed: it was not a fixed 'thing'.

Binet and his colleague **Simon** devised tests for children of different ages, based on questions (known as items) which about half of that age group would get right. Children were given the tests for each age until they started to get the answers wrong. So if an eight year old could give the right answers to the questions for eight year olds but not for nine year olds, Simon and Binet said her **mental** age was eight. If she could get most of the answers right on the test for 10 year olds, her **mental** age would be ten. However, in order to compare children's ability we need to know both their mental age and their *actual* age (called the chronological age). The **mental ratio** helps us make the comparison. This is how we calculate it, using our bright eight year old as an example:

$$\text{mental ratio} = \frac{\text{mental age}}{\text{chronological age}} = \frac{10}{8} = 1.25$$

So our eight year old has a mental ratio of 1.25. What would the mental ratio be of a child whose mental age is the same as their chronological age? Yes, it would be 1.00.

STANFORD-BINET TEST – AMERICA

C

Binet's ideas were quickly adopted and developed by researchers at Stanford University and became known as the Stanford-Binet test. The notion of an **intelligence quotient** was introduced, which multiplied the mental ratio by 100. If we use our eight year old in this new arrangement, we would find:

$$\text{IQ} = \frac{10}{8} \times 100 = 125$$

Our eight year old has an IQ of 125, and you can see where her score would be in Fig. 13.1. This curve is called a **normal distribution curve** because it shows how various kinds of human characteristics are spread throughout the population. These characteristics might be height, weight or IQ scores. The 'hump' in the curve shows that *most* of the population are in the middle of the range – and this is true of IQ scores, height or weight. The fact that the line falls quickly to a low point at each side indicates that *very* few people have *either* very low or very high IQ scores (and also that very few people are really small or really tall).

The curve in Fig. 13.1 relates to scores from *modern* IQ tests. They use questions (items) which are devised to produce a mean (average) score of 100 when tested on a large group of people. In other words, if 2,830 people took the test, the mean of the 2,830 scores would be 100. This represents a *standard* against which an individual's score can be measured. As the mean score for the population as a whole is 100, someone who scores 95 has a slightly lower than average score. The items are also designed so that two-thirds of the scores from the population fall between the range 85 to 115.

C

There are two important misunderstandings about these figures, which you need to be aware of. The first is that the IQ score is not an *absolute* figure. For example, your height and weight can be measured against an absolute standard. Your height is *not* measured in comparison with others, but against a rule. In contrast, your IQ is *only* measured in comparison with others. Nevertheless this is often overlooked and an IQ score is treated as though it is an absolute measure. This leads people to think that the difference in **intelligence** between a 100 and 105 scorer is the same as the difference between a score of 85 and a score of 90. It also makes them think that an IQ score is as unchangeable as their height.

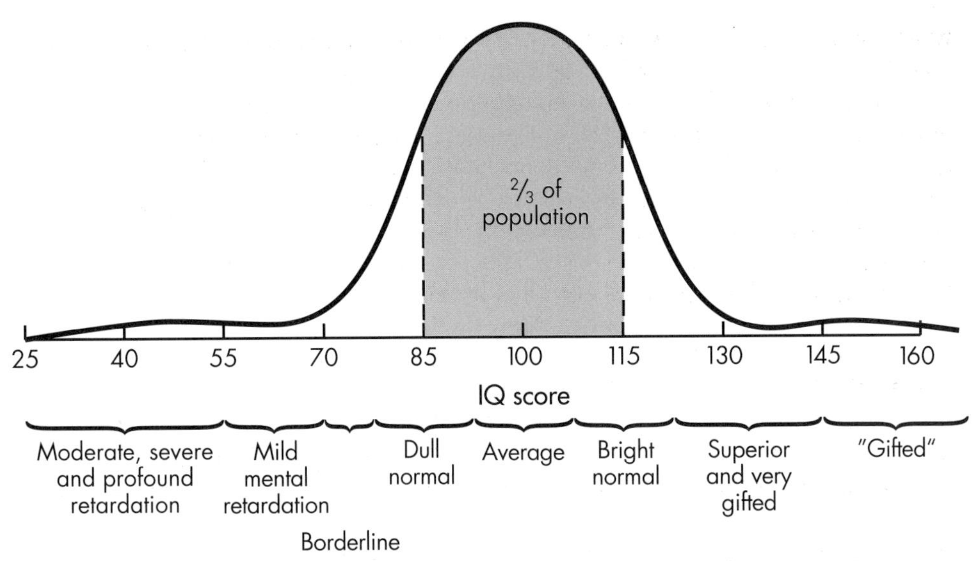

Fig. 13.1 Distribution of scores on an IQ test

The second point is that, although it appears that IQ scores *happen to be* normally distributed, just like height, in fact they are not. The questions are *specially designed* so that the right percentage of individual scores will fit in with the each part of the curve. The questions are made easy or difficult in order to produce this normal distribution. It *appears* that **intelligence** is normally distributed, but this is completely artificial. In fact we do not know how it is distributed throughout the population.

The **Stanford-Binet** test has been updated several times, and now it no longer calculates the child's mental age. Instead it uses the principle I have just described. The child's 'group' is children of the same age. The items are devised so that the mean score is 100. Tests are designed for each age between three and 16 years old. Beyond this the child's intelligence is thought to be fully developed.

WECHSLER SCALES

Some of the most widely used tests today are those devised by **David Wechsler** from the mid 1930s onwards. These, like the Standford-Binet tests, are updated every few years. Wechsler devised the Wechsler Adult Intelligence Scale (WAIS) and, later on, two scales for children. The Wechsler Pre-School Primary Scale of Intelligence (WPPSI) was devised for children between four and six and a half years old.

The Wechsler Intelligence Scale for Children (Revised) (WISC-R) is for five to 15 year olds and uses both performance tests (such as completing pictures or arranging blocks) and verbal tests (such as the meaning of words). The tests are not age related like the Stanford-Binet tests; instead the items range from very easy to very difficult. Because there are items for different types of intellectual ability, they are more useful for diagnosing learning difficulties than the Stanford-Binet tests.

BRITISH ABILITY SCALES

In 1979 the British Ability Scales (BAS) were created. They can be used for children between the ages of two and a half to 17 years of age, and are an attempt to test some

C

of the abilities thought to *underlie* **intelligent** behaviour. These abilities relate to the information processing approach to cognition, so for example there are items to assess memory or the speed of processing information.

All of these tests are *individual* tests: they require a tester to be with the person taking the test. This is partly because some items need to be constructed or sorted. However, there is now a wide variety of group tests, which can be given to many people at the same time, or to individuals without supervision. These tests use 'paper and pencil' methods.

I

The first of these were the US Army Tests – called Alpha and Beta tests. They were devised by psychologists who believed that **intelligence** was inherited, and they were used to select recruits in the American Army. In the 1920s they were also used to select immigrants who would be allowed to enter America. Those who did badly were thought to have low intelligence. Because intelligence was thought to be inherited, and therefore unchangeable, this was a way of keeping out those who were 'feeble-minded' and would contribute to 'genetic degeneracy', according to the people who *devised* the tests. You can see from the extract in Fig. 13.2 (see page 138) why immigrants and army recruits might have achieved low scores.

Ability to do pencil and paper tests depends on being able to read and understand the instructions. This is true for tests designed to select employees as well as those used in education. An example of the latter would be the 11-plus examination, which we will look at in more detail in the next section.

How have IQ tests been used?

Though **Binet**'s tests were used to identify children who needed special help, we have seen that, since then, IQ tests have been developed for many purposes. IQ tests are examples of psychometric tests, and we will look at some of their purposes in more detail.

SELECTION IN EDUCATION

IQ tests are widely used in America, particularly to select for the appropriate grade in school or for entrance into college. In Britain the 11-plus examination was taken by the vast majority of children during the 1950s and 60s in their final year of primary school. A child who passed went to a grammar school (which was very academic), one who failed went to a secondary modern school (which taught technical skills). Approximately 80 per cent of children 'failed', and this led to one of the major criticisms of the test. It **labelled** children as failures at 11 years old, and this had a long term effect on their self-perceptions (see Chapter 15). The 11-plus test was also shown to be a poor predictor of later achievement and there are now very few areas in Britain in which this form of selection is used.

DIAGNOSING PROBLEMS

IQ tests can be used to identify problems so that appropriate treatment can be given.

C

The most commonly used test for very young children is the Bayley Scale of Infant Development. Its purpose is to identify major developmental problems and it is used for children from a few weeks old to two and a half years of age. Children are tested for abilities which are appropriate for a particular age. For example, if a child is unable to following a moving object with its eyes, or sit up without help at 18 months old, then this suggests developmental problems. The Bayley Scales are not used to predict intellectual development; indeed, they have been found to be a poor predictor.

IQ tests are useful for diagnosing (identifying) a child's difficulties or weaknesses at school. For example a child might show problems with reading, but not with mathematics or reasoning. However, the tests only cover *some* aspects of intellectual ability – generally the more 'measurable' aspects. Many other abilities remain outside the scope of IQ tests. So, for example, a child who has problems getting along with others cannot be measured for social skills development and so this problem may receive less attention than one identified by the IQ test.

Tests such as the Wechsler Scale are used to measure the IQ of children who are thought to be particularly low or particular high in IQ. For example, as you can see from Fig. 13.1 (page 135), the position of a child's score on the IQ scale indicates the level of retardation it is classified with. This in turn contributes to the assessment of the child's educational abilities and needs.

Equally, a child who appears to be developing much more rapidly than his or her peers can be assessed for IQ level on various items, so that this child too can have the most appropriate educational experience. Such children are sometimes labelled 'gifted'.

Research by **S. Broman** and her colleagues has looked at IQ scores and patterns of mental retardation. Results suggest that mild retardation (roughly between IQ scores 55 to 75) is sometimes apparent in several children in a family, whereas there is usually never more than one child in a family whose IQ score is below 50. They point out that the latter case may be result of some physical damage to the child, whereas the fact that several children might be affected in the earlier case suggests family or cultural factors. They also point out that this shows mental retardation may have several causes.

EMPLOYMENT ASSESSMENT

In America, tests were devised using paper and pencil, including both words and drawings. These were much easier to administer, and as we have seen they were used to assess men recruited for the First World War. Their success led to them being developed and used in many walks of life – to find people most suited for a particular school, career, or employer for example.

Recent developments include assessment of abilities thought to underlie intelligent behaviour, such as the capacity of working memory. The British Army Recruitment Battery are tests which use computer programs and touch sensitive screens.

ASSESSMENT OF LEVEL OF INTELLECTUAL DEVELOPMENT

As we will see shortly, several programmes have been put into effect which have tried to increase children's intellectual development. IQ tests have been used to *assess* the child's development at various stages in the programme. One of the advantages of the IQ test is that it avoids the bias a teacher may have. Research shows that when teachers are assessing their pupils, they tend to over-rate girls, younger pupils and those who are more outgoing. They tend to *under-rate* boys, the older and quieter pupils.

These tests are not the same as *achievement* tests, which measure what the child has learned. However, they *are* testing learning. For example, children need to know the meaning of words in order to answer some questions, or be able to understand the relationships between numbers. IQ tests may be therefore not so much tests of intellectual ability as tests of learned skills.

What are the limitations of IQ testing?

C

You might feel that if people have been using the tests for so long, for so many important things, then they must do the job well. However, there are some criticisms of IQ tests which we will look at. They come under several headings – accuracy, fairness, validity, labelling and prediction.

ACCURACY

Because of the way IQ tests have been used, an individual's score is taken to be his or her level of **intelligence.** However, he or she may not do well because of tiredness, lack of interest or confidence, an unfamiliar type of test, a hot or noisy room. The presence of a tester in the individual tests will also have an impact. Children in particular may become shy, self-conscious, inarticulate or exhibitionist. For these types of reasons an individual's score may be lower than it could be. This in turn may affect career prospects, employment or what school children attend or class they move into.

FAIRNESS

Even if the individual does as well as he or she can, are the tests fair? There has been criticism that IQ tests are culture specific. This means that they 'make sense' only to people who understand that culture. For example, IQ tests were given to immigrants arriving in America in the early part of this century. Some groups, whose way of life was very different from that in America, did badly. You may be able to guess why if you look at some of the test items given in Fig. 13.2. As a result of this bias, immigrants belonging to those groups found it much harder to enter the country.

Fig. 13.2 What is wrong with these pictures?

A more subtle cultural bias is apparent from research into comparison of IQ scores between black and white subjects. Black people tended to score lower and several psychologists, such as **Arthur Jensen** said this was evidence of racial inferiority. These psychologists reasoned that because IQ was hereditary, black people would always be inferior; nothing could be done about it.

I

But examination of test items showed they were biased towards white middle-class culture, so members of any other group might be disadvantaged. This is an important point when set beside *other* definitions of intelligence which stress culture and environment. **David Wechsler** and **Jean Piaget** for example both said that **intelligent** behaviour is adapting or dealing effectively with the environment. Any attempt to assess an individual's intelligence should therefore use items from that individual's environment. These IQ tests were best fitted to a white middle-class environment; therefore they were not fair. Since the early tests, when there was considerable evidence for cultural bias, psychologists devising the tests have been much more conscious of the need to avoid biased items.

S

It has been argued that, though they are not perfect, IQ tests are fair in one respect. That is they do reduce bias in some situations. We have already seen that teachers may be biased against certain students, but so might interviewers for jobs or university admission tutors. At least the IQ test provides a more objective measure of the individual's ability.

VALIDITY

If you look carefully you will see that so far I have said *only* that IQ tests give a score, I have *not* said they measure **intelligence.** Why? If a test is valid then it measures what it is *supposed* to measure, but there is a lot of argument about whether IQ tests actually *do* measure intelligence.

One view is that they do because those who get higher IQ scores *also* do better at school and get better paid jobs (these two can be considered as indicators of intelligence). But you can see that this is a correlation – the higher the score, the better the school work. We know that correlations can only show a *relationship* between two variables, we cannot conclude that one variable (the score) *causes* the other variable (the quality of school work). It could be that a child who is good at IQ tests is also good at school work. This doesn't necessarily mean that the child is intelligent. Albert Einstein was apparently rather *poor* at school work!

C

The other view is that IQ scores are *not* a test of intelligence, because we do not even know what intelligence is. Many of the abilities which are widely accepted as intelligent, such as creativity, planning or adaptability are not measured by such tests. The critics say IQ tests do not measure these abilities, and therefore do not measure intelligence.

LABELLING

Although **Binet**'s test was designed for selection purposes, and he said that what was being measured was always changing, IQ tests have frequently been treated as an index of some final, absolute ability. A child's score may become a label, defining its ability and consequently its future. **Labelling** can be a first step in the **self-fulfilling prophecy** (see Chapter 15). The 11-plus exam, it was argued, created a generation of children who thought of themselves as failures. The child who is treated as a failure may see himself as a failure, begin to behave like a failure, and may become a failure.

PREDICTION

Despite the rather gloomy sequence I've just described, research shows that IQ tests are not very good predictors of intellectual ability as an adult. A test which was a good predictor would show a high correlation between the scores a child achieved at any two points in its development. Both the Stanford-Binet and the Wechsler Scales are quite good predictors for children's scores when tests are taken one or two years apart. However, this correlation gets weaker as children go into their mid-teens so that eventually the IQ test is not a very good predictor of later ability. I am sure you can think of some reasons why. They do not take into account things like motivation, commitment, environment, ambition, creativity, social awareness or emotional stability. All of these may be important influences on later ability.

This brings us full circle – can we measure **intelligence?** The answer must be no. First of all, we do not know what intelligence is. Secondly, IQ tests are only ways of comparing people's performance on various tests of mental ability, which have been devised so as to produce a **normal distribution** of scores. This treats intelligence as though it was a physical attribute like weight or height. So IQ tests have contributed to the false idea that intelligence is a 'thing' which is predictable, stable and can be measured. Having said all that, we are now going to look at the influence which heredity and the environment may have on intelligence, and you will see that, in researching this, psychologists have used IQ tests widely. You need to remember these criticisms.

What is the hereditarian view of intelligence?

I

According to the hereditarian view, intelligence is inherited. That is one of the reasons why there are differences between black people and white people in IQ scores, and why bright children tend to come from bright parents. According to this view, the closer the genetic relationship between two people, the more similar their IQ scores should be.

For this reason, some research has focused on twin studies because identical twins have identical genes. Another aspect of research has looked at adopted children, to find out if their IQ scores are closer to their birth parents (evidence for the hereditarian view) or to their adoptive parents (evidence for the environmental view). Let us look at this research and see what conclusions can be drawn from it.

Does research support the hereditarian view?

TWIN STUDIES

I

Because identical twins (monozygotic twins or MZs) come from the same fertilised egg they have exactly the same genes. On the other hand, fraternal twins (dizygotic twins or DZs) are no more alike than any brother or sister: they share 50 per cent of their genes. If identical twins prove to be more alike on IQ scores than *fraternals*, this would be evidence in favour of the hereditarian view.

There have been many twin studies and in 1980 **Robert Plomin** surveyed the results. These were usually in the form of a correlation between IQ scores for each twin. For example, a *strong* correlation would mean that if one twin had a high IQ score, it was very likely the other would. If one twin had a *low* score, it was also very likely that the other would. **Plomin** found that results consistently showed a *stronger* correlation between IQ scores for *identical* twins than fraternal twins. Even so, he noted that fraternal twins showed some correlation.

However a note of caution is necessary. Although the results appear to support the hereditarian view, identical twins tend to be dressed alike and *treated* alike by parents, siblings and teachers. In addition, because they are temperamentally alike they will probably spend a lot of time together. This means that their *environment* is likely to be more similar than fraternal twins, and this may be another reason for closer IQ scores.

Fig. 13.3 The experiences which these identical twins have will be more alike than the experiences of fraternal twins

One way to separate the environmental effects from the effects of heredity is to search out identical twins who have been reared *apart*. Some researchers have done this and the data surveyed by **Plomin** shows there was still a high correlation. When this research is examined in more detail though, it shows some important flaws. As **Leon Kamin** has pointed out, in two-thirds of the pairs one twin was reared by its mother and the other by a grandmother or aunt. Many went to the same school, and the majority were brought up together for several years before they were separated. The criteria for 'separated' twins was at least five years in different homes. You can see why the correlation in IQ scores for these twins was similar to that for twins reared together.

However, the smaller number who *were* reared apart had much lower correlations of IQ. This suggests that those twins who were genuinely separated were more dissimilar than those reared in more similar environments. So both types of twins showed a correlation in IQ scores – which supports the hereditarian view – but the evidence that the lower correlations came from twins who were reared in different environments supports the environmental view of intelligence.

The Minnesota Twin Study, which started in 1979 has been researching adult twins between 19 and 68 years of age. More than 50 pairs have been enrolled from several different countries using advertising and media coverage. This study is looking at twins who have been separated, and the length of separation varies from one year to 60 years.

I

The results also show a strong correlation between IQ scores, thus supporting the genetic view. However there has been criticism of the sampling methods and of evidence that some of the subjects had not been as separated as they claimed.

ADOPTION STUDIES

I

Adoption studies have taken the IQ scores for birth parents, adoptive parents and child. The results show that the IQs of the birth parents are a better indicator of the child's IQ than those of the adoptive parents. This supports the hereditarian view. However, there is a correlation between the adoptive parents' and child's scores. This applies to younger adopted children. From adolescence onwards this relationship is not found. Evidence from families with *two* adopted children shows their IQ scores are more closely related than you would expect as a result of chance. This suggests environmental influence.

S

Research such as that by **A. Dumaret** in France looked at children who were born to mothers from fairly poor or uneducated backgrounds. Results show that children who were adopted into upper class homes tended to have a higher IQ than their siblings who stayed with their birth mothers. Dumaret also compared siblings who were reared in institutions or foster homes, and *their* IQ scores were lowest of all. This is evidence for the environmental view. You can see the comparative IQ scores, using the **Wechsler Scale,** in the bar chart below.

S

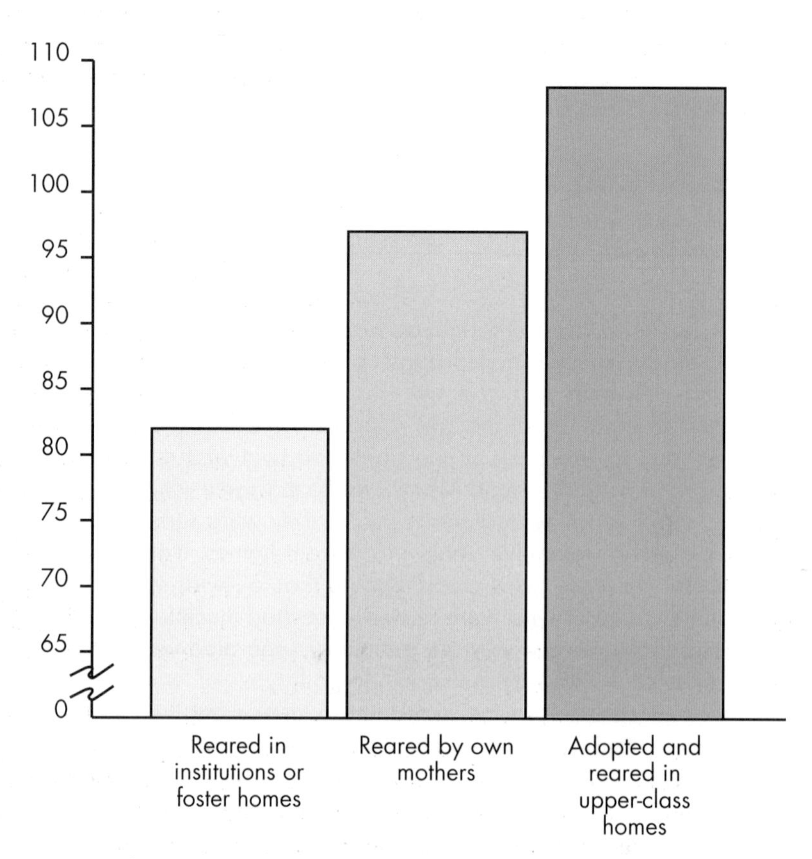

Fig. 13.4 Bar chart showing IQ of siblings reared in different environments (from A. Dumaret 1985)

As far as the hereditarian view is concerned then, there seems to be considerable evidence coming from twin studies which supports the genetic side. Nevertheless, it appears that environment may well play a part, and research from adoption studies suggests that the role of the environment may be considerable. Let us look more closely at research in this area now.

What is the environmental view of intelligence?

The environmental view of intelligence proposes that it develops as a result of the individual's experience. According to this view then, intelligence changes – and so do IQ scores! It proposes that we can increase an IQ score by, for example, giving the child additional stimulation and attention. If the environmental view is to be supported then, we need evidence that this type of change can occur. We have already seen results which suggest this is the case, particularly in the adoption studies. But studies have also focused on particular *aspects* of the environment, so let's see what they have found.

Does research support the environmentalist view?

Environmental factors which seem to be related to IQ scores include nutrition, pre- and post-natal health of the mother, emotional stress, time in school, social class, family influence and special intervention programmes. We will look at the last three factors in some detail.

SOCIAL CLASS

Although there are no apparent differences between children's IQ levels during the first two years, the differences become apparent soon after and *increase* with age. From this point, research shows that children from poor, working-class or relatively uneducated families have lower than average IQs than do children from middle-class families. However, one of the difficulties in looking at the effect of class on intelligence is that of defining class. Studies use different definitions, such as father's profession or family income. We have already seen that some of the research takes account of the *mother's* level of education. It appears that level of education of one or both parents (rather than father's job) and the degree of poverty or affluence both seem to be important factors which are related to IQ scores.

There has been research into which biological factors at the time of birth may be related to lower **intellectual** development. These factors include maternal stress, poor diet and nutrition for both mother and child, smoking and birth difficulties. They are all correlated with lower class status and *also* with poorer intellectual development, although the reasons for this relationship are complicated.

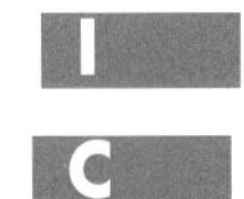

Another view of intellectual development comes from researchers who have looked at language. There are some very strong arguments from psychologists which propose that language and intellectual ability are closely related. However, **Basil Bernstein** proposed that there was a relationship between language and class. He said working-class children tend to hear less complex language and fewer abstract ideas than middle-class children and as a result they have lower **intellectual** ability. He called the difference between the two types of language **restricted** and **elaborated** codes.

Although he has received criticisms that his work was biased because he tested children's ability to understand **elaborated** codes, rather than see how they used language in their own environment, there is an important point here. The education system uses the elaborated code – teachers use standard forms of English, expect children to understand verbal instructions and value elaborated rather than restricted codes. This disadvantages any child who is not brought up to use and understand the elaborated code, and as Bernstein found, these are more likely to be children from working-class homes.

FAMILY INFLUENCE

Helen Bee has reviewed research into families whose children achieve high IQ scores and concluded that they shared five characteristics:

- **appropriate play materials** for the child's stage of development were provided. It is their *appropriateness,* not the quantity of toys, which were important. This links with Piaget's ideas for cognitive development (see Chapter 16)
- **emotionally responsive and involved parents** answered questions, listened to and encouraged the child. They spent time with the child, creating a warm environment
- **parent's language** when talking to their child was rich and accurate
- **high expectations** were shown: parents expected their child to develop rapidly and do well in school
- **room to explore** and even make mistakes was allowed. Excessive restriction or control was avoided

There are a number of studies which show strong correlation between these five characteristics and high IQ. However, **Bee** notes that one study showed that the fifth factor was probably more important than the others because mothers who were punitive had children with *lower* IQs.

We have already seen that because this research only shows a correlation we can not say what *causes* IQ. But one study tested for the possibility that the link was genetic. **Robert Plomin**'s study in 1985 looked at family interactions and *adopted* children. He still found a correlation between quality of interaction and the children's later IQ. Although the correlation was not so strong, it was still good evidence for the importance of family interactions.

This suggests that heredity is not the crucial variable affecting the correlation, but we must remember that factors related to heredity could still be involved. For example **temperament** is likely to affect the way the parent interacts with the child, and the way the child responds to its environment. The child's intelligence may be a factor in the interaction – a bright, articulate, responsive child will encourage the parent to spend more time with it, take more time in talking and explaining, and so on.

SPECIAL INTERVENTION PROGRAMMES

Special intervention programmes are schemes which help children who may live in particularly unstimulating environments. They offer these children an **enriched** environment from a young age, with the aim of enhancing their development so that they can also benefit from the formal school system. Many programmes were started in America in the late 1960s under **Operation Head Start**. The programmes varied: for example sometimes teachers would visit children at home; others offered different types of stimulation

Early results from Head Start programmes showed, on average, a jump in IQ of about 10 points for children in the first couple of years. However disappointment followed, when it seemed that this effect 'wore off' as they went through early school years. But as these children moved into early teens the gains seemed to reappear. When these children were compared with those from similar backgrounds who had no **enrichment,** then the enriched children were doing better. This reappearance of the benefits of the enrichment programme has been called the **'sleeper effect'**. The graph in Fig. 13.5 shows clearly how the scores of the enriched group are similar to the non-enriched group until about 11 years of age.

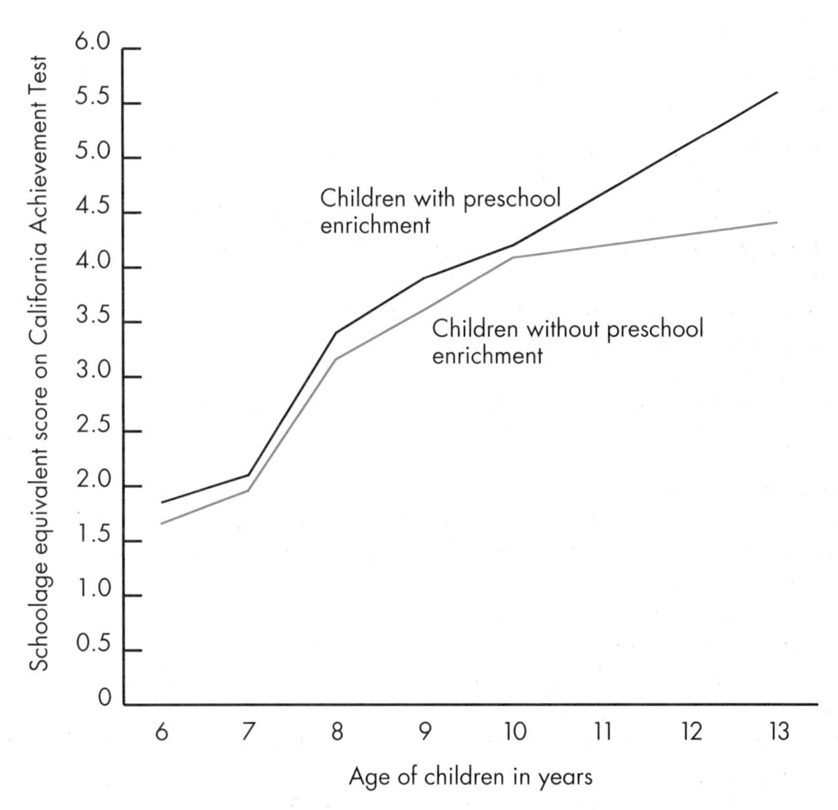

Fig. 13.5 Scores of children from enriched and non-enriched pre-school programmes (from H. Bee 1992)

These results are typical for 12 American studies which were surveyed by **Irving Lazar and Richard Darlington**, who highlighted the 'sleeper effect'. They also found that children who had been part of the pre-school **enrichment** programmes were less likely to have to repeat a year in school, or enter a remedial class. So, although the scores appear similar in the early school years, the children may have been able to cope with school better.

Darlington is one of several psychologists to note that a possible reason for these results is not so much to do with the programmes themselves, but more to do with the difference the programme makes to the *parent's* attitude. Parents became more interested in their child's development, and learned better skills to help the child, and Darlington says it is this factor which has the most impact on the child's improvement.

S

Some programmes have focused on children from particularly deprived environments, and have taken them in special day-care **enrichment** programmes five days a week, all day. One study, run by **Craig Ramey** and his colleagues, took children whose mothers also had low IQs. The children started when two to three months old and the programme provided an environment similar to that which **Bee** described as a good home environment – warm and stimulating. **Ramey** found a considerable increase in the IQ levels of the enriched children throughout the programme and into school.

So what have these studies told us about the influence of the environment? Because children's IQ scores can increase, and that increase persists, this suggests that the environment does have some influence. However, correlational studies again form the largest base of evidence and these show only that a more stimulating and physically healthy environment is correlated with greater **intellectual** development. We are still unsure just how this occurs.

What is the outcome of the nature or nurture debate on intelligence?

Research into this topic is particularly prone to problems. We have already seen that psychologists cannot agree on what intelligence is, that we are not able to measure it, and that, because research takes place in the field, there are many variables which can affect results. Much of the research has produced correlations, that can only show relationships, not cause and effect.

It appears that both heredity and the environment play a part in the development of **intelligence** and though some psychologists say heredity is more important, the majority are more interested in just *how* these two influences interact. We have seen how often in the research that these factors seem to be intertwined. Psychologists have pointed out that the genetic aspect of intelligence provides a *potential* but, as in other areas of our ability, it is the environment which influences how much of this potential is reached. It has been called the 'rubber band' hypothesis. Briefly, this says that intelligence is like a rubber band, the genetic aspect of intelligence determines how *long* it will be, and the environmental aspect determines how *far* it will be stretched.

A description of how this interaction might occur is offered by **T. Bouchard**. He says that our innate abilities and dispositions direct us to those experiences which interest us and are relevant to us. We may therefore pay little attention to other aspects of our environment if they do not appear to be useful to us.

Other psychologists have pointed out that in any case intelligence is abstract, and that one can only look at intelligent behaviour, which operates differently in different cultural environments. They add that our emphasis on intelligence is also cultural to some degree – a reflection of the individualist and competitive nature of Western societies.

Further Reading

Bee H (1992) *The Developing Child* (6th ed), New York, Harper Collins

EXERCISES

1 What is wrong with the sampling method in the Minnesota Twin Study? Describe a better method.
2 Describe two limitations of IQ tests.
3 In your own words give two reasons why it is difficult to discover whether intelligence is largely due to heredity or environment.
4 Describe in your own words one study which offers support for the hereditarian view of intelligence.
5 Describe in your own words one study which offers support for the environmental view of intelligence.
6 Think about Bouchard's comments at the end of the chapter and imagine a visit to the beach. What might interest a three year old ? What might interest his nine year old sister ? Explain your answer.

Chapter 14
The Development of Gender

When a baby is born one of the first questions we ask is – 'Is it a boy or a girl?' From that moment on, the sex of the infant becomes a central part of how we see it. But the baby does not know what it means to be a boy or a girl. How does it find out? In other words, how does a child's gender concept develop?

Some adults who physically appear to be males say they have a female identity. What does this mean? It means that their sense of themselves is as a female. We would say that their gender identity does not agree with their biological label. In this chapter we are going to look at how our understanding of gender develops, and evidence and reasons for gender differences.

What is gender?

I

S

Although **gender** is often used instead of **sex**, the two do have different meanings. Generally 'sex' refers to biological aspects of the individual. For example, a child's sex is identified at birth by whether or not it has a penis. In contrast '**gender**' refers to the psychological or cultural aspects of maleness or femaleness. So, when we refer to **gender differences** we mean the differences which a society sees between males and females – the jobs they do, the way they are treated, the clothes they wear, the personality traits they have.

Another term you will come across here is **gender identity**. It is the name for the first stage in the development of **gender concept**, but it is also used to mean the *inner* sense that we have of our maleness or femaleness. You can see I have used this term in the second paragraph at the top of this chapter.

Most of the ideas and work we will be looking at comes from Western societies – chiefly Britain and the United States. When we talk of what is typical or appropriate for males or females, we are referring to these societies.

What is gender concept and how does it develop?

Our **gender concept** is our sense of what it means to be male or to be female. For example, when a child has developed a gender concept it knows what sex it is, that one's sex does not change and it knows the features which its society associates with males or females. This knowledge includes awareness of its own behaviour and preferences, as well as those of others.

It appears that a child's **gender concept** develops in three stages: gender identity, gender stability and gender constancy. These three stages have been proposed by **Lawrence Kohlberg**, whose ideas we will return to later. However for now we will look at each of the stages in a little detail.

GENDER IDENTITY (UP TO THREE YEARS OLD)

S

By about 18 months of age the child knows what 'label' it is – a boy or a girl (its **gender identity**). By the age of two and a half years old it can 'label' other children as well, but this is largely due to their appearance. The child will look at clothes and hair for instance in order to decide what label to apply. Knowing the right label means the child can identify the sex of the person. However it thinks that this is changeable. For example a girl may think that she can grow up to be a daddy, or that a man who put on a dress would become a woman.

GENDER STABILITY (THREE TO FOUR YEARS OLD)

C

The child has **gender stability** when it understands that it will be the *same sex* throughout its life. So a four-year-old girl, when asked whether she will be a woman or a man when she grows up, will know that she will become a woman. However, she is less sure about others and can still be deceived by appearances.

For children, one of the most important clues about judging a person's sex is how they look. In the 1950s, only men had short hair and wore trousers, only women had ponytails and wore earrings. Forty years later, these gender clues have disappeared. Nevertheless, psychologists still use appearance as one way of testing a child's understanding of gender.

In **Sandra Bem**'s 1989 study, she showed her subjects photographs of a male and a female toddler with no clothes on the lower part of their bodies. (Bem had to be very careful about the ethics in this study – see below). It was clear which sex they were because their genitals were visible. However, on the *top* part of their bodies they wore clothes for the *other* sex. In this way the cultural definition of sex (clothes) was in conflict with the biological (genitals).

Ethical concerns in research

Psychologists must make sure that when they study children, they first get the consent of the parents or guardian. These people are treated as though they are themselves the subjects. They can withdraw their child from the research at any time, and the research must not cause distress to these adults or their children.

For example, in **Sandra Bem**'s study, the parents of the subjects and of the toddlers who appeared in the photographs all saw the photographs first, and gave their written consent to their children's participation. In addition, when subjects were shown the photographs, it was in their own home, with at least one parent present.

Results showed that the majority of subjects were still at the stage of **gender stability**, because only 40 per cent of three to five year olds knew that changing clothes made no difference to the sex of the child. Cross-cultural research also shows that even when children know their sex cannot change, they can still be confused about gender stability in others.

GENDER CONSTANCY (FROM FIVE ONWARDS)

In **Bem**'s study, the 40 per cent of subjects who correctly identified the sex of the toddler had achieved a complete concept of gender – called **gender constancy**. This means that they knew that a person's sex stays the same throughout their lives, regardless of any other changes. However, another study showed different results – when children saw photographs of their classmates dressed in other sex clothes, almost *all* three to five year olds knew their classmates were still the same sex. The difference could have been because they knew their classmates well, but Bem's study used *strangers*.

Children's behaviour and its relationship to gender

C

What have psychologists found out about a child's behaviour in relation to gender? Alongside the development of **gender concept**, which is the child's understanding of what it means to be male or female, is the development of the child's *behaviour* and *attitudes* related to gender in their society. Let's look at some of the research which tells us what children know and how they behave at various ages. We can then look at some theories for how this knowledge develops, and can see how well each theory explains these research results.

S

It appears that quite young children can differentiate between the two sexes and prefer things related to their own sex. Observational studies have shown that at two or three years old children play more with toys 'appropriate' for their sex – girls with dolls, boys with guns. **Carol Jacklin and Eleanor Maccoby** showed that at this age children are much more sociable with playmates of the *same* sex. In spite of this, two year olds cannot say what type of toy another girl (or boy) would like to play with. Other research found that at two and a half to three and a half years old children could say which behaviours were shown by boys and which by girls.

Diane Ruble and her colleagues found that choices for 'appropriate' playmates and toys became stronger at about five to six years old. Details of their study appear later in the chapter. This tendency to show gender-appropriate behaviour seems to be stronger in boys. They tend to make other boys conform to 'appropriate' boy behaviour. Four or five year old boys may make fun of boys who play with dolls, who cry, or who dress as girls. However, girls show less concern at such cross-sex behaviour. It seems from these studies that by four or five years of age children have a clear idea of what behaviour is associated with each sex but boys are more concerned to enforce it.

C

In addition, children's **stereotyped** ideas of what is correct for *males* appears to develop earlier, and be stronger, than stereotyped ideas about females. The stereotypes for both sexes seem to get stronger up to about seven years old; we can see the beginnings of this in **Ruble**'s study. However the stereotypes seem to get weaker as the child approaches adolescence.

Fig.14.1 These toys encourage the child to adopt gender-related behaviour

L

Research into the way nursery school teachers may affect a child's behaviour was conducted by **Beverly Fagot** in 1985. She found that teachers rewarded both boys and girls for behaviour which was co-operative and quiet, in other words behaviour associated more with girls than boys. Despite this, boys continued to show **stereotypical** male behaviour, and only changed when *other boys* showed disapproval or approval. In contrast a girl's behaviour responded to reinforcement from the teacher and other girls.

Several studies have looked at children raised in one-parent, two parent or homosexual homes and found no evidence of problems with **gender concept** or behaviour. For example one study comprised an experimental group of 37 children aged five to 17 years who were raised in lesbian homes. The control group comprised 38 children of the same age, raised in single parent heterosexual families. The researchers found no difference between the two groups on any of the measures of gender role which they used, and concluded that children who are brought up in homosexual families are not confused about their **gender identity**.

Now that we have some conclusions from research, let's look at some explanations for how children learn to be a male or a female in their society – this is known as **gender acquisition**. We will examine four theories – the psychodynamic, social learning, cognitive-developmental and gender-schema explanations in turn. We will then see how well the research we have just looked at is explained by each theory.

Psychodynamic explanations for the acquisition of gender

According to **Freud**'s **psychoanalytic** theory (see Chapter 12) the child acquires the appropriate features of its gender during the **phallic stage** of psychosexual development.

I

At about four years old the **libido** focuses on the genitals and the child becomes attracted to its opposite sex parent. This creates conflict between the child's desire for its opposite sex parent and fear of punishment from the same sex parent and in boys is called the **Oedipus conflict**. Freud claimed that a boy thought he would be castrated by his father. In order to reduce fear of his father and gain possession of his mother, a boy **identifies** with his father. This means the boy tries to become like his father by taking on his behaviours, speech and attitudes. This is how the boy adopts the correct behaviours and attitudes for a male in his society.

The conflict for girls is called the **Electra conflict** but it works differently from boys. A girl thinks she has already been castrated, she blames her mother, and transfers her affections to her father because he has a penis and the girls wants one. However, because a girl's fear of her mother is less strong than the boy's of his father, the girl experiences less conflict. Thus, according to Freud, she identifies less strongly with her mother. A girl, therefore, may have a weaker sense of what it means to be female, and how to be a female.

According to **Freud** then, children of both sexes should start to show gender-appropriate behaviour by about five years of age, and the differences between the two types of behaviour should be clear. The evidence we looked at earlier shows that gender-appropriate behaviour *is* more apparent from about five years old onwards. Nevertheless children do show preference for same-sex toys and friends a long time before the **phallic** stage is reached. According to Freud's ideas this should not happen.

Another criticism is that a boy brought up in a family without a father would have a weak **gender identity** because he had no father to identify with. As we have already seen, research on one parent and homosexual homes shows no evidence of this. Overall then the **psychodynamic** explanation does not appear to be very useful.

Social learning explanations for the acquisition of gender

According to social learning theorists a child acquires the appropriate features of its gender by the major processes of social learning – modelling, reinforcement and punishment, and self-efficacy.

MODELLING

L

Bandura proposed that the child learns by observing others and modelling their behaviour. The child is more likely to model itself on those who are **nurturant, powerful** or **similar**, and it is this last factor which has the most influence on gender- appropriate behaviour because this means those of the *same* sex will be more important. Some of these models will become more important than others, and the child will attend less to a specific behaviour and more to the many ways that model behaves. Eventually the child will **internalise** that model's behaviours so that it will be able to act as that person would act in a situation it has never seen the model in. This explanation suggests the importance of the same sex adult in the family.

L

We saw earlier that *boys* discourage other boys from cross-sex play. The social learning theory explanation is that these boys are modelling the behaviour of their fathers, or other adult males.

Children's toys also provide opportunities to model same sex behaviour. Adults tend to give girls items such as tea-sets, dolls houses, make-up and Barbie dolls. Boys are more likely to get soldiers, weapons or football club outfits. But as we have seen, children *also* show a preference for gender-related toys. These toys enable the child to model sex-related behaviour more completely. They are also giving the child messages about what kind of models the adult *approves* of and this brings us to our next topic – reinforcement.

L

REINFORCEMENT AND PUNISHMENT

There is evidence that people *expect* boys to be different from girls. Parents describing their newborn babies said the boys were stronger than the girls, and the girls were smaller than the boys. In fact both sexes of babies were very similar in size and weight. The growing child will learn these expectations from the patterns of reinforcement and punishment which it experiences.

L

C. Smith and B. Lloyd dressed infant boys and girls in blue, gave them boys' names, and observed how strangers (who were also experienced mothers) interacted with them. They then dressed the same babies in pink and gave them girls' names, and observed how stranger mothers interacted with them. The results showed that when the babies were thought to be boys, they were played with more physically and given toys such as a hammer shaped rattle to play with. When they were thought to be girls, they were held and talked to more, and given soft toys to play with. From these results Smith and Lloyd concluded that the subjects (the adults) were responding to the baby according to what sex they *thought* it was, not according to its *actual* behaviours and needs.

Theorists such as **Walter Mischel** have argued that the child learns the appropriate behaviour by the pattern of reinforcement we give it. By this he means that when the child shows sex-appropriate behaviour it is rewarded and approved of. When it shows opposite sex behaviour, it will be ignored or even punished. Research shows that *fathers* are more concerned that children show the appropriate behaviour, particularly in their sons. They will discourage boys from 'girls' activities but are less troubled if girls play 'tomboy' games.

L

SELF-EFFICACY

Bandura said that through the process of internalising a model's behaviour, learning which settings or circumstances are rewarding for which kinds of behaviour, the child achieves **self-efficacy**. This is related to the child's self-concept, and is when the child is able to predict outcomes of behaviour and to have certain expectations about itself. These expectations and standards form the core of personality.

Jeanne Block has looked at sex-role behaviour in terms of self-efficacy and has highlighted some important differences in the way members of the two sexes are treated. She said that boys are taught (through toys and the behaviour which is reinforced) to be

L

competent and exploratory whereas girls are taught to be more careful and dependent. Boys therefore achieve a much *stronger* sense of self-efficacy than girls and research suggests this extends to the wider choice of jobs which men feel they can do.

Fig. 14.2 These young women belong to the Tamil Tigers in Sri Lanka. How closely do they fit your idea of what is appropriate for females?

Studies of social learning ideas indicate how parents and others create an environment which shows their son or daughter what is appropriate behaviour. Reinforcement which is given by someone of the same sex appears to be more powerful. However, as we saw earlier, studies have shown that children are making gender-related choices of friends and toys *even* when there is no apparent external pressure to do so. In addition, this theory does not explain why children's behaviour seems to become more **stereotyped** at about six years of age. So, although social learning can offer many convincing explanations of some aspects of gender acquisition, it does not appear to explain *all* the findings.

C

Cognitive-developmental explanations for the acquisition of gender

According to **Lawrence Kohlberg** the child acquires its gender *after* it understands gender concept. He proposed that **gender concept** develops through the three stages which we came across earlier in the chapter (see page 149) and his ideas are based on **Piaget**'s theory of cognitive development.

Piaget proposed that at about seven years old a child would be able to **conserve**. This means it understands that something stays the same even though its *appearance*

C

changes (you can find a full explanation in Chapter 16). Piaget said a child could conserve when it understood that liquid poured into a different shaped glass was still the same in *amount* even though it looked different. A child who can conserve would also understand that a person's *sex* is the same even though the person *looks* different. Research has shown that a child who makes the right judgement about liquid amount *also* makes it about gender, and equally that a child unable to conserve liquid amount fails to show **gender constancy**. By about six years of age gender constancy has developed.

Kohlberg said that *until* the child has reached **gender constancy** its behaviour will not be sex-typed. Once it understands that gender is constant then it will start to use the appropriate behaviours, copy the appropriate models, and so on.

L

There is research which supports this idea from **Diane Ruble** and her colleagues.

Ruble, Balaban and Cooper (1981)

Subjects Subjects were 50 males and 50 females between four and six years of age. They were given various tests and were then identified as high in gender constancy or low in gender constancy. Subjects were assigned to one of three conditions, each having an equal number of subjects high and low in gender constancy.

Procedure In the two experimental conditions subjects saw a cartoon which was interrupted by a commercial. In one condition the commercial showed two boys playing with a gender-neutral toy, in the other condition two girls played with the same toy. In the control condition the subjects only saw the cartoon. Afterwards each subject had the opportunity to play with the toy and the researcher asked questions about whether the toy would be suitable for a little girl, a little boy or both.

Results Results showed that only the subjects who showed high gender constancy were affected by the sex of the children in the commercial. When other sex models had been playing with it, they avoided spending time with the toy and said it would be appropriate for an opposite sex child.

Ruble and her colleagues concluded this was evidence that a child's attitude to a choice of toy changes at about five or six years old, once it has **gender constancy**. When this has occurred, the child is then *active* in searching out gender-appropriate toys and behaviour. Until then, she says, the child is only *passively* influenced by reinforcement and information relating to gender.

L

Although these stages in the development of **gender concept** are supported by evidence from some of the studies we looked at earlier, there is still an inconsistency. This is that children show differences in choice of toy and playmate *before* the time when they understand the label 'boy' or 'girl'. **Kohlberg** did not explain this.

Gender schema explanation

C

This explanation is cognitive, like the previous one, but has a different approach and has developed through the 1980s. We have come across schemas several times. They are mental frameworks which we create and which we use to make sense of what we experience.

C

Carol Martin and Charles Halverson have proposed that when the child has acquired basic **gender identity** at about two and three years old, it starts to organise its experience and perceptions around its own gender – in other words it starts to develop a **gender schema.** Initially it is a simple schema comprising an 'in-group' (those of my sex) and an 'out-group' (the rest). When **gender constancy** develops, by about six years old, the child starts to pay much more attention to information which is *relevant* to its own gender schema. Also, because its cognitive development at this stage includes understanding and applying rules, the child has fairly fixed ideas about what is 'right' and 'wrong' behaviour for its sex. Gradually as its schema becomes more complex and flexible, it is able to understand gender in a more flexible way.

Psychologists such as **Sandra Bem** have found that those adults who have a **stereotyped** gender schema do see the world through a male or female 'lens'. For example, a woman who sees herself as feminine and adopts traditionally female behaviours, is more likely to remember more 'female' words (such as bikini) from a word-list than 'male' words.

C

Gender schema theory explains why a young child knows what sex it is but is still confused about others – it is because it has a simple schema. It also says that stages in the development of the **gender concept** are evidence of the gender schema becoming richer and more complex. Once gender concept has developed it is as though the child fully realises the implications for him- or herself and pays much more attention to the gender-related behaviour of others. The child **assimilates** this new information by trying to adapt its environment to its schema – and we see that this means a rather *rigid* view of gender behaviour. Finally it starts to **accommodate** and become more flexible – 'it's OK for a girl to be a soldier, it's just that I don't want to'.

Overall, this is the most comprehensive explanation, of the four, for how a child acquires its gender. Where it is weakest is in the early years. It says why children choose same sex toys and playmates from an early age, because our schemas affect what we pay attention to, but if our schemas are so vague then why are children so consistent in their preferences at such a young age? This is better explained by social learning ideas.

It appears then that the child acquires its gender through the interaction between itself and its environment. As its understanding of its world changes, so does the child's own behaviour and gender concept.

What evidence is there for gender differences?

There has been a lot of research comparing males and females, and in 1974 **Eleanor Maccoby and Carol Jacklin** surveyed more than 1,500 studies in their book *The Psychology of Sex Differences*. Sometimes there was conflicting evidence, but overall they concluded that, according to the research, the only consistent differences between males and females were:

- males were more physically and verbally aggressive than females

- boys were superior on visuo-spatial tasks and arithmetic reasoning
- girls were superior on language skills

Since then research has continued, still with contradictory findings, but we will look at some which support the first two of the differences listed above and another one:

- males tend to over-estimate their ability, females to under-estimate it

AGGRESSION

Studies of aggression often involve observing the child's behaviour – whether in a natural setting or, like **Bandura**'s work, in a laboratory setting. Aggression can be very difficult to measure. For example studies which have asked parents to describe their children's behaviour have shown how often comments are made about the *energy level* of boys. When comparing studies of aggression one study may include *verbal taunting* but another may not. This is why a report of a study must say how the researchers measured aggression.

J. Langlois carried out an observational study on pairs of children playing in a well-stocked playroom. Some pairs were of the same sex and others were boy and girl. Their play and interactions were observed, and results showed little difference in levels of aggression at three years old. By five years old however, boys consistently showed more aggression than girls – but only towards other *boys.*

This is one of several studies which show that less aggression is shown towards girls than towards boys. One explanation could be that children have learned that females are not acceptable targets for aggression or it could be that girls know aggression but do not show it. For example, in **Bandura**'s studies of modelling, boys showed more aggressive behaviour towards the Bobo doll than girls (see Chapter 11). However when the children were rewarded for showing the behaviour they had observed, girls showed that they could remember as much as boys.

L

VISUO-SPATIAL TASKS

Research has shown consistently that boys get better scores on visuo-spatial tasks than girls do. Two examples of visuo-spatial tasks are given in Fig. 14.3 on the next page.

C

This ability is one of the abilities assessed by **intelligence** tests, and as part of the standardisation of the **Wechsler Scale** (see Chapter 13) in the mid-1960s, over 2,000 six to 16 year olds were tested in America. Results showed that up to adolescence boys were slightly better at visuo-spatial tasks than girls. However, by the mid-teens, boys scored higher than girls on all types of visuo-spatial tasks. In an attempt to find out some reasons for this difference, **M. Allen** studied *how* males and females went about solving these types of problems. Results showed that they both used the same strategies for solving the problems, but females were less successful. Allen concluded that failure to solve the problems could have led the female subjects to guess.

Another explanation for this could be related to girls' experience with maths at school. Research in America and Britain has shown that in the middle of this century the majority of maths teachers were male and that the lack of a female role model may have affected girls' perceptions of their own ability. Other research in education showed that these teachers tended to *expect* girls to do less well and to have more difficulties than boys. Poor results and low confidence could have occurred as a result of the **self-fulfilling prophecy.**

L

S

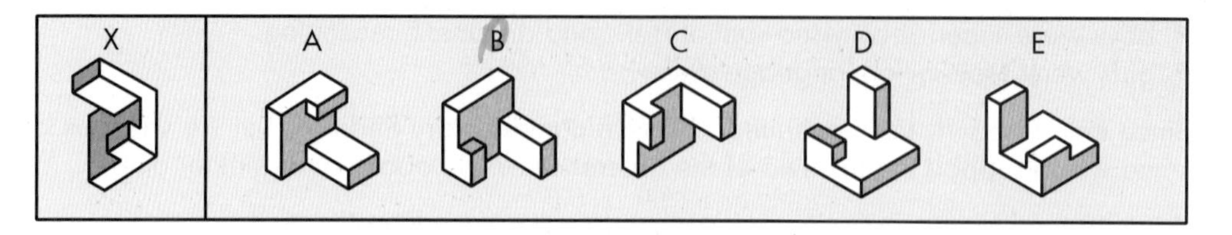

Look at figures A–E. Which of these shows figure X viewed from a different angle?

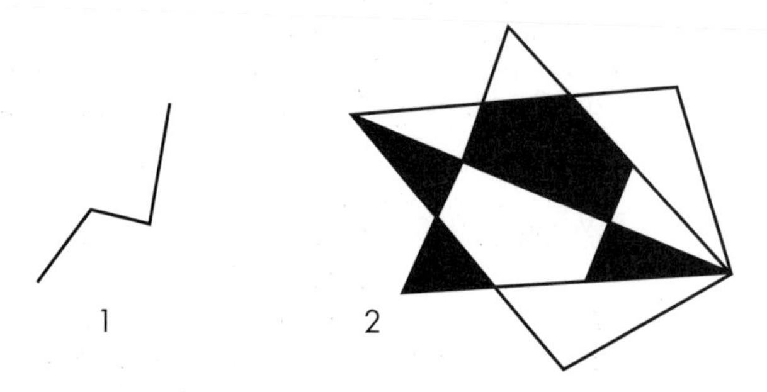

Find the figure 1 in the pattern shown in figure 2.

Fig.14.3 Two examples of a visuo-spatial task

So, although the evidence suggests that girls *are* poorer at visuo-spatial tasks, it could be that any difference in ability has been exaggerated by girls' experience.

ESTIMATING ABILITY

There is some research which shows that women tend to under-estimate their own ability and men to over-estimate theirs. When asked how well they are going to do in a test, for example, men predict higher grades for themselves than women, even when the women do better than the men in the test itself! More consistent findings come from research which has compared male and female explanations for success or failure. These show that when they succeed, men say it is due to their *skill* but women are more likely to say their own success was due to *luck*. Equally, when they fail on a task, men tend to say it was due to the task *difficulty* and women tend to say they weren't any good at it. Can you see the pattern here? To over-simplify a little, when men succeed it's because they are competent, when they fail it's not their fault. When women succeed it's because they were lucky; when they fail it is their fault.

There have been several possible explanations for this, such as women fear success or women have low self-esteem. Research on these explanations shows contradictory findings. Another possibility is that women have learned to see themselves as having less power and being inferior, and this explains their attitude to their own ability. **David Burgner and Miles Hewstone** wanted to see whether this sex difference was apparent at a young age and also to see whether it might be due to feelings of inferiority. They provided a task which a subject could do easily (the successful outcome) and one which was extremely difficult (the unsuccessful outcome). Here are some details of their study.

Burgner and Hewstone (1993)

Subjects Subjects were several groups of boys and girls, with a mean age of five and a quarter years. Some were white and some were Asian.

Materials A seven-piece jigsaw of a clown was provided for the successful outcome. For the unsuccessful outcome, there was a small loop which had to be moved along a twisted wire. If the loop touched the wire a buzzer sounded. A third task was provided which was similar to the wire and loop task, but was very easy. The results on this last task were not part of the experiment. The tasks were completed on a small table with the experimenter and child sat either side. A tape-recorder was hidden underneath the table to record the child's responses.

Procedure The experimenter demonstrated the jigsaw puzzle, then broke it up and asked the child to complete it. When the child had finished it was asked 'Why did you think you could do/not do that?' The same sequence was repeated with the difficult loop and wire task. Finally each child completed the easy task.

Burgner and Hewstone found that the results followed the expected pattern. Boys took credit for success and blamed something else for their failure. Some girls said success was due to luck and some to ability, and some said failure was due to lack of ability and others to task difficulty. The researchers concluded that this shows the differences found for adults are evident at five years of age.

You will remember that one explanation for these results is that girls feel inferior to boys. Burgner and Hewstone reasoned that Asian children might also feel inferior, so that is why they were included in this study. If inferiority was the cause, then the results from *Asian* children should be similar to the results from *girls*. They found no evidence of a difference between Asian and white children and so concluded that the reasons for girls' explanations for success and failure were *not* due to a sense of inferiority.

S

We have looked at only a tiny number of the studies of sex differences, and I have already mentioned that results frequently contradict each other. In addition, results suggest that differences which were thought to be evident 30 years ago may no longer be apparent. This is probably due to changing cultural expectations of men and women as well as greater sensitivity to gender stereotyping.

A final comment on research into sex differences is that it *emphasises* the differences between men and women. In reality many of the differences which have been studied have been found to be fairly equally distributed amongst men and women. By stressing the gender differences we ignore what we have in common and the way in which we differ from individual to individual.

How are gender differences promoted and reinforced?

THE MEDIA

We have seen from social learning theory that people model themselves on others, particularly those who are similar to them, or who are seen as powerful or rewarded for their behaviour. Children, who are particularly open to learning in this way, will gain a lot of information from what they watch or hear or read. What is of concern here is that males and females are sometimes portrayed in the media in **stereotypical** ways.

Aletha Huston found that adverts for boys' toys were loud and fast, whereas those for girls' toys were soft and fuzzy. When six year olds were shown ads for a 'neutral' toy, but in either the 'fast' or the 'fuzzy' style, they could tell whether the ad was aimed at a girl or a boy by the style it used. In television advertising, several surveys in America and Britain have found males are usually the authority figures, the voice-overs, those who act independently and give arguments for buying products. These adverts portray men as more important and influential than women.

Television also shows society's role models and these are predominantly male – politicians, sports people, lawyers, programme presenters, police officers and so on. A child whose home and school environment includes a wide range of role models will still see that 'out there' men have most of the action and the power. Nevertheless, television does offer less traditional role models, for example in programmes like Gladiators.

Fig. 14.4 Gladiators – challenging gender stereotypes

In young children's books there is still some **stereotyping.** Fairy stories (Snow White, Sleeping Beauty, Cinderella, Rumpelstiltskin) all have beautiful helpless heroines who are rescued by strong adventurous princes. History books are filled with male models – heroes, kings, explorers, adventurers, scientists.

The 'Janet and John' learn to read books which were popular in the 1960s showed John helping Dad build a tree house while Janet and Mum made the sandwiches. They showed Mum setting the table for tea and Dad coming home from work with his briefcase. Not only were these books showing gender **stereotypes** for boys and girls, men and women, but they were also promoting the idea of a **stereotypical** family – mother, father and two children, all white. Such stereotyping is less evident today, partly as a result of pressure by parents and teachers.

C

PARENTS

Parents have a crucial influence on their children's gender development. **Jeffrey Rubin** and his colleagues found that within 24 hours of their baby's birth, parents described their girls as softer and smaller than parents of boys, who thought their boys were more alert, stronger and better co-ordinated. There was no apparent physical difference in size, weight or response. Fathers tended to see greater differences between the sexes than mothers did.

Several studies have shown that parents respond differently to their child's behaviour depending on the sex of the child. **Robert Sears** and his colleagues found parents tolerated **aggression** in their sons much more than in their daughters – this could strengthen the difference in aggression which has been found. Parents are more likely to punish a boy if he hits a girl than if he hits another boy.

L

We have already seen in this chapter that the toys we buy, clothes we provide and whether we approve or disapprove of certain behaviours all affect the child's development. Our attitudes and expectations may affect children's abilities. I have already referred to differences in maths ability and in children's explanations for success and failure. A study by **Susan Holloway and Robert Hess** showed how parents may reinforce these differences. They found that *mothers* of girls *also* explained their daughter's success in maths as due to effort and good teaching, but for boys it was due to ability. Failure in maths was due to lack of ability in daughters, but lack of effort in sons.

S

SCHOOL

When it is playtime in school, if girls are told to form a line and boys another line, then sex differences are being highlighted. Research in the 1970s showed differences in the way teachers treated children – they spent more time talking to boys than girls. This seemed to be partly because boys were more disruptive in class, but also teachers were found to have higher expectations of boys than of girls. Teachers rewarded girls who were well-behaved, but rewarded boys when they tried. This is how gender differences may be identified and reinforced.

L

The role models which teachers provide are also influential. The majority of primary teachers are female, yet a greater proportion of headteachers are male. In secondary schools, there are more males in senior positions than females. The predominance of male teachers in maths and sciences may also affect a child's expectations of the kind of jobs which are appropriate for men and women.

Finally then we have seen how children develop their idea of what it means to be male or female in their society, although none of the theories explain fully how it occurs. We have also seen that there appear to be differences between males and females, but because of the cultural emphasis on differences, the similarities have been hidden. Society itself is also changing, stereotyped ideas of the male as breadwinner are no longer true and many of the gender stereotyped jobs – typists and shipbuilders for example – are disappearing. This makes it harder to study gender differences.

Further Reading

Bee H (1992) *The Developing Child* (6th ed), New York, Harper Collins
Deaux K, Dane F and Wrightsman L (1993) *Social Psychology in the 90s* (6th ed), Pacific Grove, Brooks/Cole
Nicholson J (1984) *Men and Women – How Different Are They?* Oxford, Oxford University Press

EXERCISES

1 What was the IV and the DV in the Smith and Lloyd study?
2 What was the purpose of the control condition in the Ruble study?
3 If you were to replicate the Burgner and Hewstone study, what would your experimental hypothesis be?
4 What was the purpose of the final task in the Burgner and Hewstone study? (Think about ethics and 'distress'.)
5 Describe one difference between any two explanations for the development of gender.
6 Imagine you run a playgroup. One three-year-old boy goes straight to the dressing-up box as soon as he arrives and spends the rest of the morning in a large pink hat, a flowered skirt and several bracelets. Explain his behaviour, using one of the four explanations of the acquisition of gender.

Chapter 15

Towards a Concept of Self

In this chapter we are going to look at the idea of 'self'. Philosophers and psychologists have discussed the peculiar situation which results from thinking about ourselves. When we study ourselves we are both the object being studied and the person doing the studying. Imagine we have a dilemma – shall we go out tonight with friends or stay in and study? As we are making our decision we can, at the same time, observe how we are responding to our friends' persuasion, deciding whether to spend money now or wait until the weekend, thinking about how we'll feel tomorrow after a late night. We can evaluate what we are doing as we do it.

As we will see, this type of evaluation seems to be one of the ways in which we learn about ourselves – about the kind of person we are, and how we feel about ourselves. This chapter will look at our self-concept and how it is related to our social relationships.

What is a concept of self?

Self-concept has been defined as the set of views or beliefs which the individual has about him- or herself. Our self-concept is generally considered to consist of two parts – our **self-image** (what we know about ourselves) and **self-esteem** (how we feel about ourselves). Let us examine these two concepts in more detail.

SELF-IMAGE

Our **self-image** is what we know about ourselves, the kind of person we think we are. It consists of the facts and characteristics which we would use to describe ourselves. Let us look at how it is related to our self-concept.

Development of self-image

Research shows that when asked to describe themselves, typical nine year olds will mention their age, sex, name, height, hair colour, their school, brothers and sisters, and some likes or dislikes. By the age of 17 years old, their answers would include fewer facts but *more* about personality traits, nationality, relationships with others, religious and political beliefs. The later description includes many more abstract traits and this reflects changes in cognitive development. It also shows increasing awareness of the social aspect of self – our relationships with others and the society we live in.

S

Diane Ruble proposed that children self-socialise. By this she means that at an early age they construct rules about themselves and about their social environments. This information in turn influences their behaviour and how others respond to them. For example, imagine a child who decides she is no good at ball games. This decision is partly a result of trying to play ball games and watching others do so. How will this affect her behaviour? According to **Ruble**'s research, she will choose not to play ball games or get involved with those who do. She has therefore avoided a situation that might lower her **self-esteem,** and created an environment that is likely to raise her self-esteem.

S

How do we come to know what traits we have? In part we learn from others. **Charles Cooley** used the term 'the looking glass self' in 1902. By this he meant that our **self-image** is a reflection of the way others see us – we see ourselves as others see us. However others may not all see us the same way. One study found that female college students relied more on evaluations of *peers,* but males looked to *parental* appraisal. So in the creation of our **self-image** not only do *others* vary in the attitude and behaviour towards us, but we *value* some of these people more than others.

Personal bias

Research shows consistently that most individuals see themselves in a good light. When asked which adjectives apply to them, they chose mostly positive ones. One study found that people even put a higher value on the letters which appear in their name when compared to others in the alphabet! They value activities which they are good at more than those they are not, and those negative aspects of themselves are considered less important than the positive.

Overall we see ourselves in more flattering ways than others see us. We also tend to see ourselves as having control when we have none. For example when gambling, subjects felt they had control over the outcome, which was in fact completely due to chance. **Shelley Taylor** argues that these biased perceptions of our **self-image** are important for promoting mental health. Several psychologists have said people who have successful life-adjustment are those who are positive, in control and feel they can be effective.

Self-observation

Daryl Bem proposed that we also develop our **self-image** as a result of observing our own behaviour. He said that when we are not sure what we feel about something, we watch how we behave and then decide. Thus, by observing our own behaviour, we build up elements of our **self-concept.** For example, if you were to go bowling for the first time and find yourself trying very hard to get a high score, you might reflect that you didn't realise you were so competitive. This idea would start to creep in to your self-concept. However, our knowledge of ourselves also accumulates as we notice the outcomes of our actions. If you regularly obtain reasonable marks in your studies, your **self-image** starts to include the notion that you are a good student.

Important traits

As we saw at the start of this section, visible characteristics also form part of **self-image** from a very early age. They are evidently a key part of self-knowledge for children and appear to be more central to the child's **self-image** if they are distinctive. For example, researchers found that children included information in their **self-image** which is more unusual – if the rest of the family was female, a girl was less likely to mention her sex than a male was. Children who were much older or younger than most of their classmates were more likely to mention this in their self-image. **Michael Argyle** suggests how these distinctive features not only form part of our **self-image,** but may be quite persistent. He found that girls who were taller than average at 13 years of age still saw themselves as taller later in life, even though they were average height then.

We have seen how those features which are important to us may be identified by comparison with others. However, another reason why they may become important is through seeing how others behave towards us. If they treat us in a **stereotypical** way because of our race or gender for example, this is more likely to make race or gender a central aspect of our **self-image.** We will look in detail at this later under the **self-fulfilling prophecy.**

Self-image as a schema

According to the ideas within the social cognition perspective, the self-concept is made up of schemas – knowledge about oneself – and these are called **self-schemas**. Schemas organise and guide the information we attend to and take note of: we notice what we expect to see, and ignore that which is not part of our schemas. The effect of the schema was demonstrated in a study by **Hazel Markus** who initially gave participants questionnaires to complete. From the results she divided them into three groups – very independent, very dependent and neither one extreme nor the other.

Several weeks later, as part of another study, they were presented with various adjectives and had to press a button – 'me' or 'not me' – to show whether they thought the adjective referred to them. **Markus** found those classed as independent responded to 'independent' related adjectives more rapidly than to 'dependent' adjectives. The dependent subjects showed the opposite response and the 'in between' subjects took an equal amount of time to respond to independent or dependent adjectives. **Markus** concluded that our **self-schema** affects how we process information. Those aspects of our **self-image** that are most central will in turn affect what information we take in about ourselves.

Research has shown that we use our **self-schemas** to perceive others as well. **Hazel Markus** and colleagues found that subjects with a strong masculinity schema remembered more information from a film about another person's masculine behaviours. Whether this is because their masculinity schema is easily triggered, or whether that is a schema they use both for themselves *and* others is unclear. However, additional research has found that we tend to use *other* people's schemas if they are people we know well. The schemas they use for us become incorporated in our *own* **self-image.** This echoes what **Cooley** said – we see ourselves as others see us.

SELF-ESTEEM

Our **self-esteem** refers to our evaluation of ourselves. Our evaluation can be positive or negative. Do you like yourself? Do you think you are worthwhile? Do you think you are a failure? Psychologists have used the notion of an **'ideal self',** which is the type of person we would *like* to be. They say we compare our **ideal self** with our **self-image,** and the greater the gap, the lower our **self-esteem.** Self-esteem has been tested by psychologists on the basis of questions like 'on the whole I am satisfied with myself'.

Aspects of self-esteem

Susan Harter proposed in 1982 that we assess ourselves in four different areas of ability – cognitive, social, physical and general self-worth. She gave eight year olds questions about themselves in these four areas and also asked teachers and others about them. **Harter** found the child's **self-image** was very similar to the assessment by others. Not only did this show considerable accuracy in their own evaluations, but it also showed that children already evaluated their abilities differently in each area, because they said they were good in some and not in others.

As physical attributes are part of our **self-image,** so satisfaction with our appearance increases our **self-esteem.** The self-evaluations of men have been found to be related to muscular strength – the greater the muscle strength, the higher the self-evaluation. But what happens when our bodies change? Adolescence is a time of rapid change, and research with boys suggests that those who are late maturing have less self-confidence than early maturers. The early maturers were seen as less childish and tended to be treated in a more adult way; they were seen as more confident and given more responsibility than the late maturers. This treatment affected their **self-image** and their **self-esteem.**

Context

Research suggests people's *self-descriptions* change with context, although their *self-knowledge* does not. What does this mean? If you were doing some psychological research as part of your coursework in a group which was not taking it very seriously, you might see yourself as being fairly responsible. However, if you were in a group that was very intense and thorough about the work and spent a lot of time meeting and planning it, you might feel rather irresponsible in contrast. So are you responsible or irresponsible? Because knowledge about ourselves **(self-image)** is built up of many such incidents, our self-image is the result of an accumulation of information. But if we were to be asked *at any one time* whether we would describe ourselves as responsible or irresponsible, the way we answered would depend in part on how we were behaving at that time. This is important because psychological research often involves asking people to describe themselves and this tendency to change our self-descriptions may distort psychologists' results.

Social identity

S

Henri Tajfel proposed that our **social identity** is another factor in our **self-image.** We gain our social identity from the group we belong to, for example the school or college we attend. If it has a good reputation then it is likely to increase our **self-esteem.** However, if it has a poor reputation, then according to **Tajfel** we would be likely to distance ourselves from it, so as not to threaten our self-esteem.

There are occasions when we want to identify with another group. In these cases we will try to show that membership of our own group is weak and also show evidence of our closeness to the other group. The photograph on the next page is an example of this.

Self-efficacy

Another aspect of our **self-esteem** is how effective or able we are, and relates to **Albert Bandura**'s idea of **self-efficacy**. He said that four psychological processes were affected by self-efficacy. These are:

Fig. 15.1 This policewoman is on duty at the International Clown Convention. She is creating distance between herself and her role by wearing a clown's red nose and moustache

- **cognitive** if we believe we are able this can affect our thought patterns and therefore our behaviour
- **motivational** we are more likely to persist if we have high self-efficacy
- **affective** those high in self-efficacy show less stress and anxiety
- **selection** those high in self-efficacy will choose challenging tasks which they can manage

These ideas have been supported by research. For example, children with high **self-efficacy** on a maths task solved problems more rapidly, and were more likely to go over answers and correct them, than those with low self-efficacy *regardless* of their actual ability. **R. Weinberg** and his colleagues manipulated the self-efficacy beliefs of their subjects and gave them endurance tasks. Those with high self-efficacy performed better, and when they failed they tried harder to recover in comparison to those with low self-efficacy. Interestingly, the researchers manipulated **self-efficacy** so that female subjects thought they were high and males thought they were low. **Weinberg** found that normal gender differences on physical endurance tasks disappeared almost entirely. **Bandura** points out that girls are raised to think of themselves as having poor endurance. It seems then, that if we have high **self-esteem** about our abilities, this will influence the outcome of our actions.

Parental influence

Stanley Coopersmith's study in 1967 looked at **self-esteem** and its relationship to parental influence. This was a longitudinal study of white middle-class boys in the USA, which followed them from 10 years old up to adulthood. As a result of questionnaires, tests and interviews with teachers, Coopersmith identified high self-esteem and low self-esteem boys, although there was no difference in intelligence and physical attractiveness between the two groups. He also interviewed the mothers and asked the boys about their parents' child-rearing methods.

He found that the high **self-esteem** boys were more popular and were more successful than the low self-esteem boys when they reached adulthood. They were also more likely to come from homes which gave them a lot of responsibility but created firm guidelines. Their parents had high self-esteem and created a warm accepting environment. However this is only correlational evidence from a restricted sample of white middle-class boys. How would girls, or black people have fared in this study?

Some research has shown that boys tend to over-estimate their ability and girls tend to under-estimate theirs and have lower **self-esteem.** There are several possible explanations for this, some relating to the social expectations and treatment which girls receive in contrast with boys and others to do with the lower status of women in our society. This topic is considered in more detail in Chapter 14.

Important traits

We have already seen that some parts of our **self-concept** may be more important or *central* than others. For example your role as a son may be more important to your self-concept than your role as a table-tennis player. When we judge ourselves we are more concerned about these important parts. If we fail on a central part of our **self-concept,** this affects our **self-esteem** more. For example, if you forget to send a Mother's Day card your self-esteem will suffer more than if you lose a table-tennis game.

S

Culture also plays a role in our **self-esteem,** because different cultures value different attributes. Those traits which are highly valued in your own culture will be more important to you than less valued traits. In a competitive culture, those who achieve are more likely to have high self-esteem than if they lived in a culture in which mutual co-operation was valued more than individual achievement.

Social comparison

S

One source of **self-esteem** is how well we do compared to others. **Leon Festinger** has proposed in **social comparison** theory that we compare ourselves with others in order to evaluate ourselves. Research shows we compare ourselves with those we see as important, particularly if we would like to be like them, or accepted by the group that they are in. We also compare ourselves with those individuals or groups seen as *similar* to us in that ability because this gives us more accurate information. If you went ice-skating with a group of friends, you would be more likely to compare your ability with them than with Torvill and Dean. What if you are unrealistic about your comparison person? If you insist on comparing your ice-skating ability with the champions you are likely to have low **self-esteem** about your ice-skating ability.

Psychological well-being

The difference between our **self-image** and our **ideal self** can lead to anxiety and depression, according to **Tory Higgins**. He proposed in his **self-discrepancy** theory that we think about what we are, what we would *like* to be and what we *ought* to be. The bigger the gap between our ideal self and our self-image, the lower our **self-esteem.** This may be one reason why, as research suggests, we tend to avoid situations in which we will do badly: we avoid negative feedback about our abilities. Nevertheless some people consistently set themselves excessively high standards – remember your ice-skating? This can lead to the type of problems which interested **Carl Rogers**.

High **self-esteem** is generally equated with being psychologically healthy, and low **self-esteem** with distress. This is **Tory Higgins**' point, and also a key aspect of **Carl Rogers**' attitude to psychological well-being. He says we all need to be thought well of by others but at the same time we also need to think well of ourselves – to have high **self-esteem. Rogers** called this part of us our 'self' but he also claimed that in our attempts to think well of ourselves, and have others think of us this way, we may *deny* aspects of ourselves such as our anger or insecurity.

Nonetheless, these other parts 'belong' to us and form part of our whole experience. **Rogers**' aim is to enable people to integrate *all* of their experience, and this usually involves getting people to acknowledge the parts of themselves they have denied. He does this by offering 'unconditional positive regard' – acceptance – whilst they go through this process of integration. If successful, the individual's **self-image** will be fairly accurate and will be close to their idea self. They will then have high **self-esteem** – or high 'positive regard' in Rogers' terms.

How do social roles contribute to an individual's self-concept?

Social roles are part of our **self-concept.** We know ourselves through our interactions with others. The different roles we play require us to use different abilities so we acquire more aspects to our **self-image.** But equally, how *successful* we are in each of our roles will affect our **self-esteem.** Social roles therefore play an important part in enlarging our self-concept and enhancing, or lowering, our self-esteem.

S

HOW DO SOCIAL ROLES BECOME PART OF OUR SELF-CONCEPT?

Research suggests our **self-concept** does not include many social roles when we are young, but roles play an increasingly important part in our self-concept as we reach adulthood. **Kuhn** asked seven year olds and undergraduates to give 20 different answers to the question, 'Who am I?'. The seven year olds averaged five answers relating to roles, whilst the undergraduates gave ten. This reflects the number of roles we take on as we move out into the world. Many roles imply a partner – father-daughter, student-teacher, doctor-patient; or membership of a group – football player, train passenger, supermarket shopper. These roles are the social setting we operate in and the role determines how we should behave in that setting – it is related to the social norms.

S

Irving Goffman said we develop a core self through three stages of role development:

- the **first stage** (infancy) is when we imitate those around us, without knowing the meaning of what we do
- the **second stage** is where we act out various roles – those of significant others in our world, those who have an important effect on us. By playing these roles we start to understand the context in which different roles are played, and what is appropriate and inappropriate. A child feeding his teddy-bear or a group playing at fire-fighting are acting out adult roles, and learning when to be brave and when to be gentle

S

S

- the **third stage** is when we integrate all the roles into a coherent whole – we internalise them as our core self. According to **Goffman**, the origins of this core self lie in the social roles we have learned to play, so our **self-concept** is created by society and needs social support to maintain it

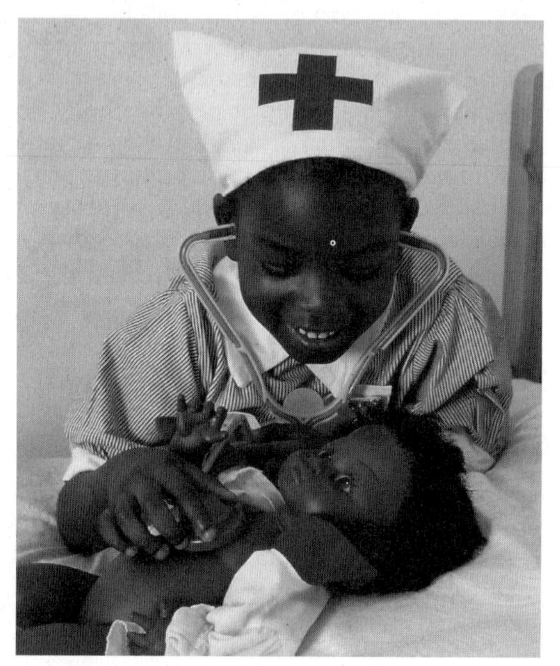

Fig. 15.2 Some of the abilities which this little girl brings to her nurse role may become important to her self-concept

How *others* treat us in our role will affect our **self-concept.** People are often quite hesitant when they first perform a role, but research shows that if others treat them in accordance with the demands of the role, then they quickly come to adopt the role, and thus it becomes part of their self-concept.

HOW MUCH INFLUENCE DO SOCIAL ROLES HAVE ON OUR SELF-CONCEPT?

One very powerful study of the influence of roles was carried out by **Philip Zimbardo** and his colleagues (see opposite).

Zimbardo noted the 'frightening' results of this study. Within six days prisoners had become withdrawn and obedient, guards had become aggressive and punitive. Some guards were excessively punitive and verbally aggressive and any attempted rebellion was punished. Several guards commented on the 'high' they felt at having power, and a few were disappointed when the study ended abruptly. Even the less hostile guards never challenged the aggressive ones; a high level of aggression was the group norm.

S

Very few direct instructions had been given to subjects so that they could respond to the demands of their role – which was what the researchers were interested in. Although subjects were very similar at the start of the study and had been assigned to their role by chance, there was a rapid change. Behaviour between the two groups

Zimbardo *et al.* (1973)

Aim of study	The aim of the study was to see whether the dehumanising effects of prisons were due to the nature of prisoners, the nature of prison staff or to the prison environment.
Hypothesis	The hypothesis was that there would be a difference in behaviour between subjects in the 'prison guard' role and subjects in the 'prisoner' role.
Design	This was an experiment using independent measures design and the observational method.
Sample	From a population of 75 respondents to an advertisement, 21 subjects were selected on the basis of sound physical and mental health, maturity and the lowest involvement in anti-social behaviour. All were white middle-class males. The subjects were randomly assigned to two groups: 10 prisoners and 11 guards.
Procedure	A mock prison was built in the basement of Stanford University. After being assigned to their groups, the guards met to receive uniforms and basic instructions on their duties, and were explicitly directed that there was to be no violence. Prisoners returned to their homes but did not know when the experiment was to start. They were 'arrested' early one morning, taken to the prison, shaved, dressed in loose gowns and put in cells. Observers watched and recorded behaviour over the next few days. The experiment was terminated before it was half-way through due to the extreme reaction of the prisoners.

differed greatly, and the differences became more marked as the study progressed. The subjects increasingly conformed to the role they played, to the point where **Zimbardo** found the majority were eventually unable to differentiate between themselves and their role. The fact that guards spent eight hours in the 'prison' and the remaining time continuing with their normal lives did not seem to weaken their sense of role.

Regardless of their roles, **Zimbardo** reported drastic changes in subjects' feelings, self-evaluation and behaviour. He gave an example of a 'parole board' when prisoners were asked if they would give up their pay (which they were receiving to take part in the experiment) so they could be 'released'. Each prisoner said they would, and so in effect they ended their participation in the experiment right then. By making this offer, the researchers were also reminding prisoners how *artificial* the situation was. Nevertheless, each prisoner meekly went back to his cell under escort while he waited to hear what the 'parole board' had decided.

The Prison Simulation experiment shows the power of roles, not only to influence behaviour, but also our **self-concept.** If we were to use **Bem**'s **self-perception** theory, we could see how the behaviour of one of these subjects might change their

S

perception of themselves. 'I am the sort of person who could treat someone very badly', or perhaps even more importantly 'I am someone who enjoys treating people badly'. The various roles we play therefore give us an opportunity to observe ourselves in various settings and to note our own behaviour. From this we infer what kind of person we are, so the roles we play contribute to our **self-concept.**

INTEGRATING ROLES

We saw earlier that **Goffman** proposed that the third stage was when we integrated all the roles into a 'core self'. The characteristics associated with each role become incorporated into the **self-concept.** Depending on what role we are playing, some characteristics will be prominent and others will not. So the practical parent may become the flirting party-goer. Nevertheless the individual can bring to each role the same personality characteristics – such as the reliable friend, son and car driver. How do we juggle all these roles, and know which one to play? The explanation from the social cognition approach may be useful.

C

This approach says that the behaviours associated with each role can be seen as schemas. When we are going to a party, our party-going schema is activated, and so the appropriate behaviours are more easily accessible. Our parenting schema has been pushed lower down the hierarchy of schemas and is therefore less accessible. This reorganisation of schemas has been called the **working self-concept** by **Hazel Markus**. It means that the role we are playing at any one time will bring to the forefront aspects of our identity which are activated by the role. A large number of roles, and therefore a more complex self-concept, appears to be beneficial for our well-being.

S

ROLES AND SELF-ESTEEM

Patricia Linville has found that a more *complex* **self-concept** is related to greater ability to cope with stress. She proposes this is due to the number of roles which are related to self-concept – damage to our **self-esteem** in one role can be offset by self-esteem in our other roles. For example, if your self-esteem is very dependent on your popularity with the opposite sex, then rejection will damage your self-esteem. But if you have positive self-esteem in your role as friend or shop assistant, then your self-esteem relating to these roles will cushion the blow to your self-esteem in another role. **Linville** found this also happens with success. People with highly complex **self-concepts** are less affected by success in *one* area than those with less complex self-concepts.

S

If you perform a role which is highly valued in your culture – for instance as a doctor – then this role enhances your **self-esteem.** Many feminists argue that the child-care role, which is performed mainly by women, is held in low esteem in Western society and that this is why women staying at home to care for children experience low self-esteem.

The self-fulfilling prophecy

S

A **self-fulfilling prophecy** is the process which makes someone's expectations about another person come true. If you have certain expectations of people, you treat them in a way which relates to those expectations. In turn *they* respond to the way you treat them, so that in fact their behaviour fulfils your expectation of them – they behave as you thought they would.

Why does it matter? Let's look for an answer in the study carried out by **Robert Rosenthal and Lenore Jacobson** in 1966. They felt that teachers unwittingly conveyed their *expectations* about students to those students. This in turn had an effect on student's *behaviour* – the **self-fulfilling prophecy.** At the beginning of the school year the researchers gave IQ tests to children aged six to 12 years old in one school. The test was unfamiliar to the teachers, who were told that it was a way of identifying 'bloomers' – children who were about to show a rapid increase in their learning abilities. The teachers learned of the names of their students who had come out in the top 20 per cent. This information was false: the names had been randomly selected from each class by the researchers. At the end of the academic year all the children in the school were tested again. Here are the results.

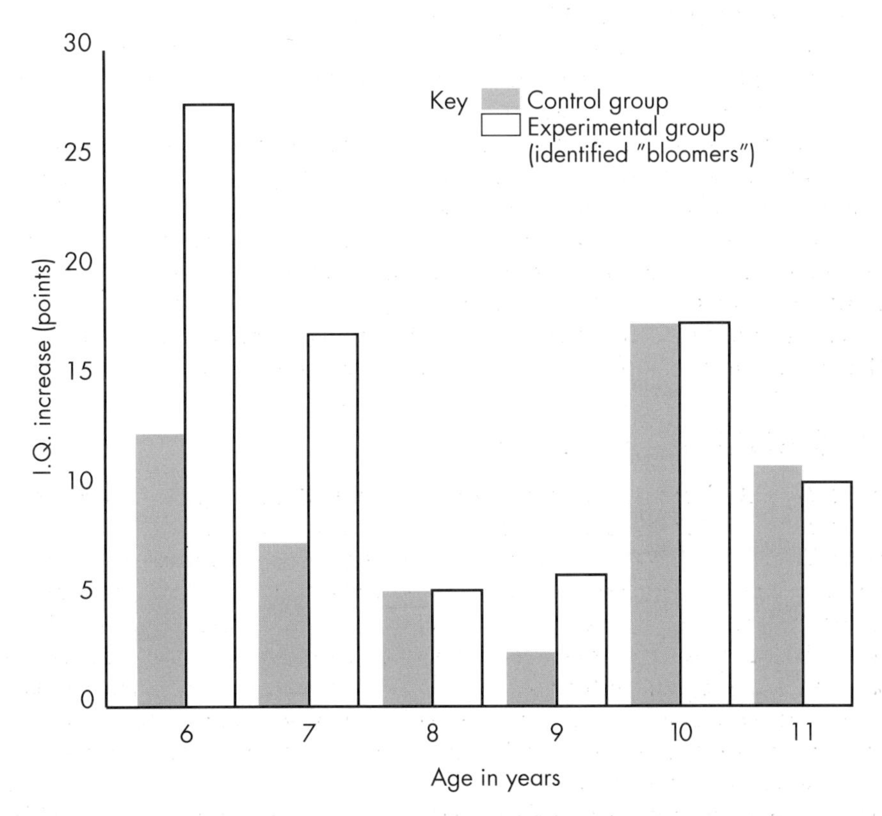

Fig. 15.3 Bar chart showing percentage increase in IQ score for students in each year (from R. Rosenthal and L. Jacobson 1966)

As you can, see the increase in IQ scores was considerable in the first two years of school. **Rosenthal and Jacobson** concluded that it was the teachers' expectations which had caused the increase in IQ scores and therefore that the **self-fulfilling prophecy** did occur in a real-life setting. They also noted that it was most evident in the early years of school but not later on. They suggested this could be because the teachers had not yet formed expectations of the children, so were more influenced by the false IQ information. Alternatively, younger children may be more easy to influence and more open to the non-verbal ways of communicating information.

S

How did the **self-fulfilling prophecy** develop? **Rosenthal** has emphasised four factors:

- **climate** – the expectations lead to a different treatment of the target person. In this study the teacher's warmer behaviour towards the 'blooming' students would be due to their higher expectations. **Mark Snyder** and his colleagues have noted the power of non-verbal behaviour – eye contact, smiling, nodding, posture, tone of voice and so on – in the transmission of expectation
- **feedback** – more differentiated feedback is given to the target person. For example the teachers would give more accurate information to these students about their work, perhaps saying where they could improve it rather than just giving a general 'well done'
- **input** – teachers give more demanding material to the high expectation students: they push them more
- **output** – teachers give 'blooming' students more chance to respond, to answer questions in class for example

In Fig. 15.4 below you can see the stages which **J. Darley and R. Fazio** say must take place before the self-fulfilling prophecy can occur.

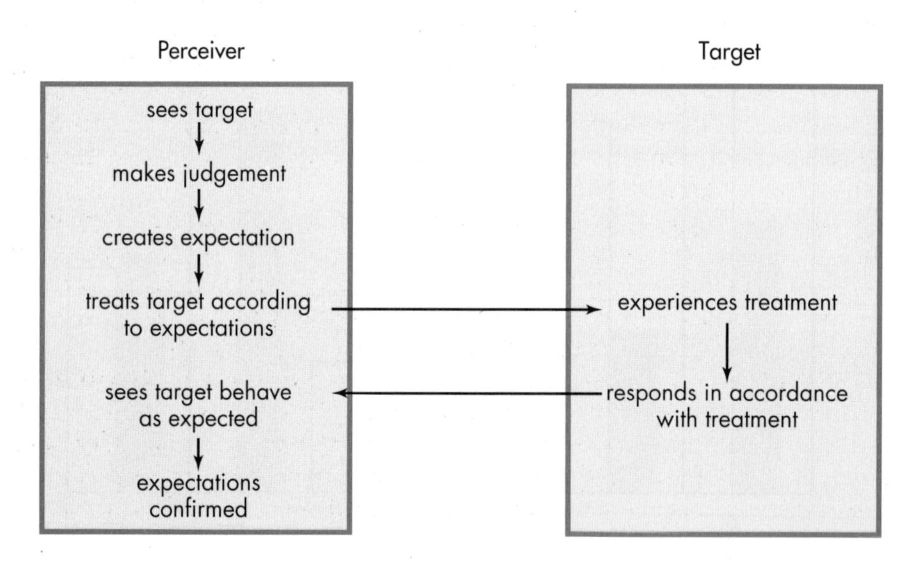

Fig. 15.4 The stages in the self-fulfilling prophecy process

Let us return to the question we asked before the **Rosenthal and Jacobson** study. Why does the **self-fulfilling prophecy** matter? If we hold expectations about people, then the way we behave towards them can 'prove' that we were right. When we are interacting with someone we know very little about we tend to fall back on our **stereotypes,** and the stereotype will trigger certain expectations. You can see how stereotypes can, through the self-fulfilling prophecy, actually be *confirmed*. This is why the **self-fulfilling prophecy** is closely related to the maintenance of **prejudice** and **discrimination.**

C

The **self-fulfilling prophecy** also matters because it affects how people see themselves – their **self-concept.** Once the individual understands what the other's expectation is, he or she may **internalise** the expectation. This means they acknowledge the expectation as true, they behave in the appropriate way and this knowledge forms part of their **self-concept.**

Imagine how the 'blooming' students felt in the **Rosenthal and Jacobson** study? Imagine the effect on **self-esteem** for the non-bloomers! Many other studies have shown that the **self-fulfilling prophecy** is true for both positive and negative expectations, on various target persons and situations. We can look at a study of adults to examine this process again.

Mark Snyder and his colleagues arranged for male students to have phone conversations with female students. In some instances they were led to believe the female was attractive, and in others that she was unattractive. The male subjects were much livelier in their conversations with the 'attractive' female. All the female sides of the *conversations* were judged for how attractive the speaker was likely to be, and judges found that the females who shared in the lively conversations were judged to be more attractive. So, one factor determined how the female speakers were treated, and how they were treated in turn affected how they *behaved.*

Self-fulfilling prophecies are important even if we do *not* **stereotype.** The study mentioned above is related to the way we form impressions of people (see Chapter 19) and these impressions will affect our expectations. Let's look at an example. According to the **halo effect** we see attractive people as having other positive qualities. Therefore we are likely to treat attractive people in a pleasant way, thus eliciting a pleasant response from them, thus reinforcing our impression of them as pleasant *and* encouraging them to have pleasantness as part of their **self-concept.** So you can see how the self-fulfilling prophecy can have a powerful effect on both the *perceiver's* expectations and the *target's* self-concept.

C

Mark Snyder has pointed out that at any stage the self-fulfilling prophecy can break down. How can it? Research suggests this is possible if the *perceiver* tries to compensate for an expectation he holds or if the *target* contradicts the expectation. These strategies are important in real life. For example, teachers should be active in their efforts to avoid creating and acting on their expectations of their students.

Equally, when those who have been the targets of **prejudice** and **discrimination** behave in ways which are *inconsistent* with the expectations, such expectations are less likely to be confirmed and the self-fulfilling cycle may be broken. This has been one of the aims of the Black Power and the feminist movements in the last two decades – to encourage members to challenge stereotypical expectations and break the cycle.

Labelling

Labelling is the term used when we classify someone on the basis of a particular feature – often one which is unusual. For example, we might label a child 'difficult' or a man 'schizophrenic'. Labelling is frequently seen as negative, and can lead to poor **self-esteem** in the individual and of course this directly affects their self-concept. Let's look at some aspects of labelling.

LABELLING AS A SOCIAL STIGMA

Thomas Szasz has proposed that when people want to exclude others they give them *stigmatizing labels* – foreigner, criminal, mentally ill and so on. These are used for people who do not conform to the social norms of their society. **Irving Goffman** says

S

labelling disqualifies a person from full social acceptance, and therefore allows us to treat them in a less human way. In the **Zimbardo** prison study we looked at earlier, any sign of rebellion by the 'prisoners' was labelled as typical prisoner behaviour and was therefore punished. Whether it was justified was not important.

DOES LABELLING MATTER?

C

It does, because it affects the individual's **self-concept** and it also determines how he or she is treated. **Arnold Sameroff** suggests how this process works. He says parents who label a child as 'difficult' may come to treat him as such, regardless of his behaviour. As the child advances in his cognitive development and comes to understand the value the world places on him, he will accept 'difficult' as part of his **self-image.** The child has learned to *internalise* his label so it forms part of his **self-concept.** You can also see from this example that **labelling** can be the first step in the **self-fulfilling prophecy** cycle.

Research into mental retardation has shown that the more aware children who are classed as mental retards know of their **label** and are depressed by it – they have lower **self-esteem** than those children who are more retarded. These children prefer to keep a greater social distance from the more retarded children too, which shows their awareness of the **label** as a stigma. However there is another side to this. Research on children who are not mentally retarded shows they accept *deviant* behaviour far more from mentally retarded subjects if they are *labelled* mentally retarded than when they are not labelled. In other words, special allowances are made for children when they are **labelled.** This is a complex situation and has implications for mainstream education.

HOW LABELLING AFFECTS PERCEPTIONS

S

Another criticism of **labelling** relates to its use for unusual behaviour. By labelling someone, the implication is that the difficulty is with *them*, not with the society or circumstances in which they live. This can lead to two outcomes. One is that the *individual* is treated, not their environment; the other is that once a person is **labelled,** there is a tendency to treat *all* behaviours as confirmation that the label is right. It is as though labelling creates a schema through which to view behaviour. **David Rosenhan**'s study highlights this.

Rosenhan arranged for eight researchers to request admission to mental hospitals throughout the USA on the basis that they were hearing voices. However, from the moment of their admission they acted normally and said that they no longer heard voices. **Rosenhan** was interested to find out how each of these 'patients' was treated.

The 'patients' were diagnosed as schizophrenic and kept in from 7 to 52 days. None of the staff challenged this view: the patients' behaviour was interpreted as if they were schizophrenic. All of them took notes for the research and this was entered on their daily record sheets as 'engaging in writing behaviour'. The other (genuine) patients however challenged them with 'You're not crazy, you're a journalist or a professor', because of their note-taking.

The researchers noted how the hospital routine and lack of activity led to behaviours that were quite normal responses (for example frustration) in the patients, but the staff perceived them as evidence of mental disorder. In other words, the **label** each patient was given then determined the lens through which their behaviour was interpreted.

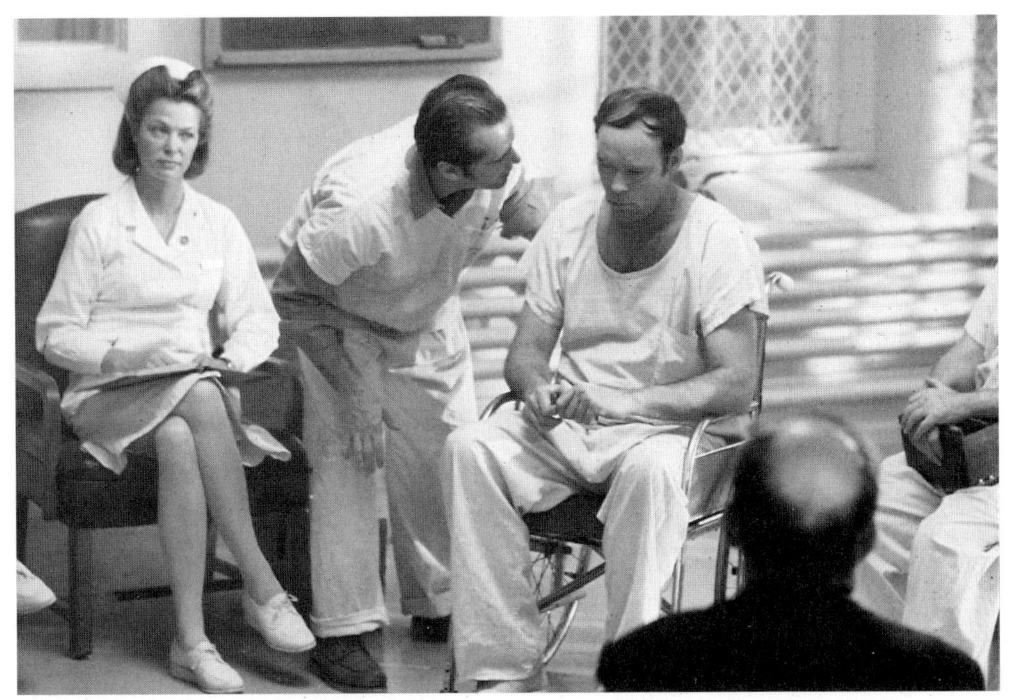

Fig. 15.5 A scene from 'One Flew Over the Cuckoo's Nest' – a film which vividly expresses the consequences of labelling in a mental hospital

Labelling has many consequences. The label may act as a **self-fulfilling prophecy,** it may also act as a central trait through which all other traits are viewed. Because of its negative tone, and the way that labelling distances other people from us, we are more likely to treat them differently, not to accept them fully, and thus to contribute to their negative **self-concept.**

Further Reading

Gross R (1992) *Psychology – The Science of Mind and Behaviour*, London, Hodder & Stoughton
Hayes N (1994) *Foundations of Psychology,* London, Routledge

EXERCISES

1 What is the difference between self-image and self-esteem?
2 Think of your own example of a social role. How would it affect someone's self-concept?
3 What was the IV and the DV in Zimbardo's experiment?
4 Explain one criticism of the Zimbardo experiment.
5 Find an example of a self-fulfilling prophecy from another chapter in this book.

COGNITIVE AND SOCIAL COMPETENCE

SECTION E

Introduction

In Chapter 16 of this section we look at two aspects of cognition – intellectual development and the development of visual perception.

The remainder of this section examines how we come to understand ourselves and others in a social setting. We also consider how that understanding is affected by other people, by the media and by our own mental bias. This information appears throughout the last three chapters, but in particular Chapter 19.

We also study various explanations of how our moral and helping behaviour develops, and how other people affect that behaviour. These topics are covered in Chapters 17 and 18.

Chapter 16
Cognitive Development

ANYTHING WHICH IS COGNITIVE IS RELATED TO HOW WE THINK, SEE, REMEMBER AND UNDERSTAND OUR WORLD. SO COGNITIVE DEVELOPMENT IS THE CHANGE THAT TAKES PLACE IN THESE MENTAL ACTIVITIES AS WE GROW. IN THIS CHAPTER WE WILL LOOK AT HOW THE CHILD COMES TO MAKE SENSE OF ITS WORLD. IN THE FIRST HALF WE WILL EXAMINE A VERY INFLUENTIAL EXPLANATION OF HOW THE CHILD'S INTELLECTUAL DEVELOPMENT OCCURS, AND IN THE SECOND HALF OF THE CHAPTER WE WILL LOOK AT THE ROLE OF HEREDITY AND THE ENVIRONMENT IN OUR ABILITY TO MAKE SENSE OF WHAT WE SEE.

Piaget's stages of cognitive development

Jean Piaget, who was Swiss, created a theory of the **cognitive development** of children. He was interested in how humans *adapt* to their environment. In his early work with children he asked them questions, and was interested to find that many children gave the same *kind* of wrong answers. So he and his researchers began to study how children's thinking developed. Piaget started studying his own children when they were a few weeks old, using naturalistic observation. He noted how they used reflexes to start exploring their world. He used clinical interviews with toddlers and older children, playing games with them and asking them questions. Later on Piaget and his researchers tested his ideas through experiments.

I

From this research **Piaget** said that children were actively trying to make sense of the world – to explore and test it by interacting with it. He called them little scientists. He proposed that children do not think in the same way as adults. He said their knowledge is *structured* differently from adults and he showed that their understanding developed through four stages – in each one the child's thinking has different characteristics from the stage before. The four stages, with their characteristics and the ages to which they roughly relate, are as follows.

C

1 SENSORY MOTOR STAGE (BIRTH TO 18 MONTHS)

During this first stage the child's understanding of its world is gained by using its senses in combination with movement. You will see its skills become more complicated. At first the infant watches moving objects, then it reaches out to something of interest, then it is able to grasp an object, then it brings the object to its mouth, then it may shake or bang the object. Eventually it will start putting objects into one another, or piling them up. Once the infant starts to crawl around its world becomes much bigger – there are so many new things to manipulate and experiment with!

What are the characteristics of this stage?

Senses and movement

The child learns about its world through the information it gets through its senses: by what it sees, hears, touches, tastes and smells. It also learns about its world through the development of bodily movement – motor movement. **Piaget** said that reflexes such as grasping and looking are the **innate schemas** which form the basis for the child's cognitive development. For example it adapts its *grasping* reflex to hold, then to twist, stroke and so on. As it develops, the infant uses its sensory motor skills in increasingly complex ways. In the early months it may grasp an object and immediately put it into its mouth. But towards the end of the first year it will hold the object, look at it carefully, turn it over and perhaps *then* put the object in its mouth.

I

Egocentricity

The infant is born **egocentric** in Piaget's terms. This means that it has no sense of the world as being *separate* from it. The child's world is simply an extension of itself so it only sees things from its own point of view. Look again at the example of the child's exploration of an object – in the early months the object is put straight to the mouth as if it is merely an extension of the infant. Gradually the infant seems to gain an understanding that the object is separate from itself. The infant becomes interested in the object as a separate entity and this is the beginning of a reduction in **egocentricity**. Evidence for this change is shown in the next characteristic.

Object permanence

If you shake a rattle in front of a five-month-old baby, it will reach out for it. If you cover the rattle with a cloth, the baby immediately loses interest. It is as though the rattle never existed. If you do the same thing with a one year old, the baby will continue to reach for the rattle, and may show distress that it has disappeared. The one year old has **object permanence**, according to Piaget. This means that the baby appears to understand that, although it can no longer *see* an object, the object still exists. So, in the early part of the sensorimotor stage the baby has not developed **object permanence**, but towards the end of the stage it has.

During its second year the toddler starts to develop language and its thinking shows new characteristics. It has moved into the second stage of cognitive development.

2 PRE-OPERATIONAL STAGE (18 MONTHS TO SEVEN YEARS OLD)

The child at this stage becomes able to represent objects or events by symbols or signs. The toddler's ability to use and understand language enables it to talk about things and express ideas. **Piaget** said that language skills develop as a result of the child's cognitive development. Its ability to talk also allows us to find out more about the child's

C

understanding of its world. It can talk about the future – 'Janey go swings today'; about things it cannot see – 'Ali gone school'; about possibilities – 'Me drive car?' Let's look at the characteristics of the pre-operational stage.

Symbolic thinking

The child begins to show **symbolic** thinking. This means that it can make something 'stand for' something else. For example, it will use a cardboard box as a house, car, boat or a shop. Language is symbolic thinking, because the child knows that when you say 'table' the word 'stands for' an actual table – he could draw one, or point one out in the room or tell you how you could use a table.

C

Animism

Children in the early part of this stage show **animism**. This means that they think inanimate objects have feelings like they do. A three year old might say 'my shoes are sad' because her shoes are dirty. By about five years old animism has largely disappeared.

Egocentricity

The child is still **egocentric**. Have you ever played 'hide and seek' with a three year old who just covers his eyes when he is hiding? Because he cannot see *you* he thinks you cannot see *him*; this is an example of egocentrism. A child showing egocentric thinking is unable to take someone else's view.

C

Piaget set up the 'three mountains task' to test **egocentric** thinking. In this task there was a large, table-top model of three mountains – one with a cross on top, another with snow and another with a green field. First Piaget asked the child what he could see when he was stood at one side of the model. Then he introduced a doll and placed it at various positions around the table. The child was shown photographs of the mountains taken from these different positions, and asked to indicate which photograph showed the view that the doll would see. He found that four and five-year-old children thought the doll's view would be the same as their own.

Fig. 16.1 A child doing a version of the 'three mountains' task

Centration

Another limitation is that the child seems to be unable to take account of more than one feature of a situation at one time. **Piaget** called this characteristic **centration** – the tendency to attend to only one aspect of a situation. This can be seen in the development of gender concept, when a child thinks a man is a woman he puts on a dress. The dress is what the child attends to, not the sex of the person.

Once the child can take into account more than one aspect of a situation it can **decentre**. This changes the way it understands the world, so the child has moved on to the next stage of cognitive development.

3 CONCRETE OPERATIONAL STAGE (SEVEN TO 11 YEARS)

C

The child has entered the **concrete operational stage** when it can **decentre** and think **logically**. How do we know it can do this? There are several experiments which **Piaget** devised to assess the child's understanding. We will refer to them as we look at the characteristics of the concrete operations stage.

Conservation

If you show a four year old two identical glasses, each filled with liquid to the same level, he or she will tell you that there is the same amount of liquid in each. However, if you pour the liquid from one glass into a *different* shaped glass, the child will tell you that there is a *different* amount of liquid in the second container. Because the *appearance* of the liquid changes, the child thinks the amount has changed. However, if you did the same task with a seven year old, he or she would tell you there was the *same* amount in the different shaped glass. In fact they might look at you as though you were stupid, because you asked such a stupid question! Once a child understands that although the *appearance* changes, the *amount* does not, then the child can **conserve**.

C

This experiment is an example of **conservation of liquid**. **Piaget** studied children's ability to conserve number, length, mass, weight, volume and area as well. He found that children's ability to conserve started with liquid, and as they progressed through the **concrete operational** stage, these other conservation abilities appeared in the same order. When the child can conserve it is able to take account of *more* than one aspect of a situation – the matching levels of liquid at the start of the task, and the *new* level, as well as the fact that no liquid has been added. This is an example of **decentring**.

Loss of Egocentricity

C

Remember the 'three mountains' task which showed the child's egocentric thinking? When **Piaget** gave the task to seven year old children, they showed they *were* able to take the view of the doll. They could say which picture corresponded with the view from the doll's position. This means the child was no longer showing **egocentric** thinking.

Reversibility

If you were to do the **conservation** study with a seven year old you could ask her how she knows the amount of liquid is the same. A lot of children would answer 'because if you pour it back into the first glass, it will be level with the other one.' These children can *imagine* what would happen if you reversed the procedure. The ability to reverse a procedure *in your head* is called **reversibility**. The child can understand the logical sequence and can reverse it mentally.

Rules

Piaget noted that children started to create their own rules during this stage, and these became more complex as children advanced through the stage. The ability to create and apply rules shows logical abstract thinking.

Seriation

This means that the child can put things in a logical order, but during the **concrete operational** stage he needs something 'concrete' to help it understand. For example, if you asked a child to imagine that a spotted block was bigger than a striped one, but smaller than a plain one, he could not tell you which was the biggest. But if you *gave* him the three blocks he could work out the answer. So, during this **concrete operational** stage the child becomes able to understand many things, but often needs to experience them in a 'real' (concrete) way first.

By the time a child has reached 11 years old, he will be able to solve the block problem in his head (in the abstract). This means that he can think **logically**. Once he can use **logical abstract** thinking, he has moved on to the final stage.

4 FORMAL OPERATIONAL STAGE (11 YEARS AND OLDER)

The child has entered the **formal operational stage** when it can solve problems logically in its head – it can perform abstract thinking.

Abstract thinking

Abstract thinking means, for example, being able to do sums, to imagine the impossible, to think through a sequence. The child is able to manipulate ideas in his head, just as it was able to manipulate objects. **Piaget** and his colleagues set complicated tasks for adolescents and noted how they solved them. The tasks included features we are looking at when we design experiments – variables. The task would be to find out which variable, of several operating at the same time, was the one that caused a particular effect.

In the 'pendulum' task **Piaget** gave the child a piece of string hanging from a hook and several weights. She was told she could vary the length of the string and could attach any of the weights to it to make a pendulum. The child was also told she should push the weight (to make it swing). The task for the child was to find out which of the factors (the length of string, the strength of push or the amount of weight) affected the length of time it took to make one complete swing of the pendulum. The researchers found that younger children would try all kinds of combinations in a haphazard way and this showed they were still thinking in the **concrete operational** way. But those showing **formal operational** thinking would systematically test all the possibilities in a *logical* way until they found the answer.

According to Piaget, once the young person has achieved **formal operational** thinking, there is no further **structural** change; thinking becomes more complex, flexible and abstract with experience.

How do children progress through these stages?

Piaget proposed that children move through these stages by using specific mental processes. These enable the child to understand and adapt to its environment, and to move from one stage of cognitive development to the next. Four of his most important ideas are the schema, assimilation, accommodation and equilibration. So how do these work?

SCHEMA

Piaget said that each of the infant's reflexes is a schema. A schema is a mental structure, an internal representation of experience. So, for example, the infant's grasping reflex is also a very simple **action schema** for grasping. As the infant matures, and interacts with its environment, so its schemas develop and become more complex. The infant will start to use its grasping reflex to grasp fingers, rattles and blankets.

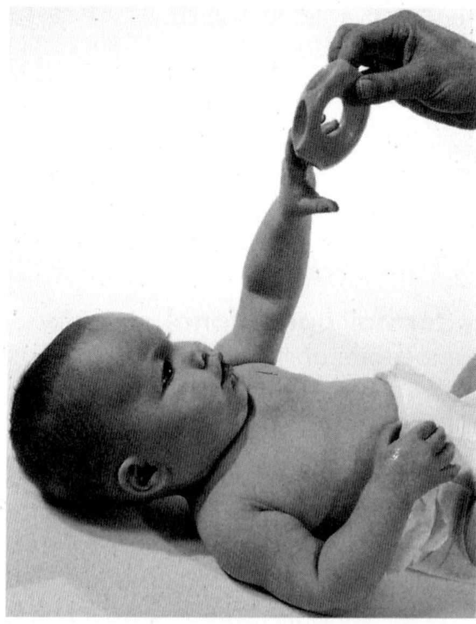

Fig.16.2 The baby's grasping schema in action

ASSIMILATION

Piaget called the process of using a schema **assimilation**. This is when the infant tries to fit its environment into its schema. A favourite schema for babies is 'dropping things on the floor'. If it can find someone to pick up the objects, the baby shows endless fascination with repeatedly dropping different things. It is assimilating its 'dropping things' schema.

However, there are times when the baby cannot fit something into its schema very easily. For example, its grasping schema will need to *change* a little in order for the infant to grasp a block, instead of a blanket. A different process occurs here.

ACCOMMODATION

Piaget called the process of modifying a schema **accommodation**. So accommodation takes place when the schema has to be changed because it is unable to cope with the new experience or information. Sometimes the new information may be so *different* that the child creates an entirely *new* schema. For example, some objects will be too large for the infant to grasp, but through the processes of **accommodation** and **assimilation** it will find that these objects can be *held* with two hands. It will then have a schema for *holding*.

EQUILIBRATION

When the child has **assimilated** the schemas for all its experiences, it is in a state of **equilibration**, according to **Piaget**. This is a state of cognitive balance. But because of its continuing exploration of its world it will come across new experiences for which it has no schemas. This will create cognitive imbalance. The need to reduce the imbalance drives the child to restructure its schemas in order to regain cognitive balance. This is how the continuous process of adaptation ocurs.

To summarise **Piaget's** theory of cognitive development, he saw children as scientists, actively exploring and trying to make sense of their environment. He said that intelligence develops as we adapt to meet the needs of our environment. Successful adaptation is evidence of intelligent behaviour: the better the adaptation the more intelligent the behaviour. For Piaget, intelligence was not a quantity, which you could measure, but a process. Adaptation to the environment takes place through assimilation and accommodation and the child's efforts to maintain equilibration.

Although there has been some criticism of his theory, mainly that children show these abilities at a *younger* age than Piaget claimed, his ideas created a framework which has greatly increased our understanding of cognitive development. His ideas have *also* been widely adapted to enrich children's cognitive development. We will look at some examples now.

What influence have Piaget's ideas had?

Piaget's ideas have been used in many areas of child rearing – in toy design, playgroups, and recommendations to parents as to how to encourage children's cognitive development. Adults need to be aware of the child's stage of development in order to provide the appropriate toys or experience. First we will consider providing materials for different types of play, then we will look at the other important factors.

MATERIALS FOR DIFFERENT TYPES OF PLAY

Sensory motor play

There are many babies' toys which aim to develop **sensory motor** skills. Some attach to a cot and have knobs or handles for manipulation. These in turn may produce the sound of a bell or the movement of a dial. As it gets older, the baby needs a wider range of toys which give it an opportunity to manipulate objects and to recognise shapes, to create noise and move things about.

Constructive play

From about two years old the child's ability to put things together, for example to pile blocks on top of one another, and its interest in materials such as water, sand and mud, lead it towards exploration and construction. This involves **sensory motor** skills, but also the creation of things with a purpose in mind, using skills and past experience so see what happens.

Imaginative play

Once in the **pre-operational** stage, the child's **symbolic** thinking enables it to create its own world – clothes are used for dressing up, blankets make houses, boxes become cars, chairs become trains. Imagination is also expressed through drawing and painting, so children need to have lots of paper and crayons or paints. This kind of play further develops **sensory motor** skills.

Problem solving and rule games

As 'little scientists' children like to solve problems. Toys which give them this opportunity will develop their problem solving skills. Jigsaw puzzles, picture dominoes and other simple rule games will also encourage the development of sensory and cognitive skills, such as matching colours or shapes.

Fig. 16.3 Problem solving play

PROVIDING APPROPRIATE EXPERIENCES

Accommodation

There should be variety and challenge in the range of toys a child can play with. This means the child has opportunities to try out new experiences which will create **disequilibrium** and therefore the accommodation of its schemas. A child could start playing with Lego using the large blocks and then some small blocks could be introduced. As it finds out how to use them it will become more confident and we can see that it will have **assimilated** this new information into its schema for Lego. Providing blocks with some special features like wheels will require **accommodation.**

Assimilation

There should also be a few toys or activities which are of a similar level of difficulty. This allows the child to **assimilate** experiences into its schema. For example, there could be two or three jigsaws with about the same number of pieces, similar in size and with pictures that are equally complicated.

Egocentricity and decentring

Piaget highlighted the child's **egocentricity** for the first seven years or so. One of the ways in which this limitation can be reduced is by giving the child the opportunity to hear or see things from another view.

When a small group of children are working together to solve a problem, they learn from each other because they hear other ideas and have to discuss their own. This leads to **accommodation** of their schemas, and also an increasing awareness of the viewpoints of others. Equally, adults can play an important role by, for example, pointing out another feature of a situation and encouraging the child to consider it. This helps the child to **decentre.** The opportunity to play with their peers, and sensitive guidance from adults benefit the child's cognitive development.

There are many aspects of children's play which can be linked to Piaget's ideas. We can see how it is possible to help children's cognitive development and by watching how they go about their play, we can see what level of cognitive development they are at.

The development of visual perception

Perception is the process of interpreting, organising and combining sensory information. So when we study **visual perception** we look at how we make sense of the information which comes into the brain through the eyes. As you look at this page, it is your visual perception which enables you to organise the pattern of light waves entering your eye into black and white marks which you understand as letter shapes.

Psychologists have long been interested in the development of visual perception. Some say that our ability to organise and make sense of what we see is largely innate because we are born with certain abilities and their development depends solely on maturation. These represent the hereditarian view. Others say that the infant is unable to make any sense of its visual experiences at birth, and visual perception develops through experience in the environment. This is the environmentalist view. So the development of visual perception is a key area of study for those interested in the nature or nurture

debate. Let us look at some of the evidence from these two perspectives to see if we can decide which is the most convincing.

Evidence for the hereditarian view of the development of visual perception

I

Psychologists have studied newborn infants to find out what they see and understand. Anything which is evident in newborns must be innate, and the sooner an ability appears, the more likely it is to be due to innate factors. Let us look first at the perceptual abilities infants have.

BASIC VISUAL PERCEPTION

Research has shown that infants have several basic visual skills. They have a fixed focal length of about 20 cm; this means that the objects they can see most clearly will be approximately 20 cm distance from their eyes. If the image is much nearer or further away then it is blurred. Interestingly, this is the approximate distance of the mother's face when she is breastfeeding.

In the first few weeks of life, the infant appears to scan its world until it sees something of interest; then it will fixate on the object. For example it may fixate on a slowly *moving* object, which shows it can see the difference between **form and background.** Or it may fixate on the *edge* of objects. This shows that the infant can tell the difference between light and dark, because the sharpest contrast is at edges.

Initially these basic visual skills appear to be rather poor but by the time the baby is two months of age research shows they have developed considerably. The baby stops scanning the world for interesting movement or contrasts, and starts to *look* at objects.

Fig. 16.4 This baby is obviously looking, and grasping!

Babies rapidly begin to notice and remember patterns and sequences of movement. Are these new skills, evident soon after two months of age, due to the physical maturation of the eye, or to experience, or to the interaction between them? Psychologists do not know for sure.

Robert Fantz has studied many aspects of the infant's visual abilities, and one series of studies examined their ability to recognise pattern, which is an aspect of **form perception.** This is what he did.

Fantz (1961)

Aim of study The aim of the study was to see whether infants preferred a complex stimulus more than a simple one.

Type of study This longitudinal study took place over 15 weeks.

Method The method used was the experimental method.

Subjects The subjects were 30 one-week-old infants.

Procedure Once a week each infant was shown a set of patterns. The patterns were presented in pairs to each infant. The length of time the infant fixated on each pattern was recorded.

Results The results of the experiment are shown below.

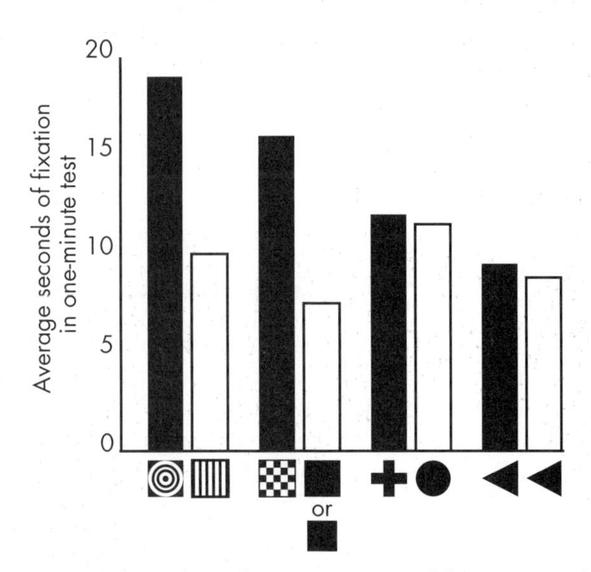

Fig. 16.5 Bar chart showing amount of fixation time for each pattern (from R. Fantz 1961)

It can be seen that infants spent more time looking at the more complex pattern in the pair. Where patterns were similar, or the same, in complexity there was little difference in the time spent looking.

Conclusions Fantz concluded 1) that infants could *differentiate* between two patterns and thus show form perception and 2) that they *preferred* looking at the more complex pattern.

Fantz' results suggest these abilities are present very soon after birth and are therefore likely to be innate.

COMPLEX VISUAL PERCEPTION

These basic visual skills are combined and organised in the more complex visual judgements which we are able to make. These include judgement of distance, direction and depth. What evidence do we have that these more complex abilities may be innate?

Distance and direction

If we look at the ability to judge **distance** and **direction**, this requires integrating information about the changing size and shape of objects. Close this book and hold it at arms' length in front of you. Bring it slowly towards you as if you are going to pass it over your left shoulder. See how its size and shape change? These changes are *visual clues* which tell you the distance and direction of the book's movement. The *speed* with which these changes occur tell you how fast the book is moving. Are these more complex perceptual skills innate or learned?

Studies carried out by **Tom Bower** suggest that an infant's ability to judge **distance** and **direction** are innate. When an object is moved towards an infant's face it shows a defensive response – it will raise its hands as if to protect its face, and may appear disturbed. **Bower** thought this did not necessarily show the infant could *see* the object moving towards it, because the infant could be responding to the movement of air. In order to find out which of these two explanations were correct, **Bower** devised a study with three experimental conditions:

- condition 1 – the infant saw a cube moving towards it and felt a rush of air at the same time
- condition 2 – a film of the cube moving towards it was shown (so there was no rush of air)
- condition 3 – the rush of air was presented, but no object

Infants from three weeks old showed the defensive response most in condition 1, less in condition 2, and not at all in the third condition. **Bower** also found that when the direction of the object was to the *side* of the infant, there was no defensive response. He concluded that infants could perceive **distance** and **direction** from three weeks old. This suggests that these visual abilities are present at, or very soon after, birth and are therefore strong evidence in support of the hereditarian view.

Depth perception

Another ability which has been investigated is called **depth perception**. This is the ability to recognise that the ground 'drops away' – just as it does when you look over a cliff. Depth perception has been investigated in animals and babies on the same apparatus, with interesting results.

Eleanor Gibson and **Richard Walk** used the **visual cliff** apparatus. This consists of a board which goes across the centre of a large sheet of glass. *Immediately* under the glass on one side of the board is a check pattern – called the 'shallow' side. But under the glass on the *other* side of the board the check pattern 'drops' several feet – the 'deep drop'. Gibson and Walk placed their subjects on the centre board and encouraged them to move *off* it and onto the glass which was over the deep 'drop'.

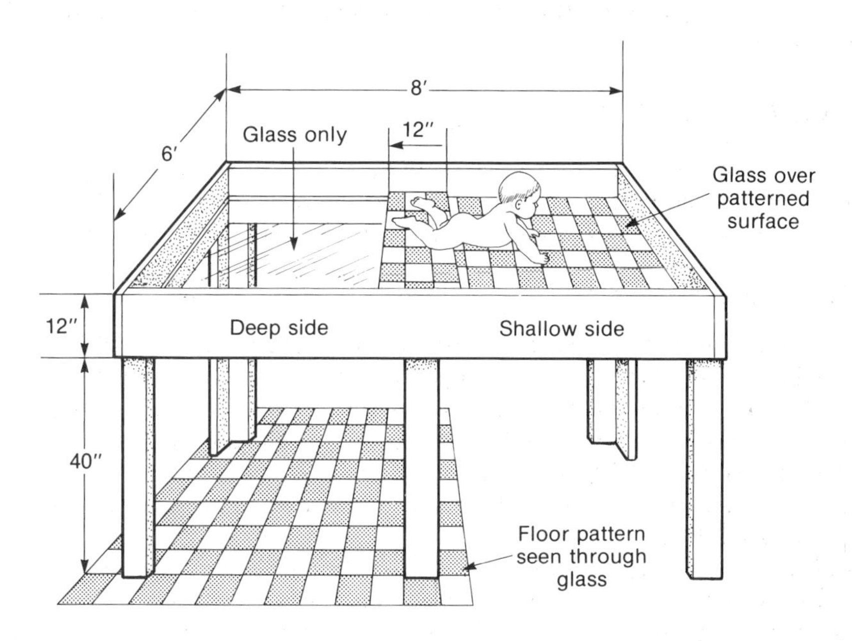

Fig. 16.6 Gibson and Walk's visual cliff apparatus

Results showed that very young animals, such as chicks and kittens, would not move over the deep drop but would readily move over the shallow side. If they were placed on the deep side they *froze* – and could not move. These results showed that animals appear to have innate **depth perception**.

I

However, it was not possible to run this study with new born infants; because they cannot move about by themselves. When it was done with babies about six months old, **Gibson and Walk** found that they too would not move over the deep side towards their mothers, but would move over the shallow side. Because the human subjects were several months old, it could be that they had already learned the visual cues which show depth perception. For example, through interaction with their environment they had come to understand that an abrupt change in the size of the pattern on the ground meant that the ground 'dropped away'. Subsequent research has proposed some answers.

S

Joseph Campos and his colleagues studied babies on the visual cliff by attaching heart rate monitors to them. If heart rate slows, it is an indication of interest, if it speeds up it is an indication of fear. **Campos** and later researchers found that heart rate changed, depending on the age of the baby. Their findings are summarised in Table 16.1.

Age of baby	Change in heart rate	What change indicates
under 2 months	none	no perception of depth
2–9 months	slows	interest
9 months +	increases	fear

Table 16.1 Table showing age and change of heart rate in babies on deep side of visual cliff apparatus (after J. Campos et al. 1970)

S

We could conclude from these results that very young infants cannot perceive depth, but those over two months can because there is a change in heart-rate. By nine months old the baby appeared to understand the *implications* of depth. Because this took much longer to develop, the baby was likely to have learned that depth means danger through experience in its environment.

So the **visual cliff** experiment shows **depth perception** is innate in animals but possibly *not* in humans. However, evidence from monitoring heart-rate suggests that depth perception *might* be innate in humans, although the *implications* of depth may be learned.

We have seen, through the results of the research in this section, some strong evidence that infants are born with basic visual abilities. Some of the more complex abilities, even if not present at birth, are certainly evident at a very young age. In all, this is strong evidence for the hereditarian view. The Gibson and Walk study is less conclusive, but highlights an important distinction we need to make in studying visual perception – that is the distinction between what people see and how they *understand* it. We will return to this point later on.

Evidence for the environmentalist view of the development of visual perception

S

Various types of studies have investigated the role of environmental factors on the development of visual perception. We will look first at adults who have gained sight for the first time and then at efforts to find out if visual abilities can be changed.

NEWLY SIGHTED ADULTS

S

I

Adults who have gained their sight for the first time can be seen as similar to infants, in that they have 'unused' visual abilities. This makes them very interesting to researchers because they can also *tell* researchers how and what they see (which infants cannot). If newly sighted people are not able to make sense of what they see, then this suggests that they need experience to enable them to do so. Therefore we might conclude that the environment is the main factor in the development of visual perception. On the other hand, if such people can correctly interpret what they see once they gain sight, this suggests that most of our visual abilities are innate.

In the early 1930s **von Senden** brought together evidence from 65 studies of people who had gained sight for the first time as adults. It appeared that most showed the abilities we have already noted in infants – the ability to separate form from background, to scan and follow moving objects. But he also noted that most were *unable* to recognise simple objects or shapes which they knew by touch. Some people learned to see quite well, usually the better-educated patients. Others gave up.

These findings are reflected in a detailed case study done by **Richard Gregory and Jean Wallace** of a man known as SB (remember ethics – the subject must be anonymous). He could see for the first time after an operation at 52 years of age. He was able to recognise and judge the distance of objects he was familiar with by touch, but had difficulty with unfamiliar objects. He could recognise people's emotions by the sound of their voice, but never learned to recognise emotions from facial expressions. He was too frightened to cross a busy street on his own, but had confidently done this when he was blind. He liked bright colours, but became depressed when light faded.

Despite his initial excitement at gaining sight, he eventually became depressed and died three years later.

It is difficult to draw conclusions about the influence of heredity or the environment from such studies. For one thing, the patient's visual system is not the same as an infants – it may have deteriorated from *lack of use*, not because of lack of stimulation from the environment. Another complication comes from years spent using *other* senses to compensate for lack of sight. Newly sighted people have become very dependent on touch and hearing, for example, and it is very difficult to *unlearn* this knowledge. For example, SB preferred to spend evenings sitting in the dark, even when he could see!

CAN VISUAL ABILITIES BE CHANGED?

If an ability is innate, then it cannot be altered, so if visual perception can be *altered* this suggests that it is not innate. Several psychologists have devised ways of altering perception in humans in order to test this.

At the turn of this century **G. Stratton** devised a lens which made everything appear to be upside down. He wore this all the time for several days and kept his other eye covered. He found that he learned to adjust to the 'upside down' information he received – imagine drinking a cup of coffee wearing this lens! However, it is not clear whether his perception changed or he was able to *adapt* his movements. For example, he reported seeing a fire in one place, but the sound of its crackling came from another point. Other clues in his environment could have helped his adjustment to the new world. He reported that when he removed the lens he soon saw things as 'normal'.

A more recent study by **W. Kohler** in the 1960s related to colour. He wore lenses which were half green and half red. He found that soon after putting them on, he had adapted and colours seemed 'normal'. When he took them off again though, he saw red where the lens had been green, and green where it had been red. In other words, his brain had been compensating for the colours.

The studies in this section do suggest that environment plays a part in the development of visual perception. We have seen how the visual system seems to be able to adapt: it is flexible. However, it is difficult in these studies to separate out what people *see* and how they *understand* it.

How can we decide between the influences of heredity and environment?

It is clear from the studies we have looked at so far that the development of visual perception is the result of *both* heredity and environment. Some abilities appear to be innate and others learned. However we have also seen that it is difficult to tease apart which factors are important and why. For example, it seems that some abilities develop only after time, but whether this is due to environmental factors, or to maturational factors is less clear.

There is a type of study which can be used to answer these heredity versus environment questions – the cross cultural study. Researchers into the development of visual perception have studied different cultures, in order to identify differences and similarities between them. If some abilities appear in many cultures then they are probably innate. If an ability is only found in a few cultures then it is likely to be learned.

EVIDENCE FROM CROSS-CULTURAL STUDIES

M. Segall and his colleagues reported studies of visual perception carried out with subjects from the Philippines, South Africans of European descent, Americans and members of several African tribes. The researchers tested the participants on these two visual illusions:

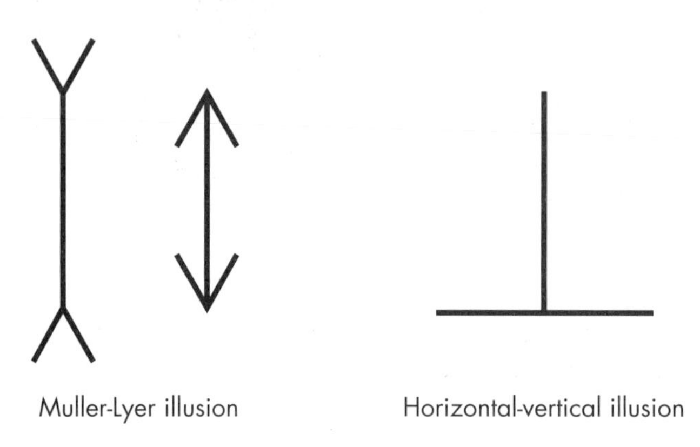

Fig. 16.7 Visual illusions

In the Muller-Lyer illusion the vertical lines are the same length, but you will probably 'see' the line with the fins pointing outwards as the longer one. In the horizontal-vertical illusion, again the two lines are the same length, although the vertical one usually appears longer to Western eyes.

Segall and his colleagues found that the Africans and the Philippinos were less able to see the Muller-Lyer illusion than the other participants. This suggests that it is something in our environment which creates this illusion. **Segall** proposed the 'carpentered world hypothesis' as an explanation. This means that people familiar with a world of right angles, buildings, and perspective 'understand' the Muller-Lyer illusion as a three-dimensional picture showing the *inner* corner of a room and the *outer* edge of a building. Both lines appear the same length on the retina of the eye, but we 'compensate' because the *inner* line is further away, according to the visual cues, so we 'understand' it as longer. This is the explanation offered by **Richard Gregory**, and it is based on Western perceptions of people's environment. Those who are not familiar with this environment will not 'see' the illusion.

S

The role of the environment is more clearly suggested in the results the researchers obtained from the second illusion. They found that participants from two of the African tribes were the most likely to see the horizontal-vertical illusion. Members of a third tribe were the *least* likely to see it, and the rest of the participants were in between. **Segall** looked at differences in the environment of the three tribes and found that the first two lived in high, open country where trees were important features, and could be clearly seen from a distance. In contrast, the third tribe lived in a jungle environment, and so had little opportunity to see vertical objects clearly. He concluded that it was the environment which had caused different interpretations of the stimulus. Was he right?

S

Other cross cultural studies have found conflicting results. It has been argued that what these studies are testing is how *cultures* represent their world in pictures. For example, the first picture shown in Fig. 16.8 uses **depth** cues (such as the smaller an object is, the further away it is) to help the viewer understand its meaning.

Fig. 16.8 A picture to test depth perception

Researchers found that members of African tribes were unable to understand this picture. For example they thought the man was about to spear the elephant. They were therefore considered unable to use depth cues. However, later research amended the picture by adding *other* depth cues. When these cues were added, as they have been in the second picture (Fig.16.9), then the subjects' ability to understand the picture improved markedly. Can you pick out what the cues are?

Fig. 16.9 The same picture with additional depth cues

In a culture which does not represent its experience like this, these pictures do not 'make sense'. However, we learn the depth cues given in Fig 16.8 from a very early age in our culture and this is why we can understand them. Look at the example on the next page, which is taken from a child's 'Learning to Read' book.

S

Fig. 16.10 'It looks like a toy train' says Jane

S

Where has this point taken us? It underlines the difficulty of studying people of other cultures, because we are bound in the conventions of our *own* culture. Therefore our studies may not be valid. This means we are not testing what we *think* we are testing. We *think* we are testing depth perception, whereas what we are really testing is *cultural conventions* of how to represent experience in two dimensions. This is not to say that cross-cultural studies have no value, but that we should be aware of their weaknesses, and try to compensate for them.

So what conclusions can we come to?

Throughout this section we have found that whenever there appears to be evidence for *one* view, there are always some aspects of the *other* view which are involved. Overall, we see clear evidence of some abilities which are innate and also evidence for the importance of the environment for those abilities to develop.

In reality the nature or nurture debate in psychology is no longer the predominant debate. Psychologists largely adopt the interactionist view. This is that *both* have a role to play, but it is how nature and nurture interact which is of most interest and most difficult to tease apart.

These are two reasons then, why the nature or nurture debate on visual perception is likely to remain inconclusive. One is that interest is no longer focused on nature or nurture, but on the interaction between them. The other reason relates to methodology – it is difficult to isolate the many variables which are involved in studying the development of visual perception.

Further Reading

Bee H (1992) *The Developing Child* (6th ed), New York, Harper Collins
Sylva K and Lunt I (1982) *Child Development, A First Course*, Oxford, Basil Blackwell
Gross R (1992) *Psychology – The Science of Mind and Behaviour*, Chapter 10, London, Hodder and Stoughton

EXERCISES

1. In you own words describe object permanence, egocentricity, conservation and decentring.
2. Say what stage and age the above terms are related to.
3. Write a paragraph describing the development of attachment (Chapter 8) in terms of object permanence.
4. What is the difference between assimilation and accommodation?
5. Suggest how a selection of empty plastic cartons could be used by an 18 month old child and a four year old child. In your answer use the terms schema and equilibration.
6. Write an experimental hypothesis for the Fantz study.
7. What is the IV and what is the DV in the Fantz study?
8. Using your own words, describe a study which suggests visual perception is innate.
9. Using your own words, describe a study which suggests visual perception is due to environment.

Chapter 17

The Development of Moral Behaviour and Moral Judgements

ANYTHING THAT RELATES TO MORALS RELATES TO HOW WE OUGHT TO BEHAVE. IN THIS CHAPTER WE WILL LOOK AT HOW MORAL BEHAVIOUR AND MORAL JUDGEMENTS DEVELOP. WE WILL SEE THE WAYS IN WHICH PARENTS AND PEERS ARE IMPORTANT IN THIS PROCESS.

What are moral behaviour and moral judgements?

Moral behaviour is what we do and **moral judgements** are the decisions we make about an action – is it right or is it wrong, fair or unfair? Consider someone who cheats in an exam: cheating is the behaviour and in this case we would say it was wrong – that it was immoral. If I asked you *why* it was wrong, then you would be giving your moral judgements. How does this sense of right and wrong develop? We will start by looking at three different theories, each of which attempts to answer this question.

Psychodynamic explanation for moral development

I

Freud said that the moral part of the personality was the **superego** (see Chapter 12 for details). So how does the superego develop? During the **phallic stage** of psychosexual development the boy experiences the **Oedipus conflict**. This occurs between three to five years of age. His longings for his mother conflict with his fear of his father. He **identifies** with his father in order to avoid the father's anger. Through this identification the boy takes on his father's attitudes, behaviours and moral standards – he takes on his father's views about what is right, wrong, good, bad.

In this way the boy **internalises** his father's **moral** standards. Freud claimed this internal parent was represented by the superego. He divided the **superego** into two parts, the ego-ideal and the conscience:

- the **ego-ideal** represents the kind of person the child *wants* to be; the ego-ideal is the rewarding and approving parent, the source of pride when we do the right thing

- the **conscience** watches the child's behaviour, stops it from doing the wrong things; it is the punishing parent, the source of guilt when we do the wrong thing

According to **Freud** then, once the boy resolves the **Oedipus** conflict, he no longer needs an external influence to make him behave morally – the influence is *internal.* Freud felt that once the child had left the phallic stage successfully it was morally mature.

As you will remember, the girl experiences the **Electra** conflict. She does not fear her mother so much, although she does fear loss of her love, so her identification with her mother is weaker. Freud claimed that this led to females having a weaker moral sense than males.

There are criticisms of the **psychodynamic** explanation of **moral development.** For example, children show moral behaviour when they are *younger* than five years of age, when they typically enter the phallic stage. But they are *not* morally mature by seven years old, when they leave the phallic stage. Research which has compared the moral sense of boys and girls suggests that girls may develop a moral sense *more* rapidly than boys, which is opposite to what Freud's explanation would predict.

Freud also sees the two-parent family as the key influence on the child's moral development. This may have been true for the small group of women whom Freud studied at the turn of the century. However, it is less relevant today, when there are many one parent families and a wide range of other influences – through television, computers, videos, playgroups and schools.

S

Since Freud, other psychoanalysts have stressed the importance of the **ego** in the individual's **moral development,** rather than instincts as Freud did. They say that the development of the ego (or self) takes place over many years, and depends not only on parents but on 'significant others'. These may be teachers or peers for example.

Learning theory explanations of moral development

Learning theory explanations focus on the child's environment, and its effect on **moral development**. We will look at the contributions from classical conditioning, operant conditioning and social learning theory.

L

CLASSICAL CONDITIONING

Classical conditioning can create moral behaviour, according to psychologists such as **Hans Eysenck**. He said that if a child is naughty and is disciplined immediately, it learns to associate the naughtiness with the unpleasantness of discipline. Let us put this in classical conditioning terms.

A naughty act brings punishment, such as shouting, pain or withdrawal of affection. The child associates punishment (the unconditioned stimulus) with anxiety (the unconditioned response). If the naughty act is paired with punishment several times then the anxiety becomes the conditioned response to the naughty act (which is now the conditioned stimulus). So, even when the child *thinks* about being naughty it feels anxiety. This is what stops it being naughty again – and is therefore how moral development takes place.

L

Classical conditioning has also been used to explain why children *help* others. The infant associates the distress of being hurt with aspects of the injury – crying, blood, and so on. When it sees an injured child or hears another child crying, these same feelings of distress are triggered. This is because they have been conditioned in the child. It has been suggested that this is one reason that children behave in a helpful or moral way – in order to relieve this distress in others (see page 214).

OPERANT CONDITIONING

The operant conditioning explanation says that moral behaviour is like any other behaviour: it can be strengthened by reinforcement and weakened by punishment. Reinforcement includes receiving approval, thanks, congratulations and attention. These are examples of positive reinforcement.

Negative reinforcement can also strengthen **moral** behaviour. When a parent says to a child, 'If you hit baby again, then you'll be in trouble', the desire to hit baby will create anxiety in the child. This anxiety is unpleasant, and the way to end the unpleasantness is to decide *not* to hit baby and do something less controversial. Because the unpleasant experience – anxiety – is stopped, then the decision to do something else is an example of negative reinforcement.

Recent research shows that adults do not reinforce moral behaviour very often, but they punish *wrong* behaviour more frequently. Punishment alone is not very effective in changing behaviour because it shows the child what it *should not* do, not what it *should* do. Also, according to learning theorists, behaviour which is *not* reinforced should become extinguished. Therefore if the child does something wrong, the reaction should simply be not to reward it! More importantly, certain kinds of punishment may give messages to the child about hostility and rejection which create those feelings in the child itself.

There are criticisms of the ideas behind operant conditioning, one of which is that punishment *does* appear to work in some circumstances. Equally, some children *do* continue to behave unkindly and selfishly even when they are reinforced for the right kind of behaviour. We will look at this again when we examine the role of parents in **moral development.**

SOCIAL LEARNING THEORY

Social learning theory proposes that **moral development** occurs as a result of the child observing and modelling the behaviour of someone who is important to him or her. The model may be **similar** to the child, **powerful** or **nurturant**. A child is also *more* likely to imitate the behaviour of a model who is reinforced (Fig. 17.1) and *less* likely to imitate the behaviour of a model who is punished. This is called vicarious reinforcement or vicarious punishment.

Does social learning theory explain why children may show **moral** behaviour in one situation and not in another? It does, because it says that the *situation* will affect the child's behaviour. Consider a situation where a girl watches another girl helping her little brother on a climbing frame and sees the girl's mother saying how good she is. The watching child may help *her* little brother next time her own mother is present, but may not help him if there is no-one watching.

Bandura made the point that through modelling children learn what they are able to do. He called this **self-efficacy**. Initially the child may be told it is a helpful child, because of its helpful behaviour. Gradually he comes to think of himself as helpful, and

Fig.17.1 This model may help the child's moral development

behaves accordingly. His helpful behaviour confirms his **self-efficacy**, which is rewarding for the child. This is called **internal reinforcement** because it is within the child.

Criticisms of social learning theory explanations note the artificiality of some of the experiments, where models are often adults, sometimes on film. They say this is an artificial situation. In real life, children frequently interact with models and have a personal relationship with them; indeed many of their models are not even adults. We will return to this in the final section of the chapter.

Another criticism is that this approach predicts children will learn moral behaviour as a direct result of what they experience. Therefore there will not be a consistent pattern in children's **moral development**. The next explanation says that there is a general pattern in moral development.

Cognitive-developmental explanations of moral development

Cognitive-developmental explanations of **moral development** propose that children's moral development follows certain patterns. This is because their moral development is part of their general cognitive development. There are two major theorists in this area, **Jean Piaget** and **Lawrence Kohlberg**.

PIAGET'S IDEAS ON MORAL JUDGEMENTS

Piaget used several way of finding out more about children's **moral judgements** and we will look at two of them. He wanted to know how children understood rules. However, he did not want to examine the rules imposed by adults, but the child's *own* rules. In order to do this he used the clinical interview method. He played marbles with children whilst asking questions about the rules they created, and what would happen if they were broken, or did not work very well. The ideas he gained can be seen in his theory of **moral development**.

Another method he used was to tell children two stories. In one, a naughty child causes a little damage, in the other a helpful child causes a lot of damage. Then he asked the children some questions. Here is an example.

An example of Piaget's stories

A little boy called John came running into the kitchen. He didn't know that there was a tray of cups behind the door. When he pushed the door he knocked the tray on the floor and lots of the cups were broken.

A little boy called Henry wanted to take some jam while his mother was out of the room. When he climbed up on the cupboard to reach the jam he knocked a cup onto the floor and it broke.

Sample of questions

Which boy was the naughtiest, John or Henry?
Which boy should be punished more?
Why?

Piaget found that children under about eight years of age said that John was the naughtiest because he broke more glasses. He was the child who should be punished more. By eight years old, children were able to make the correct judgement, because they took *intent* into account. This is an example of **decentring**, because the child can take into account both the damage caused and the intent behind the action.

Piaget said that up to about three or four years old the child was unable to make moral judgements because she does not understand rules, so she cannot understand breaking rules. Once she understands rules she is in the first stage of moral development. Piaget said there are two stages of moral development, and these relate to the child's cognitive development. They are heteronomous and autonomous morality.

C

Heteronomous morality

Heteronomous morality means morality based on rules imposed from outside. Rules are made by parents, teachers, God, and are also unchangeable. The child makes moral judgements based on rules. If you do something which is wrong, you will be punished. At this stage the child also bases judgement about the rightness or wrongness of behaviour on the *consequences* of an action. **Piaget** called this **moral realism**, and children show it up to about eight years old.

Autonomous morality

Autonomous morality is morality based on your own rules. This kind of thinking appears when the child is able to judge the *intent* behind the action as well as the consequence – in other words when it can **decentre**. The child also understands that rules can be flexible to suit the situation. For example, when playing hide and seek the small child will be allowed by other children to count to a lower number. At this stage children make up their *own* rules as they apply to their group at the moment. **Moral judgements** are based on awareness and respect for other people's views which are helped by the increase in co-operation with their peers. At this stage, because the child's thinking is more flexible, and can take account of other people's perspective, Piaget said the child's thinking showed **moral relativism**.

There have been criticisms of **Piaget's** points: for example other research has shown that when the *intention* is emphasised, even three year olds can make the correct judgements. Another criticism is that his stages are rather general, because research shows a difference in the **moral** thinking of the child of, perhaps 12 years old who is just in the **autonomous morality** stage, and the thinking of a 42 year old, with many years of experience as well. This was addressed in the next cognitive-developmental explanation.

KOHLBERG'S STAGES OF MORAL DEVELOPMENT

Kohlberg's theory was based on Piaget's, so it is cognitive, but it identifies more stages in the development process, and continues into adulthood. Kohlberg was interested in **moral reasoning**. To assess people's moral reasoning he told them a story – a moral dilemma – and then asked them questions.

One of the best known **moral dilemmas** is the story of Heinz.

Heinz' dilemma

Heinz' wife was dying of cancer. Doctors said a new drug might save her. The drug had been discovered by a pharmacist in Heinz' town but he was charging a lot of money for it – ten times what it cost him to make. Heinz couldn't afford to buy the drug, so he asked friends and relatives to lend him money. But still he only had half the money he needed. He told the pharmacist his wife was dying and asked him to sell the drug cheaper, or asked if he could pay the rest of the money later. The pharmacist said no; he had discovered the drug and was going to make money on it. Heinz got desperate so he broke in to the pharmacy and stole some of the drug.

Sample of questions

Should Heinz have stolen the drug?
Would it change anything if Heinz did not love his wife?
If the person dying was a stranger to Heinz, would it make any difference?

Kohlberg noted people's answers and analysed them. From this he proposed three **levels** of moral reasoning, each containing two stages.

Level 1 pre-conventional morality

Here authority is imposed from outside the individual. This level covers answers which are based on the results of actions. The first stage of reasoning is based on the punishment of actions. If an action is punished it must have been wrong. People who have greater power are obeyed. The later stage of reasoning is based on behaviour which is carried out because of personal gain such as a reward or to get help from someone else: 'the pharmacist should have let Heinz pay later, because one day he might need something from Heinz.'

Level 2 conventional morality

S C Here authority is **internalised** but not questioned. This level covers reasoning which is based on the norms of the group to which the person belongs. The first stage answers say that people like you when you do good, helpful things and are based on what the wrongdoer *intended*, not the consequences. The later stage reasoning is based on respect for law and order – not the authority of specific people like parents, but a generalised social norm of obedience to authority and doing one's duty.

Level 3 postconventional morality

C Here individual judgement is based on self-chosen principles. Reasoning at the first stage says that, although laws are important, to be fair there are times when they must be changed or ignored. For example, in Heinz' dilemma the protection of life is more important than breaking the law against stealing. In the final stage people assume personal responsibility for their actions, based on universal ethical and moral principles which are not necessarily laid down by society. Kohlberg doubted few ever reached this stage.

C As with all **stage theories**, Kohlberg claimed that the individual's reasoning progresses through each stage. Therefore reasoning cannot 'go backwards' from level 2 to level 1. He did not tie the levels to a specific age, although research has suggested that level 1 is about up to ten years old, level 2 is ten years up to adulthood; very few adults show level 3 reasoning.

Kohlberg has been criticised because his studies only used male subjects. However more recent work has shown similar results with girls' moral thinking. Critics have also noted that it is very difficult for subjects to put their reasoning into words, particularly when they include abstract ideas of justice. Subjects therefore may have an *intuitive* understanding relating to the higher levels, but be unable to express it. Finally, S Kohlberg's theory has been criticised because it is ethnocentric: he viewed morality from the viewpoint of Western society. Other cultures have different values which would lead to different types of reasoning and judgements, whereas Kohlberg saw the values in his research as *the* moral standards.

There are some general criticisms of the **cognitive developmental** theories of moral development. One is that although the child's *social* context is acknowledged, these explanations do not say *how* the social context has influence. They also fail to S differentiate between *moral* and *social* transgressions, which more recent research has highlighted. We will return to this in the last section.

How does pro-social reasoning develop in most children?

C Many of the ideas we have looked at so far have examined what children think about doing *wrong*. More recently psychologists have looked at the judgements children make about *good* behaviour. Pro-social reasoning is making judgements about helping behaviour.

In the early 1980s **Nancy Eisenberg** ran a longitudinal study using dilemmas. These were not like Kohlberg's dilemmas, because she wanted to find out whether her participants would put their *own* interests before someone else's interests. This is another example of a clinical interview. One dilemma asked the child to imagine he was walking to a friend's birthday party but passes a child who has fallen over and is hurt. If he stays to help, he might miss the fun of the party. What should he do?

From the answers, **Eisenberg** proposed six stages of **pro-social reasoning,** which were related to age.

C

Stage 1 – self-focused, showing the child satisfying its own needs or only helping if the other could help him. 'I'd help because she'd help me next time' (up to six years old).
Stage 2 – needs of others, showing the child's awareness of the other child's needs. 'He needs help'.(up to 10 years old).
Stage 3 – approval of others, behaving pro-socially because others will like you, or you should do it. 'He'd like me more if I helped' (up to 13 years old).
Stage 4 – empathic orientation, showing empathy with others' feelings. 'I know how he feels' (adolescents).
Stage 5 – transitional, showing some evidence of acting on internalised norms or responsibilities. 'I'd feel good if I helped' (adolescents and some adults).
Stage 6 – strongly internalised, showing clear relationship between behaviour and the need to act according to one's principles – I'd feel bad if I didn't help' (rarely seen other than in adults).

These six levels can be compared with **Kohlberg**'s six stages, but the child's reasoning seems more advanced. Eisenberg suggested that this was because the ideas were about *pro-social* (or helping) behaviour, and not about what the child should *not* do.

Is she right? **Eisenberg**'s evidence for pro-social reasoning at a younger age may be due to the kind of dilemma the child is given. Perhaps Eisenberg's stories are easier to understand because they are related to the child's own experience. If that is so, then her results may be due to the way her research was designed.

C

How is the individual's moral development and behaviour related to others?

As we have examined each of these explanations for children's **moral development**, we have come across the part that others play. Recent research has looked more at the *interaction* between the child and these others. For example, instead of viewing the parent just as a person who delivers reinforcement, the *meaning* of that reinforcement for the child has been examined. We will look at research which has studied the child's interaction with the parent and then research related to its interaction with peers.

THE ROLE OF PARENTS IN MORAL DEVELOPMENT

The explanations we have examined *all* give a key role to parents, whether as the person the child **identifies** with, is reinforced or punished by, or models her behaviour on. Although parents play little formal part in **cognitive-developmental** explanations, recent research suggests they are important in this explanation too. Let us start by re-examining some of the ideas we looked at earlier in the chapter.

Punishment – how does it work?

L

A child who seeks attention from its parent may find the quickest way to get it is to be naughty, and thus bring on punishment. In this situation, the punishment is actually rewarding for the child, because it brings the attention it desires. By looking at the child's perception we can see why punishment may not work.

C S

In addition, **Ross Parke** has shown that if an *explanation* is given with punishment, mild punishment is just as effective at weakening behaviour as strong punishment. This suggests that increasing the child's understanding of its behaviour will mean there is less need to punish. Parke also found that if there was a warm affectionate relationship between adult and child, the punishment was much more effective. Why should this be? A warm affectionate relationship suggests a strong attachment. Punishment may increase feelings of guilt, or may include withdrawal of affection, both of which are more likely to be effective in a strongly attached child.

Reinforcement – is it used?

L

Reinforcement should strengthen behaviour, and again the evidence shows that a warm affectionate relationship enhances the effects of reinforcement. However, it also appears that parents are not very good at rewarding the appropriate behaviour. In fact they are more likely to punish bad behaviour than reward good behaviour. This finding suggests that children know more about the consequences of *bad* actions than they know about the consequences of good actions.

Fig. 17.2 This little girl is receiving positive reinforcement from her mother, and negative reinforcement by giving her spinach away

Modelling – how influential is it?

Parents constantly act as models. How influential will they be on the child's **moral development?** One factor of importance is whether the parent is *consistent* in what he does and what he says. The greater the consistency, the more likely it is that the child will model the moral behaviour. What if the behaviour the child sees is contradictory? Research has shown that where an adult says one thing but does another, the child will model what is *done* not what is *said*. This reflects **Piaget**'s idea that the child at the pre-operational stage can only attend to one aspect of the situation at a time. What the child *sees* appears to be most important.

Bandura says the most effective models are those who are **powerful, similar** and **nurturant.** We have just seen that parents who are 'warm' are able to punish and reward more effectively, but according to Bandura they are also more likely to be imitated. This kind of parent appears to have a positive influence on their child's **moral development.** Equally, it is argued that the punishing parent may have a *negative* impact on their child's moral development. However, **Judith Smetana** has found that parents may not have such a direct influence and we will look at her work shortly.

Several of these ideas are incorporated in results found by **Martin Hoffman** in the 1960s. He carried out research on the relationship between a child's **moral** behaviour and the way the parent used discipline. Hoffman did this by asking children questions about topics such as which classmate was most likely to help another. He also asked parents questions relating to discipline, such as how they would react to various examples of their child's wrongdoing. From the results Hoffman proposed three types of discipline:

- **power assertive** discipline where the parent used threats or force or withdrew privileges
- **love withdrawal** which involved ignoring or isolating the child
- **inductive** discipline which meant reasoning with the child, encouraging the child to think about its behaviour, its consequences and how his or her parents felt

Other research supports Hoffman's findings and there seem to be two types of moral behaviour that result from these styles:

Internalised moral behaviour

Internalised moral behaviour is shown by the child who behaves morally even when there is no *external* pressure to do so. Such children show greater consideration of others and express more guilt when they do wrong than those whose parents use power assertive techniques. This behaviour is related to the **inductive**, and to a lesser degree the **love withdrawal** styles. Inductive techniques appear to encourage **empathy** for others and the **internalisation** of morality, according to Hoffman.

Externalised moral behaviour

Externalised moral behaviour is shown by the child who behaves morally in order to avoid punishment. Children who behave like this tend to show less concern about others and this behaviour is related to the **power assertive** style of parental discipline. Hoffman suggests this is because power assertion creates hostility and provides a model which shows the child they should direct hostility *outwards* and also that the morality of actions is *controlled* from the outside.

For example, **Susan Londerville and Mary Main** found that the mothers of two year olds who used **power assertive** discipline had children who were more disobedient and unco-operative. However, these results are correlational, as they are in most of these studies examining parental discipline and **moral behaviour**. We cannot conclude therefore that a parent's disciplining style *causes* particular moral behaviour. Nevertheless **Hoffman's** points show how the child's moral development is related to the emotional, behavioural and cognitive aspects of its relationship with its parent.

Despite these ideas about parental influence on **moral development**, some research shows the influence may not be so straightforward. **Judith Smetana** compared children who were suffering from physical abuse with some suffering neglect and another group who were not maltreated. In all three groups she found the children gave similar decisions on what was right and what was wrong. It seems that different parental models had little effect on their children's moral sense.

S

Other research on parents and moral behaviour has highlighted the difference between *moral* rules and *social* rules. Social rules are the norms which guide our behaviour, and are a reflection of the society in which we live. For example, saying 'please' is a *social* not a *moral* rule. It appears that parents and teachers are more concerned when children break a social rule than a moral rule. It also appears that children learn the difference between the two at a very early age. In this next section we will look at this topic in more detail.

INFLUENCE OF PEERS ON AN INDIVIDUAL'S MORAL BEHAVIOUR

S

Once children start at playgroup or school, their social world becomes much larger. They move from the family environment where there is adult supervision and few other children. The child has usually established its position in the family structure. In a playgroup, he is surrounded by others with less adult protection. He has to negotiate with his peers – to learn to give and take and to have mutual respect. These abilities develop as the child matures.

C

Successful **moral development** requires taking the perspective of others, and cognitive psychologists have found that when children have conflicting views about things, their attempts to understand each other and reconcile those views encourage cognitive development. This shows the importance of the influence of peers on the child's cognitive and therefore its moral development.

C

This link with cognitive development is evident in a cross-sectional study by **J. Youniss** in 1980. He gave stories to children about the behaviour of a child of the same age as them towards its friends. His participants gave these types of responses:

- 6 to 8 year olds talked of giving and sharing with others and 'playing nicely'
- 9 to 11 year olds said the child should help friends out to make things fair
- 12 to 14 year olds said friendship involved things like encouraging friends or consoling them when they are disappointed

C

Youniss pointed out that the child's responses moved from **moral** concern on the physical level to the psychological level. We can see here how children's knowledge of how to behave towards friends echoes cognitive developmental ideas. Increasingly they show awareness of the *others'* situations, and consideration of more abstract ideas.

According to social learning theory, a child's peers will provide important models. **Bandura** found children consistently model themselves on their peers, which is why Bandura said models who were *similar* were more likely to be imitated than those who were dissimilar. Research shows that boys tend to be more concerned about the opinions of their peers, and are more likely to imitate their peers than girls are. Boys are more likely to model the behaviour of older or more influential boys, and respond to approval from other boys. But both boys and girls respond to the norms and values of their peers.

L

We have already noted that children's **moral development** may not depend so heavily on parents as we once thought. Let us return to the evidence that parents tend to ignore moral transgressions but punish social transgressions. **Michael Siegel and Rebecca Storey** thought that if children did not learn morals from their parents they might learn from their peers. They set up a study in Australia (see page 212).

As a comment at the end of their report, **Siegel and Storey** also noted that staff intervened more when social rules were broken than when moral rules were broken. In other words, their response to rule breaking was similar to parents' behaviour.

The greater concern which adults show about breaking *social* rules, as opposed to *moral* rules is highlighted by an observational study of disputes in the family home. It is unusual, and difficult, to do this kind of research, but it is very valuable because it tells us about behaviour in a natural setting. So what did this study show? Disputes between parents and children seemed to be about breaking '*house* rules', such as being untidy. Disputes between *siblings* tended to be about sharing and ownership. These children were clearly more concerned about the breaking of *moral*, rather than *social* rules.

S

Fig. 17.3 Caring for a little brother

Siegel and Storey (1984)

Aim of study The aim of the study was to see whether children's moral development was the result of greater social exposure to their peers.

Independent variable The IV was the length of time the children had attended the daycare centre.

Dependent variable The DV was the answers the children gave.

Sample There were 40 subjects with an average age of four and a quarter years. Ten boys and ten girls had been attending the daycare centre for an average of two and a half years – the 'veterans'; and ten boys and ten girls had been attending the centre for an average of three months – the 'novices'.

Materials Various pictures of 'stick' figures breaking moral rules (hitting someone else) or social rules (sitting in the wrong place at story-time) were shown. There were also four pictures of faces, showing expressions from 'happy' (smiling) to 'very, very bad' (frowning intently).

Procedure Each child was shown pictures of the figures breaking the rules, then asked to indicate on the 'face' pictures what they thought of the action.

Results The results showed both age groups thought the moral transgressions were serious, but the novices thought the social transgressions were naughtier than the veterans did.

Conclusions The results were not as expected because there was no difference between the moral judgements made by the veterans and the novices. However, because the veterans were less worried about breaking social rules than the novices, Siegel and Storey concluded that day care gave children the opportunity to distinguish between social and moral rules. The veterans had a chance to discover which were more important, whereas the novices had not.

We have seen then that children appear to differentiate at quite a young age between social and moral rules. How do they know the difference if parents and other adults do not teach it? Studies which ask children what happens when you break rules suggest that children note the *consequences* of rule-breaking. Children said that moral transgressions were wrong because of the harm and distress they caused to others. These consequences were not mentioned in relation to *social* transgressions. This could be an explanation for **Smetana**'s results which showed abused children made the same moral distinctions as non-abused children.

S

This sensitivity to the effect of behaviour on others seems to be related to *responsibility* for others. **Diana Baumrind** has noted that the more a parent expects the child to show maturity in her relationships with others, the more social responsibility the child shows.

In their cross cultural work, **Beatrice Whiting and Carolyn Edwards** studied children in Kenya, India, Mexico, Japan and the United States. They found a consistent pattern – that early responsibility for the care of others is related to more concern about others. This was true for both boys and girls. Although some psychologists have stressed that children's **moral development** is encouraged by interacting with peers on an *equal* basis, Whiting and Edwards described how older children behaved as adult carers would; they modelled the behaviour of adults towards young children. This was true even between four-year-olds and two-year-olds.

In summary then, the role of peers, both as models and reinforcers, is an important factor in the development of moral behaviour. However, the way in which the child understands and uses what it experiences has also been highlighted. We have seen that, although parents have a very influential role, in reality it is not always as we expect. It seems that in some circumstances children's moral development may occur with little reinforcement, or even when they experience parental abuse. **Jerome Kagan** has proposed that morality is a universal human competence, like memory or language. He says that this is why you can see evidence of it in two year olds. How it *develops* depends on the child's environment and cultural notions of right and wrong. In studying these factors, research which concentrates on how children *understand* their social worlds is beginning to show us the complexity of the interaction between the child and its world.

Further Reading

Bee H (1992) *The Developing Child* (6th ed), New York, Harper Collins
Hayes N (1994) *Foundations of Psychology*, London, Routledge

EXERCISES

1. If you were to replicate Piaget's 'two stories' study, you would need to counterbalance. What does this mean and why would you do it?
2. Why do you think Siegel and Storey used pictures in their research?
3. What are some of the problems a researcher might have in observing family interactions in the home? What can she do to try to solve these problems?
4. Why do you think children are more concerned about breaking moral rather than social rules?
5. What are the arguments against the use of punishment in the development of moral behaviour?

Chapter 18
Pro-social Behaviour

IN THIS CHAPTER WE ARE GOING TO LOOK AT BEHAVIOUR WHICH HELPS OTHER PEOPLE. FIRST YOU WILL SEE HOW CHILDREN DEVELOP THE ABILITY TO IDENTIFY WITH OTHER PEOPLE'S EMOTIONS, THEN WE WILL LOOK AT CIRCUMSTANCES IN WHICH WE HELP OTHERS AND THE REASONS WHY WE DO SO

What is pro-social behaviour?

Pro-social behaviour is behaviour which helps others. A little boy who tries to comfort his crying sister is showing pro-social behaviour, as is a classmate who offers to share revision with you. A teenager who gives up her seat on a bus to an old lady is showing pro-social behaviour, and so is someone who dives into the sea to rescue a drowning child. Pro-social behaviour is behaviour which benefits others or has positive social consequence – the term is used to cover altruism and helping behaviour.

One of the motives for pro-social behaviour appears to be **empathy,** so we will start by looking at how empathy develops in children. We will then look at studies of **altruism** and what makes bystanders help in an emergency. Finally we will look at how society's expectations, or social norms, influence helping behaviour.

S

How does empathy develop in children?

Empathy is an emotional response to someone else's feelings or situation. There is disagreement as to whether the emotions have to be *identical* to the other's, or just similar to the other person's emotions. However, there is agreement that **empathy** is a crucial factor in **altruism**. **Altruism** is behaviour which puts someone else's well-being before your own. We will look at some evidence for the importance of empathy in altruistic behaviour in the next section, but for now we will focus on how **empathy** develops. Research suggests that cognitive development and classical conditioning are key factors.

EMPATHY AND CONDITIONING

Classical conditioning explains the development of **empathy** through the process of association. When a small child hurts itself, it cries, feels pain; perhaps it sees blood.

L

In other words it knows distress. As these experiences are repeated it learns to associate a cry of pain, or the sight of blood, with a feeling of distress. Because of this association, it will eventually *feel* distress when it hears *others* cry, or when it sees blood.

In the picture below you can see that the mother is responding to the baby's unhappy expression. She is comforting the child by showing she knows his feelings; in other words she is showing **empathy.**

Fig. 18.1 Giving comfort and encouraging empathy

This baby is probably not aware of what he looks like, but he is learning from his mother that his feelings of unhappiness are associated with a particular response. In classical conditioning terms, seeing this expression in others will automatically trigger his feelings of unhappiness. In addition, as he gets older he will be able to *recognise* the same feelings in others by this expression.

L

In these examples the feeling of distress is triggered by another's suffering. However this can happen in just the same way with *pleasurable* emotions. **J. Aronfreed** found that through the association of the child's feelings of *pleasure* with *another's* feeling of pleasure, empathy develops for the feelings of others. So there is a classical conditioning explanation of **empathy** for both distress and pleasurable emotions.

However, research has shown that children's empathy changes as children develop, and the classical conditioning explanation does not account for how this change takes place. This next account does so.

HOFFMAN'S FOUR STAGES IN THE DEVELOPMENT OF EMPATHY

C

Martin Hoffman said that the development of **empathy** is linked to cognitive development and he proposed four stages in the development of empathy.

1 Global empathy

L

I

During the first year of life an infant shows empathy through its behaviour, such as crying when it hears another baby crying. This could be because the infant is still **egocentric,** and therefore is unable to distinguish between itself and others. **Hoffman** says this **empathic response** is due either to early classical conditioning or to inborn human tendencies towards empathy.

2 Egocentric empathy

C

From about one year old toddlers respond to the feelings of others. For example toddlers will try to comfort a crying child, or show fear when another child is frightened. However, because they are still **egocentric** they cannot understand what may relieve the other's distress; a toddler may offer a favourite toy to her mother who has a cut finger. The child is showing an **empathic** response but is not able to understand the cause of the other's distress.

3 Empathy for another's feelings

C

From two years of age children start to show that they can identify other's feelings, and respond in the appropriate way. They may try to mend a broken toy, or wipe up spilled juice. As they get older they may show a real effort to understand the other's emotions in order to relieve the other's distress. This is when their capacity for **'role-taking'** is developing (see the fourth stage below).

4 Empathy for another's general plight

From about ten years of age children begin to recognise the implications of someone else's *situation* – poverty for example, as well as immediate distress. They may also understand the plight of large groups of people – such as victims of war, famine or earthquakes. By this stage they also understand that people do not always show the emotions they feel.

C

You can see how, based on the notion of infant empathy, these stages follow the features of **Piaget**'s theory of **cognitive development.** Beginning in Hoffman's third stage, the child responds less to what it *sees* and more to what it infers from what it sees. That is, the child is better able to understand the *causes* of the other's distress. The child is also increasingly able to take the perspective of someone else, as **egocentricity** reduces. This ability is called **role-taking.**

Research supports the view that there is a positive correlation between **role-taking** and helping behaviour. However, this is only apparent from about seven years or older, when **role-taking** has started to develop. An interesting correlational study of role-taking and altruism was conducted by **D. Krebs and B. Sturrup**. Here are some details. Note that **Krebs and Sturrup** could not conclude that role-taking ability *caused* altruism, but only that the two were related.

Krebs and Sturrup (1974)

Aim of study	The aim of the study was to see whether there was a positive correlation between role-taking ability and altruism in six and seven year olds.
Method	This was a correlational study using observation and tests.
Sample	Participants were 12 boys and 12 girls of 6 and 7 years old.
Procedure	The children were observed over a two-month period in school and an altruism score was devised by recording the number of responses each child showed in three categories – offering help, offering support and suggesting responsibly. In addition, each child did two tasks which tested ability in taking the perspective of another, and their ability was scored. Ratings of each child's helping and co-operative behaviour were provided by the teachers.
Results	Results showed a positive correlation between the child's ability to role-take and its observed altruistic behaviour. The teachers' ratings of pro-social behaviour also correlated with the other sets of scores.
Conclusions	Researchers concluded that role-taking ability is positively correlated with altruistic behaviour.

To sum up then, although the roots of empathy are uncertain, there is evidence that it is apparent in very young children, before it could have been completely learned through experience. According to **Paul Harris** the way children understand people's emotions is linked to their moral judgements. This is likely to be because they are both closely related to cognitive development. By the time the child has reached late adolescence, empathy should have fully developed. Let us look then at how empathy is related to altruism and what psychologists have found out about altruism.

C

What is altruism?

Altruism is behaviour which puts someone else's well-being before your own; it may be costly to you, and is done without thought of reward. There is some debate about whether *any* action can be completely altruistic, because it is possible that all altruistic behaviour brings *some* kind of benefit to the actor.

Another way of defining **altruism** is that it is pro-social behaviour which the individual can choose *not* to undertake. For example, if you go out of a shop door and immediately behind you is a mother with a loaded baby buggy, social norms dictate that you hold the door open for her. In other words, you do it because of social pressures. However, if you were one of several people going down stairs alongside a mum with a loaded buggy you would feel no social pressure to help. If you did help, this could be classed as **altruistic** behaviour because you made a free choice to do so. But we could argue that this action *still* brings you benefits because you would gain approval from passers-by: it would increase your self-esteem.

S

The topic is of interest partly because so much psychological research has gone into aggression and other forms of *anti*-social behaviour, and partly because whether or not they gain benefit, people do indeed put others' safety and well-being before their own. In addition, in an increasingly anonymous world, it is important that we know how to develop and encourage altruism.

Fig. 18.2 What does this helper gain by helping?

What have psychologists found out about altruism?

Although the study of **altruism** is relatively new, a lot of research is currently being carried out. We will look at a selection of studies which fall under the headings of similarity, empathy, arousal and the role of parents.

SIMILARITY

S

Similarity between the sufferer and the person who sees the suffering seems to increase empathy and altruistic behaviour. **Jane Piliavin** and her colleagues have proposed that seeing others in distress creates **arousal**. However, it seems that we label our feelings as 'empathy' only if we see the distressed person as similar to ourselves. Although the reasons for this are not clear, research does show that the closer we are *related* to people, the more likely we are to help them. The parent-child relationship is probably the closest and parents show constant evidence of **altruism** – putting someone else's well-being before their own, without thought of reward. However, research shows even slight evidence of similarity creates greater empathy, and researchers have manipulated similarity in their efforts to create **empathy** for a 'victim' within their subjects. We shall see examples of this in the **Batson** study which follows.

EMPATHY

I have already mentioned that some psychologists doubt there is *true* **altruism**. They argue that all pro-social actions are done to benefit the actor in some way, such as increasing self-esteem or gaining public approval. Nevertheless, there is a long tradition which claims **empathy** is the basis for **altruism**, and that it is different from other pro-social behaviour because it is done without thought of self-benefit. What evidence is there that altruism might be *different* to other pro-social behaviour?

C

Research by **C. Daniel Batson** and his colleagues makes this distinction clear. They asked female subjects to watch a woman (a confederate) on closed circuit TV who was *apparently* receiving shocks in a learning experiment. As the shocks got worse, the woman told the researcher that due to a childhood experience she was very sensitive to them. The researcher then proposed that the subject, who was watching, might like to take her place. However, the researchers led some of the female subjects to think that they had similar interests to the victim (thus increasing **empathy**) and others thought they were quite dissimilar (they had low **empathy**) The researchers also manipulated the amount of *time* subjects had to watch the suffering.

Results showed that even when they did not have to watch the suffering for long, subjects high in **empathy** *still* volunteered to change places. This appears to be an example of true **altruism.** In a later study, **Batson** and his colleagues rated subjects as high or low in **empathy** from a questionnaire they completed. Even when subjects could *avoid* changing places with the victim, those high in empathy did not take that opportunity. They preferred to change with the victim and take her shocks.

These results show that subjects who were high in **empathy** *preferred* to relieve the suffering of others rather than walk away. Those low in empathy were more likely to avoid changing places. **Batson** offered a reason for this, which we will look at in the next section.

Jane Piliavin has suggested that **empathy** might actually *interfere* with the individual's ability to think and act rationally when he or she is faced with an emergency. Why? Perhaps the next area of research can offer an explanation.

C

AROUSAL

We have already seen that a major factor in **altruistic** behaviour is **empathy**. There appears to be a correlation between empathy and altruism in children, and this seems to be the case for adults too. Psychologists have proposed that the link between **empathy** and **altruism** may be **arousal**. **Arousal** is excitement in the nervous system, and it can be easily identified by increases in heartbeat or sweating, for example.

An experiment which demonstrated a link between **empathy**, **arousal** and **altruism** was carried out by **Batson** with adults who were approximately 20 years old. Each participant was linked with a 'performer' (who was a confederate of the experimenter) who played roulette. Participants were told that performers were rewarded, or punished with an electric shock, depending on whether the ball fell on an odd or even number. Participants were also monitored for measures of arousal – heartbeat and sweating. Half of them thought they were *similar* to their partners; the other half thought

L

they were *different*. Similarity increases empathy, so this is how the researchers manipulated empathy.

The researchers found that subjects who thought they were similar to performers (therefore high in empathy) showed high arousal in their response to their partners' success or failure. When the researchers gave participants the chance to share the rewards, or shocks, with their partners, they found those high in empathy were more likely to take their partners' shocks.

Batson and his colleagues offered this explanation. They argued that feeling distress causes **arousal** and leads to behaviour which *reduces* that arousal. If arousal is due to **personal** distress (such as guilt, blame, or fear of public disapproval) then you can reduce this type of distress by rationalising that it isn't your fault, it's none of your business, walking away or of course by helping. However, if the arousal is due to empathic *concern* this can *only* be reduced by helping the other in order to reduce the *other's* suffering. Once the other's suffering is relieved your own arousal will be reduced.

In summary then, it appears that **arousal** could be the link between **empathy** and **altruism.** It also appears that **altruism** does exist and may be *different* from general helping behaviour.

THE ROLE OF PARENTS

Research which has looked at the roots of **altruism** suggests that parents have a lot of influence. It shows for example that loving, nurturant, thoughtful parents have children who are more likely to show the same qualities. It has been suggested that this could be due to the parent's role as model and this is supported by findings that parents who *behave* altruistically, as well as preaching it, had children who were more altruistic. It has also been proposed that operant conditioning plays a part. Initially the child behaves altruistically but the child doesn't realise that this is what he is doing. Gradually he becomes aware that others think this behaviour is good, because of the rewards and attention he receives. Altruistic behaviour is therefore initially more likely to occur when others are around rather than when the child is alone. However, the child eventually internalises the altruistic norm.

L

S

Researchers have also suggested that children who are more securely **attached** are likely to be more **altruistic.** Again, note that this is only a correlation. **Carolyn Zahn-Waxler** and her colleagues analysed reports provided by mothers of young children. These mothers had noted what happened when someone around the child showed distress. The researchers concluded that mothers who told children the consequences of their actions and who explained the rules clearly had children who were more likely to be helpful or sympathetic to others. Similarly, research with older children shows that giving reasons for being helpful, and encouraging children to focus on how others feel, increases their altruistic behaviour.

Overall then we can see that there is a relationship between altruism, empathy and arousal. *How* they are related is still not clear, nor is the answer to the question – is there true altruism? We could argue that if we reduce arousal by taking someone's electric shocks, we are *still* benefiting from our 'altruistic' action so the action cannot be through pure altruism. The role of parents is also important in modelling or reinforcing altruism and in fostering empathy in children.

Bystander intervention – when do we help others?

Psychologists have looked at helping behaviour in public. What makes, or stops, people from helping others? Much of this work stems from concern that people are slow to intervene when another needs help. There are vivid examples of someone being murdered or a child abducted with no-one stepping in to help.

S

The focus of **bystander intervention** is how bystanders behave in an emergency. Researchers have found, for example, that the larger the number of people who witness an accident, the less likely any individual is to step forward and help. Let us examine what types of situations and what other factors affect bystander intervention.

ATTENTION AND INTERPRETATION

In order to help someone, you need to notice that something has happened. In England, the murder of James Bulger led people to ask questions about how we notice things, what is unusual and when we should intervene. Closed circuit TV cameras recorded the first stages of his abduction by two older boys from a busy shopping centre. No-one is paying attention to them here. Later in the day many people noticed them, but still no-one intervened.

Fig. 18.3 Does anybody seem to notice these three? Why?

C

Once you have noticed an event, the next stage is how you interpret what you see – what does it mean? Are those three children just playing or is the little one frightened? Is the person running towards you a shoplifter on the run or is he about to miss his bus? Are that man and woman who are arguing having a lovers' quarrel or is she about to be attacked? Is that old man who has collapsed drunk or ill? When is an event an emergency? The way we interpret or define a situation will affect whether we intervene or not.

When we are not sure of what is happening, we look to other people to see how they respond. **Bibb Latané and John Darley** devised an experiment where subjects sat in a room filling in a questionnaire. There were three conditions: in one the subjects were alone, in the second each subject was with two others, and in the third each subject was with two others but the latter were confederates (they knew what was going on). Soon after the subject started to complete the questionnaire, smoke started to pour into the room through a small vent.

Latané and Darley found that lone subjects responded quickly to the smoke, but those in the other two groups took longer to respond. The subject who was with two confederates, who showed no concern, took longest. This study suggests that when *alone* the subject quickly defines the situation as an emergency. In other words the event is not ambiguous. However, when others are present perhaps we are not so confident, and redefine a situation according to how *they* interpret it. This process of looking to others, assuming they know what is happening, and doing nothing is known as **pluralistic ignorance**. It is also fear of making a fool of yourself.

C

A study which tried to focus on ambiguity found that the sound of someone falling brought a low level of help, but when the fall was accompanied by shouts and cries of pain, subjects rapidly went to help. Not only was the *incident* less ambiguous, the subjects knew how they might help.

PERCEIVED SIMILARITY

The work we have seen so far has involved people who are strangers to the **bystanders.** What about those who are similar or familiar to us? Greater similarity seems to be related to higher empathy and therefore **altruism. Jane Piliavin** and her colleagues have proposed that seeing others in distress does create **arousal**. However, it is only if we see the distressed person as similar to ourselves that we label our feelings as empathy.

Evidence suggests that the more **similar** we are to the person in distress, the more likely we are to intervene. We are also more likely to help those we know – whether they are relatives or someone we have met recently. Research shows that even a warm smile or very brief conversation with someone will make us more likely to help. This may be because we become more emotionally aroused when someone we know, or who is similar, needs help.

What about helping those we see as different? We would, for example, expect white people to help white people more than they would help black people. Research shows this is sometimes true, but other times the opposite happens. **Irwin Katz** has suggested this is because white people may want to appear **unprejudiced,** and so may bend over backwards to help. He found this tends to happen in unambiguous situations. Where the need is not so clear, then there is less helping of black people; he found this to be equally true for helping people with disabilities.

This is one of findings in the study described next. This is an example of a field experiment, which was carried out by **Irving Piliavin, Judith Rodin and Jane Piliavin**.

Piliavin, Rodin and Piliavin (1969)

Aim of study The aim of the study was to investigate the effect of type of victim, race of victim and presence of a model on helping behaviour.

Method This was a field experiment using observation.

Sample The participants were approximately 4,500 males and females, roughly 45 per cent black and 55 per cent white. They were opportunity sampled.

Procedure Two male confederates, playing victim and 'model' helper, acted out the 'collapse' of the victim and a helper who came to his aid. This happened at the beginning of a seven and a half minute journey on a New York subway train. The conditions varied – sometimes the model was white, sometimes black, sometimes carrying a cane, and sometimes appearing to be drunk. Sometimes the helper waited one minute before helping; at other times he waited two and a half minutes. Two observers noted who helped, how long it took, what comments were made and so on.

Results Results showed that the 'cane' victim was helped immediately in almost every trial, and the drunk victim was helped 50 per cent of the time before the 'helper' intervened. The race of the victim made little difference to helping behaviour towards the 'cane' victim, but there was more same race helping of the drunk victim. Several people helped and men were much more likely to help the victim (who was always male) than women.

Conclusions People do help in an emergency to a greater degree than laboratory experiments would suggest. The absence of diffusion of responsibility could be because participants could see what others were doing and the cost of helping was low in the 'cane' condition. In the drunk condition, it was more costly to help, because the reaction and state of the drunk was unknown, thus there was greater diffusion, though still not very much.

The importance of **similarity** was highlighted. These were male victims, and received much more help from other males than females. Equally, those of the same race were more likely to help the 'drunk'. This study also showed a high level of helping behaviour. The researchers suggested this might be because subjects were face-to-face and those close to the victim could not easily pretend nothing had happened. The emergency had attracted their attention and was fairly easy to interpret. This point is also explained in terms of personal responsibility.

PERSONAL RESPONSIBILITY

The chance that someone will step in to help is related to how much he or she feels *personal* responsibility. **Latané and Darley** devised a study where there was no ambiguity about the situation. They created a setting where each subject knew that another subject (actually a confederate) was having a fit. Results showed that when subjects thought they were the *only* ones who knew what was happening they went to help. However when they thought others knew, they took much longer to help and some did not help at all. As in the 'smoke' experiment, the more people there were present, the slower the response.

S

Latané and Darley proposed that this was due to **diffusion of responsibility.** This means that the more people who know of the incident, the more responsibility to take action is *diffused* amongst them. The more people there are present, the less the individual feels personal responsibility.

Personal responsibility is also related to the *immediacy* of the emergency. In the **Piliavin** study for example, the 'victim' was in front of the participants. It was hard to escape what was happening so witnesses felt greater personal responsibility. If the 'victim' had been further away, with other people closer, then the individual would feel less personal responsibility. The witnesses could also pretend they had not seen the emergency if it was not immediately in front of them.

S

Both of these points relate to Latané's **Social Impact** theory, which says that the *closer* people are, the more they will affect our behaviour and also that the *more* people there are, the less responsibility we take for our own behaviour (see Chapter 9).

Personal responsibility can be made explicit to the individual. When we are asked *specifically* to take responsibility for something, we are much more likely to show helping behaviour. In **Moriarty**'s field experiment which took place on a beach, a confederate of the researchers left some belongings on a beach towel. In the experimental condition he asked someone nearby to keep an eye on his belongings whilst he went away for a few minutes. In the control condition he did not do this. In his absence a 'thief' stole a portable radio. The researchers found that 95 per cent of the people in the experimental condition gave chase, but only 20 per cent of **bystanders** gave chase when they had not been asked specifically to watch the belongings.

People may also be unwilling to help and therefore deny that they have **personal responsibility.** Stress, danger, time and lack of competence were all mentioned by participants in one study as reasons for not acting.

KNOWING HOW TO HELP

If people feel that they are competent to help then they are more likely to do so. A study which arranged for students and nurses to witness an accident showed that the nurses were more likely to help and the students held back. However, when there was not a nurse present, students helped as readily as the nurses had before. This suggests **bystanders** are making some calculations as to how useful they can be, before they act. One reason for doing this is the fear of evaluation from others. If you know what to do, the presence of others may encourage you to help. If you do not, you will be reluctant to appear incompetent in front of others. This is an example of **social facilitation** which is covered in Chapter 9.

S

In sum then, we have seen that people are more likely to help when they think they are the only witnesses. When there are others, several factors affect our decision to

Fig.18.4 Could you explain this picture using some of the ideas from research into bystander intervention?

help. Some of them are due to individual variables, such as our feeling of competence or similarity to the victim. Others are due to situational variables such as how other people may evaluate us or how ambiguous the situation is.

How may social norms affect pro-social behaviour?

We have looked at how others may affect our behaviour in an emergency, but what about more general situations when we help one another? One way of explaining pro-social behaviour is to say that people do what society expects of them. Social norms are the unspoken rules and expectations of the society we live in about how to behave. These norms exert pressure on us as to how we should behave in particular circumstances. Let us look at some of the social norms relating to helping behaviour.

S

RECIPROCITY

Reciprocity means that we help others when we ourselves have been helped, or expect to be helped. If you lend your class notes to a friend who misses a class, you expect her to do the same for you in the future if you asked her to. Interestingly **reciprocity** is evident amongst animals, it is called **reciprocal altruism**. In humans it is related to feelings of indebtedness or gratitude, and research suggests that the greater the help given, the greater the help which is returned. This underlines that we have a sense of balance about how much help we 'owe' someone.

S

SOCIAL RESPONSIBILITY

S

Social responsibility relates to the idea that we should help those who are more *dis-advantaged* than us – an example would be a teenager giving her seat to an old lady. We feel a moral obligation to help.

SOCIAL JUSTICE

S

Social justice is related to the norm of social responsibility, but whereas that is fairly general, the norm of social justice means that we should help those who do not deserve their suffering. We feel less pressure to help those who bring suffering on themselves. There is an example of these two categories in the **Piliavin** experiment. The 'cane' victim is seen as not deserving his suffering but the drunk victim does deserve his.

JUSTIFIED SELF-INTEREST

S

This means that we will act in our own self-interest in a situation so long as we are not disadvantaged too much. For example, we will help those who deserve help, but we will do no more than others who are like us would do.

EQUITY

S

Equity means that what we get out of a pro-social act should be equivalent to what we put in. If you visit a friend in hospital several times and all he says is 'thanks', then you might feel resentful. If on the other hand he said how much he appreciated your visits and told people what a good friend you were, this would create equity.

S

Interestingly, cross-cultural research about helping behaviour shows that the emphasis on exchange is a Western trait which may be related to individualist cultures. In more collectivist cultures there appears to be a universal norm to help, regardless of perceived need or closeness of relationship.

S

Whatever the social norms are, research in the West suggests that the degree to which we *conform* to social norms varies. There are many reasons for this – for example some of these norms conflict; it depends how strongly we have **internalised** them and we may not apply them to those we see as in the **'out-group'.** It depends on the level and strength of our **moral development.** Which social norm is the individual conforming to who jumps into an icy river to save a drowning child? In conclusion then, social norms are only a very general guide to who will help, why they do so, who they will help and in what circumstances.

Further Reading

Bee H (1992) *The Developing Child* (6th ed), New York, Harper Collins

Deaux K, Dane F and Wrightsman L (1993) *Social Psychology in the 90s* (6th ed), Pacific Grove, Brooks/Cole

EXERCISES

1. What are the IV and the DV in the Batson roulette experiment?
2. Explain why the participants in the Piliavin subway study were opportunity sampled?
3. What ethical guidelines does the Piliavin study contravene?
4. How is altruism different from pro-social behaviour?
5. Imagine two elderly women are sitting on a park bench. A woman walking her dog passes by, trips and falls badly. How likely is it that the two women will go to help? Why?
6. Imagine the scene described in question 5, only this time it is a young male jogger who falls. Would this make any difference to the women's behaviour? Why?

Chapter 19

Construction of Social 'Reality'

HAVE YOU EVER COMPARED YOUR VIEW OF SOMEONE WITH A FRIEND AND FOUND THAT YOU 'SAW' HIM DIFFERENTLY? YOU THINK DAVE IS SURLY; YOUR FRIEND THINKS HE IS SHY. WE OFTEN 'SEE' THE WORLD DIFFERENTLY FROM OTHERS – IN OTHER WORDS WE CONSTRUCT IT DIFFERENTLY FROM OTHERS. AT THE SAME TIME, OUR VIEW IS MORE 'REAL' FOR US THAN ANYONE ELSE'S VIEW. SO WE ALL CREATE OUR OWN VERSION OF THE SOCIAL WORLD – WE CONSTRUCT OUR OWN SOCIAL 'REALITY'.

IN THIS CHAPTER WE ARE GOING TO LOOK AT SOME WAYS IN WHICH WE CONSTRUCT OUR OWN REALITY. WE WILL CONSIDER HOW WE FORM IMPRESSIONS OF PEOPLE WHEN WE FIRST MEET THEM AND HOW OUR MENTAL PROCESSES MAY AFFECT WHAT WE NOTICE AND WHAT WE IGNORE. FINALLY WE WILL LOOK AT HOW INFORMATION CAN BE CONTROLLED SO THAT IT INFLUENCES THE WAY WE SEE THE WORLD.

How do we form overall impressions of others?

C

We form impressions of others constantly and without conscious thought. Psychologists have proposed that there are two types of explanation. One is that we have our own ideas of what characteristics or traits 'go together' to make a certain personality. Once we have identified one of these characteristics, we infer the others. These are called **implicit personality theories** and we will look at them shortly.

The other explanation is that one characteristic influences our impression of *all* the others and we will look at two examples of this now – **primacy and recency**, and **central and peripheral traits**.

PRIMACY AND RECENCY

Imagine a new student joins your class. She seems pleasant and outgoing. After a couple of weeks she starts to demand a lot of the teacher's time. If someone asked you what you thought of her, what would you say? Research suggests that your answer you might be 'She seems OK' That is, your *first* impression (which was pleasant) was stronger than the more *recent* one (unpleasant). If she had been demanding as soon as she joined the class, but after a couple of weeks had started to be more pleasant then your reply might have been more like, 'Oh, she can be quite a pain.' The evidence that first impressions are more powerful than later ones is very strong, and this is called the **primacy/recency effect**.

A. Luchins tested **primacy/recency** by giving his subjects information about an imaginary person called Jim. The information was in two sections, one describing Jim as outgoing, the other as shy. Luchins had four groups of subjects. One group read the 'outgoing' description and another the 'shy' description. The next two groups read *both* descriptions but in a different order: the third group read the 'outgoing' information first, then the 'shy' information. The fourth group's description started with Jim as 'shy' and ended up with the 'outgoing' information. All of the subjects then had to rate Jim for personality characteristics, including friendliness. Here are the results.

Conditions	Percentage rating Jim as friendly
Friendly description only	95
Friendly first – unfriendly last	78
Unfriendly first – friendly last	18
Unfriendly description only	3

Table 19.1 Percentage of subjects rating Jim as friendly

You can see that from the two groups receiving *both* types of information, Luchins found that what the subjects read *first* determined their judgement of Jim's personality. This is evidence of the **primacy** effect.

Do you know why some subjects only had one piece of information? That is how **Luchins** checked that his subjects could decide on Jim's friendliness from the information they were given. For example if the rating from those reading the 'outgoing' description had been 59 per cent and the rating from those reading the 'shy' description had been 52 per cent, then Jim's friendliness would not have been clear from the descriptions subjects had. This would have made Luchins' results useless.

In another study subjects watched a confederate solving difficult problems – he always got 15 of the 30 problems correct. In one condition he got most of the *early* problems right, in the other he got most of the *later* problems right. Subjects were then asked to estimate how many problems he got right. Those who saw him get most of the *early* ones right estimated an average of 20 out of 30, those who saw more of the *later* ones right estimated 12 out of 30. These results show how first impressions are the stronger – the **primacy effect.**

Solomon Asch said that our early information affects the meaning of later information; we *alter* the later information to make it consistent and may pay less attention to it. In this study for example, subjects explained the problem solver's wrong answers as due to tiredness or boredom, whereas if the early problems were wrong, his later success would be due to luck or guesswork.

C

Why does the **primacy/recency** effect occur? Primacy seems to be due to our tendency to give more weight to first information, and to the fact that once we *have* this information, it affects whatever we learn afterwards. When we are **forming impressions** of others we are creating a schema about them. The first impressions determine the initial schema, and *later* impressions are filtered through that schema. You may remember that we tend to notice information which *confirms* our schema and ignore that which is different. So later information which does not fit into our schema is not attended to, and is therefore not absorbed or remembered. This explains why the **primacy effect** is strongest for people we do not know.

C

Do we ever take note of later information? Psychologists have found that we do, particularly if we are warned against making a judgement too early on, and also if there is a period of time between receiving the two lots of information. **Luchins** found that the **primacy effect** is strongest when we are given information about someone we do not know. For those whom we know, the **recency effect** is more powerful. Recency also occurs if the first information we receive is positive but it is followed by negative information. For example, if I describe a friend as sociable and good fun and having been banned for drunk driving then you are more likely to remember the last item, and your **impression** of him will be negative.

C

Primacy and **recency effects** have importance in our lives. We all know the 'first impressions count' advice which relates to going for an interview. Research has shown the effect primacy and recency can have on information provided by witnesses in court, and on whether the case for the defence or the prosecution is heard first.

C

Fig. 19.1 First impressions count

CENTRAL AND PERIPHERAL TRAITS

C

Research has suggested that some information about people is more important than others – the important information is **central** to that person and the way we judge them. **Solomon Asch** proposed that one central trait was how *warm* or *cold* the person was described as. He gave two groups of subjects an identical list of personality traits, like this:

intelligent skilful industrious .... determined practical cautious

The difference between them was that one group of subjects had 'warm' as the trait in the blank space, and the other group had 'cold'. Afterwards the subjects were asked whether they thought this person had any *additional* traits. They were given a list of traits to choose from – generous, wise, happy, good-natured, reliable. **Asch** found that students reading the 'warm' list gave more positive additional traits than students reading the 'cold' list.

In another study **Asch** substituted the traits 'polite' or 'blunt' for the 'warm' or 'cold' traits. He found that these new traits had little impact on the subject's impressions of the imaginary person, because subjects chose the additional traits in roughly equal percentages for 'polite' or 'blunt'. You can see this is Table 19.2 below.

Additional traits	Traits inserted into description			
	Warm or	cold	Polite or	blunt
Generous	91	8	56	58
Humorous	77	13	71	48
Altruistic	69	18	29	46

Table 19.2 Percentage of subjects assigning additional traits to imaginary figure (from S. Asch 1946)

Asch concluded from these results that certain traits will be more important than others – they will actually *affect* how other traits are interpreted. Because they appeared to be *central* to the impression we have of others, Asch called them **central traits**. 'Warm' and 'cold' are central traits. The less important traits, which were coloured by these central traits, were called **peripheral traits**.

One criticism of the study was that it was not about *real* impression formation, because subjects had to *imagine* the person. However, **Harold Kelley** devised a study of real-life **impression formation**. He gave students information on a new teacher which included *either* the words 'rather warm' or 'rather cold'. All the students were in the same class with this new teacher. Afterwards Kelley found that students reading the 'rather warm' information rated the teacher more highly than those reading 'cold', and also interacted more with him. Here we can see that not only did subjects perceive the same person differently, but behaved differently towards him, all on the basis of a difference in one word. This supports the idea that 'warm/cold' are examples of **central traits**.

However, another criticism of this study was that all the other traits were 'intellectual' ones, whereas the warm/cold trait was a '*social*' one, and this was the reason for the difference. In effect, the warm/cold trait carried *different* information from the others and was therefore more relevant. **M. Rosenberg** said that if someone is already described as helpful then warm does not add much more information. It was the distinctiveness of the information which created the effect **Asch** found.

Rosenberg has proposed that there are two major dimensions which underlie our assessment of others. One is the **social/interpersonal** dimension (which applies to warm/cold) and the other is the **intellectual/competence** dimension (which applies to intellectual abilities). Traits relating to both the social and mental dimensions are central traits. They influence the way we interpret *other* traits and so affect our overall impressions of others.

IMPLICIT PERSONALITY THEORIES

These are our own theories which we have about people. We tend to think that certain personality traits go together like a package. When we see someone we do not know we identify *one* of their features and then apply the whole personality package. We are making inferences about others, normally people we do not know, from this limited information. We are not usually aware of the judgements we make, nor do we test them, which is why they are called implicit theories. We will look at two of them.

The halo effect

The halo effect refers to how we generate information about a person based on one *known* factor which is either positive or negative. The most vivid example of the **halo effect** comes from how a physically attractive person affects our judgements. **Karen Dion** found that attractive people in photographs were thought to be more sensitive, kind and interesting than less attractive people. Other research shows that attractive people are treated more leniently – whether they are writing poor essays or being tried in court.

One study looked at teachers' impressions of 11-year-old children. The teacher was provided with a small photograph of each child and information about them. Although this information was identical for each child, teachers rated the more attractive children as being more intelligent and socially adjusted than the less attractive children.

However, people who are described with a negative, unpleasant trait are seen by subjects as having other negative traits, so the **halo effect** can occur with both positive *and* negative features.

The halo effect appears to happen when an individual has a particular feature which attracts attention. For example, in the teacher study, the teachers could compare the photographs of the children. In everyday life we are less likely to make such a direct comparison, but if a person strikes us as *particularly* attractive, or *particularly* bad-tempered then we are likely to take that feature as typical of that person's overall personality. We are likely to be making some wrong inferences about how good, or bad, their qualities are, but we are also overlooking the *opposite* qualities.

Stereotyping

Stereotyping occurs when we infer someone has certain qualities because they belong to a particular group or because of a particular feature they have. If we assume these qualities because of their membership of a group then this is a **group stereotype,** if it's because of an individual feature then it is an **individual stereotype.** We will look briefly at each of these in turn.

Group stereotype

A **group stereotype** is a schema which contains information about the abilities, behaviours, personalities and so on of *any* member of a particular group. Our group stereotypes are based on some immediately identifiable feature – age, skin colour, sex, clothing, speech or physical ability, for example. When we apply a group stereotype we categorise a person as belonging to that group *because* they show one of these features and we infer that he or she has the traits we apply to members of that group. Our stereotypes may be based partly on our experience of *other* members of these groups, but may also be based on what we have been told or heard others saying.

Individual stereotypes

Gordon Allport noted that **individual** stereotypes are related to particular features. For example, redheads are seen as hot-tempered, fat people as jolly. As we know from work on stereotypes, we treat people according to the stereotype we have of them. An example of this comes from a study that looked at stereotyping according to name.

Teachers were asked to mark children's work. Although the work was identical, the child's name was manipulated – for example either David or Hubert. Work which teachers thought was produced by a 'David' got higher marks than work by a 'Hubert'. This could also be seen as an example of the **halo effect** we covered earlier.

Individual stereotypes can also refer to personality traits. If you told me your sister was shy, I would assume she might be difficult to get to know, would not say much, would be unadventurous and so on. These are other traits which I associate with shyness and I would infer them from the one piece of information you gave me. I would have **stereotyped** your sister.

C

What is important about any form of stereotyping is that it is the schema through which we see an individual. When we **stereotype** we tend to look for information to *confirm* our stereotype, and ignore information which *contradicts* it. Thus we do not see the *individual*, but only a stereotyped distortion. If I were to meet your sister I would think up topics of conversation, treat her gently, and assume that she does not have a very exciting life. I might not give her chance to show me that she is a good conversationalist and goes hang-gliding in the Himalayas. If she were to tell me that she was thinking of going to work in America I would be likely to interpret this in a way which *conforms* to my **stereotype,** perhaps thinking, she'll never go, it's just a dream. If I was asked to describe your sister to someone else, I would be unlikely to mention her American idea because it did not fit my stereotype and I would therefore discount it.

Our **stereotypes** may also show us that our inferences about others are right. If I treated your shy sister in a stereotypical way, the behaviour she showed me could confirm what I already thought: that she was quiet and unadventurous. So my **stereotype** would be right, and that would make my stereotype for shy people even more useful to me, and more resistant to change. What I have just described here is the process of the **self-fulfilling prophecy** (see page 172).

C

Stereotypes affect the way we perceive and judge people, but they also affect how we remember them. In one study, subjects were given a description of an imaginary person – Betty K. Afterwards they were given additional information; some subjects were told she married, others were told she adopted a lesbian lifestyle. When they were asked questions later, subjects recalled more of the information from her early life which corresponded to the later information they received. So, for example, the description said that she never had a steady boyfriend in high school but that she did go out on dates. Those who were told she got married remembered her dates, those who thought she was lesbian remembered she never had a steady boyfriend. This study shows how **stereotypes** affect the information we recall.

C

So, we have seen several ways in which we form impressions of people. Psychologists differ as to whether there are some key traits or features which affect our perceptions of others, or whether the order in which we receive information alters our judgements. Our tendency to stereotype means that the way we process and retain information about others may distort our impressions of them.

How do internal mental processes act as personal filters of information?

There are several ways in which our mental processes affect what we take in, and what we do not notice, or ignore. We will look at three in particular – attention, personal constructs and scripts.

ATTENTION

C

Attention is the process by which we select some information, and ignore other information. We have seen for example that we may respond automatically to a stimulus – either we categorise people or situations, or we experience the **primacy effect,** and so on. But what makes us attend to these stimuli in the first place?

Anticipatory schema

C

Ulrich Neisser proposed that we have a **perceptual cycle,** which is constantly in motion, picking up information, modifying schemas and directing our attention as a result of this. From our experience we develop **anticipatory schema**. These are aspects of our environment which we are particularly alert to. An example would be hearing your own name amongst a lot of background chatter.

Distinctiveness

C

We are likely to attend to something which is unusual, perhaps because it contrasts with other information available at the same time. So, we are more likely to attend to someone who is very tall or who behaves in an unusual way. Researchers have found that when observers watched a group discussion of, for example, one woman among several men, or one black person in an all white group, they thought the 'odd' one had more influence on the group discussion and decisions than any of the others. So if a person or event is distinctive it is likely to be remembered more easily and evaluated more extremely.

Fig. 19.2 An example of distinctiveness

If you remember earlier we looked at central and peripheral traits. One criticism was that 'warm' was considered important because it was so different from any of the other traits described. This is an example of attention being given to something which is distinctive.

Vividness

Susan Fiske and Shelley Taylor said that we attend to information which is **vivid**. This means that it is emotionally engaging, or it may be perceptually bright – for example a colour photograph as opposed to a black and white one. Not only do we attend to this vivid information, but it is often at the expense of the surrounding information. **Elizabeth Loftus** and her colleagues found that when subjects saw an incident in which a character produced a knife (which is an example of an emotionally engaging stimulus) their ability to recall *other* details of the situation was reduced. Several researchers have found that in such a situation subjects are poorer at remembering other important details, such as what the criminal looked like. This has important implications because it makes people less reliable when they witness a crime.

C

Priming or accessibility

We attend more to information which is related to a readily accessible schema; it is as though we are 'primed' for that information. **Tory Higgins and Gillian King** said there were two reasons for accessibility – either because a schema has been used *recently* or because it is one that we use *often*. If a friend has just described a great film you will notice advertisements for it, what other people say, information about the stars and so on. Your friend's description has **primed** you to attend to other information which is related.

C

The other reason suggested by **Higgins and King** relates to frequently used schemas. If you are someone who is concerned about your weight then you will notice what people eat, the quantities they eat, the kind of foods you cannot eat, and what shape or size others are. This information is relevant to you and so you attend to it. You could probably describe the cakes in a shop window in much more detail than someone who does not have a 'diet' schema.

C

D. Norman and T. Shallice have proposed that some of our attention is completely automatic so we are not aware of what we notice. Walking into your bedroom you are not aware of what you notice, but if burglars had moved things, you would notice they were different. It is the contrast between what we *expect* and what we *experience* which attracts our attention. By attending to certain things, we are less able to pay attention to others, so this information may be filtered out and lost to us. Thus we can see that what we attend to in turn determines how we construct **social 'reality'**.

C

PERSONAL CONSTRUCTS

Personal construct is the term which **George Kelly** proposed to describe the 'patterns' which people create and try to fit over the realities they come across. He said we all have our own individual worlds – through experience we develop our own theories about what the world is like. We use these theories as a guide for our own actions and responses.

Kelly was interested in the link between perceptions and behaviour, and he proposed that our **personal constructs** affect how we interpret our world *and* act as a guide to our behaviour. Kelly said we all try to understand and predict events – our personal constructs are how we do this. **Kelly** said that our main aim is *not* to achieve reinforcements or avoid anxiety (the learning and the psychodynamic explanations). It is to obtain information which confirms our *own* **constructs**. This means we look for evidence that confirms our constructs. Kelly stressed that our concern is *not* for objective truth but that things have meaning only as they are constructed by the individual.

He also said that we look for explanations for things we see. We try to understand why things happen, what causes them. We are likely to see two unconnected events as being connected. We do this for *all* aspects of our world, but Kelly felt that the most important for us was our *social* world.

These **constructs** are bipolar according to Kelly. This means we use a range with two extremes, such as friendly/unfriendly or optimistic/pessimistic. Different people use different constructs for the same people, but also the words themselves have different meanings for the individual. Because we don't normally talk about our constructs, we understand them in terms of mental imagery and when we have to express them, the differences can be seen. For example, one person's **construct** might be friendly/unfriendly, but others might say friendly/rude or friendly/shy. This shows how we differ in our personal constructs and how they affect our **social 'reality'.**

Kelly said that we are scientists, proposing hypotheses which we test constantly against what we see or experience. We have 'tight' and 'loose' constructs. Tight constructs enable us to predict; loose constructs are more ambiguous. He also said that the personal constructs which we use most often are the ones which are most important to us – he called them **superordinate constructs**.

SCRIPTS

A **script** is a sequence of events which are linked together. You have a script for what happens each time you go to psychology class. There may be chatter between the students – it will probably be more vigorous if the teacher has not arrived. Some students may speak to him, or her, informally before the lesson begins. There will be a period when the teacher gains the attention of the class, and then the more formal lesson activities begin. This **script** enables each participant to play the appropriate role at the right time. Its fine to chat, sit on the desk, talk across the room before the class starts, but once it is under way, the student's role changes.

Robert Abelson was one psychologist who developed the idea of scripts and you can see how the notion of a **script** enables us to predict what will happen next, and how to behave in various situations. Scripts are sometimes called **event schemas.** They are a way of organising and representing our social knowledge and they are based on experience. One study looked at how much children remembered of their school day. The results showed that they remembered the outline, the general sequence of activities, but not the details. It appears then that we recall information which fits in to our script, but not information which is very detailed.

However, this does not mean we recall only what is predictable. **John Pryor and Thomas Merluzzi** studied 'dating' **scripts** of American students. They found that those who dated a lot had rich and complex scripts, and could identify behaviour as belonging to a script very easily. Those who dated *less* had more simple **scripts.** So our scripts are personal, depending on our experience and interests.

Research has pointed to the influence which television and films have on our knowledge of **scripts.** We learn how to behave in various situations from what we see others do, and we will pay more attention to scripts which are of interest or importance to us. A pregnant woman will be more interested to see what happens when you go to a pre-natal clinic than an elderly man. Some researchers have found that **scripts** for aggressive behaviour have been learned through observation from television.

L

Scripts provide us with social rules, when we can speak, how we should address someone else, whether we can act casually or formally, who has power. They help us to predict what will happen and are triggered spontaneously at the start of a script sequence. For example, the five-year-old learns the 'going to school' script; the teenager learns the 'dating' script; the hospital patient learns the 'being a patient' script; and the unemployed learn the 'claiming benefit' script. Once the script is under way we notice and interpret things in terms of the event schema – the script.

S

C

These three types of mental processes filter information from the real world in accordance with our own interests and abilities. In that way they help to build our own construction of reality.

How do social filters of information work?

Social filters of information are the points in our society where information can be manipulated – it can be released, kept back or distorted. We will look at two social filters in particular and these are gatekeepers, and the media.

GATEKEEPERS

A **gatekeeper** is someone who controls the flow of information between one area and another. To take an example from politics, the senior civil servants who advise ministers have access to a lot of information. This needs to be analysed and evaluated before it is passed to ministers for decisions. What information is finally presented, and how it is presented, is within the control of the civil servant. This makes the civil servant a **gatekeeper**.

Is your teacher a **gatekeeper?** He or she is controlling the information you receive in class. However, because you can easily find out more for yourself, we would not consider your teacher a gatekeeper because the term refers to the control of information which is not easy to get hold of in any other way.

Some of the most influential **gatekeepers** are in the **media.** These are people like newspaper editors and the producers of television programmes. They are able to decide what information is published or broadcast, how important it is (by placing it on the front page or bottom of page 11), how it is portrayed (film showing 3,000 peaceful demonstrators or the one scuffle which occurred) and what 'slant' to put on it (are striking health workers 'protesting at the government' or 'concerned about patients' well-being').

People planning television schedules are also gatekeepers. At what time will that critical documentary on a company causing pollution go out? Is a programme suitable for screening before 9.00 pm when young children may be watching?

Politicians may be gatekeepers, because they can keep back or broadcast information, or manipulate it.

THE MEDIA

The **media** have an important role in filtering information. We will look at some of the ways in which they do this.

Distorting reality

C

- because of time constraints on television and radio, information is often condensed. A complex argument is usually presented by giving two opposing viewpoints, which simplifies it and reduces it to an either/or solution

C

- if a newspaper or television company has cameras and journalists present then it can 'make' a story, if not there is much less coverage in the media. The perceiver's impression of what is important is determined by what is covered
- the media interest in violence means that news issues are presented with a violent slant. Research showed that fights between striking miners and police were more likely to be broadcast than peaceful strike action

C

- the way that language is used distorts perception. The viewer understands 'terrorists' in a different way from 'freedom fighters' – each label primes a different schema, which in turn will affect the way the information is processed. This is how the viewer's impressions are formed

C

- the way pictures are used distorts perception. News items about the 1984 miners' strike showed managers being interviewed in dignified settings, but miners were interviewed wet and windblown in the streets

The oxygen of publicity

- the presence of television cameras can 'create' news. Charities and pressure groups carry out publicity stunts in order to attract media attention (Fig. 19.3)

L

- when youngsters were shown joyriding in stolen cars, this seemed to encourage more youngsters to do it. The media coverage showed models to other youngsters to imitate, so this may have made it a much larger problem than it was.

Creating impressions

C

- the way in which information is presented can lead the viewer or reader to overestimate the relationship between two variables. If two things are rare, but they appear close together, we tend to see them as linked or correlated. For example, when a news item reports that a 'gay man' was charged with a sexual crime we are likely to attend to that information (because of its distinctiveness) rather than if a 'man' was charged. As a result we will tend to think *more* gay men are associated with sexual crimes than heterosexual men, but this is purely due to the way the information is provided in the news item. This false relationship is called an illusory correlation

C

- the media tend to report the darker side of human nature and this affects our sense of what the world is really like. Research has shown that people watching a lot of television see the world in a more threatening way. However this is only a correlation
- the role of the media in forming impressions of others was shown in America during the middle of this century. American citizens in early days of the Second World War were exposed to pro-Russian propaganda. As the Cold War began and relations with Russia became very bad, the American media started to broadcast anti-Russian propaganda. Research showed that attitudes to Russians became much more negative

Fig. 19.3 Creating news

Promoting attitudes

- ethnocentrism is promoted, by interpreting issues from our own cultural perspective. This is evident in an item such as – '350 die in air crash, no Britons were aboard'

S

- the way information is presented implies what is *normal.* By inference then, what we have (the status quo) is good and desirable. Those who criticise our economic, social or political system may be portrayed as threats to the present system.
- the 'public interest' and 'public opinion' are presented as though they are something concrete, but there is often little evidence for them. Nevertheless this approach gives the individual the impression that others have this view, and so it can affect the individual's attitude as well. We know from research into the creation of norms that when people are uncertain they look to others for information

S

- the media influence in creating **empathy** for those suffering from disease, starvation, homelessness and cruelty has led to public action
- the media promotes, or challenges, stereotypical attitudes through news items, soap operas, documentaries, game shows, presenters, photographs, comedy shows and headlines

C

These examples and evidence of both the activities of gatekeepers and the media can be linked directly to some of the topics we considered earlier. For example, they can be linked to attention, **primacy,** and **impression formation.**

We have seen how we create our own, personalised, view of the world. Our tendency to infer information from very little, to attend to certain aspects of our environment and to be influenced by our own needs will distort the way we see the world. This distortion is increased by the information we receive through social channels of communication.

Further Reading

Deaux K, Dane F and Wrightsman L (1993) *Social Psychology in the 90s* Pacific Grove,: Brooks/Cole

EXERCISES

1 In Luchins' experiment, what are the aim, the IV and the DV?
2 Look at the range of scores for the 'generous' trait in Asch's research. Calculate the range in the 'warm-cold' condition and the range in the 'polite-blunt' condition. What is the difference between the two ranges and how does it relate to Asch's conclusions?
3 To find out how people's personal constructs differ, write down six personality traits and ask friends (subjects?) to write down what they feel would be the opposite. Avoid obvious opposites like optimistic/pessimistic or friendly/unfriendly.
4 Can you think of a reason why people who watch more television may find the world a more threatening place?
5 Give an example of one way in which the media has promoted a stereotype and one way in which it has challenged a stereotype.

Glossary

accommodation modifying a schema or creating a new one in order to cope with new information (Piaget) (p.187)

affiliation the need to be in contact with others (p.14)

altruism behaviour which puts someone's well-being before your own, perhaps in a way which is damaging to oneself, without thought of reward (p.217)

assimilation using a schema to act on the environment (Piaget) (p.186)

attachment a close emotional bond felt by one person towards another (p.61)

attention the process by which we notice or attend to information (p.21)

autonomous morality morals based on one's own rules and taking account of intent (Piaget) (p.204)

bar chart a way of showing data to enable comparisons to be made (p.48)

bias distortion (p.30)

bystander intervention the way in which people behave who witness an incident (p.221)

case study a detailed study of an individual's (or a small group's) background (p.29)

categorisation grouping things together on the basis of some similarity (p.23)

centration the tendency to attend to only one feature of a situation at a time (Piaget) (p.204)

child rearing style the way parents bring up children, relating particularly to affection and discipline (p.113)

classical conditioning showing an automatic response to a previously unrelated stimulus (p.8)

clinical interview a way of finding out about a subject's thinking or emotions by using the subject's replies to determine what questions will be asked next, using open-ended, unstructured questions (p.29)

concept an abstract idea, a way of grouping things (p.24)

conclusions information which can be drawn from the results of a study (p.53)

concrete operational stage third stage of cognitive development (Piaget) (p.184)

conditioned response the response which occurs when the conditioned stimulus is presented (p.8)

conditioned stimulus the stimulus which is presented with the unconditioned stimulus (p.8)

conditions the experiences which different groups of subjects undergo (p.42)

confederate someone who appears to be a subject but who is actually following the researcher's instructions, so is part of the study (p.86)

cognition anything to do with mental processes such as remembering or thinking (p.19)

conformity following the ideas or behaviour of others rather than one's own (p.86)

confounding variables any variables which may distort results (p.45)

conservation the understanding that somethings stays the same even though the appearance changes (Piaget) (p.184)

control condition/control group the group of subjects who do not experience the IV (p.41)

counterbalancing giving half the subjects the experimental condition first and the other subjects the control condition first (p.42)

correlational study a study to discover if there is relationship between two variables (p.32)

cross-cultural study a study which compares people from different cultures (p.36)

cross-sectional study a study in which different groups are studied at the same time (p.35)

debrief in ethics, giving a general explanation of the study to the subject when they have finished and ensuring their wellbeing (p.57)

decentre to be able to take into account more than one aspect of a situation at a time (Piaget) (p.184)

defence mechanisms unconscious strategies to reduce anxiety (Freud) (p.123)

deindividuation a state in which the individual becomes less aware of themselves and has less control over their own behaviour (p.88)

demand characteristics the clues in an experiment which lead the subject to think they know what the researcher is looking for (p.34)

dependent variable the outcome of manipulation of the indpendent variable, the results (p.40)

discrimination treating people differently on the basis of one particular feature or characteristic (p.91)

dizygotic twins twins from two eggs – fraternal or non-identical (p.6)

ego the part of personality in touch with reality (Freud) (p.122)

egocentric being unable to take someone else's view of the world, understanding the world as an extension of oneself (Piaget) (p.182)

empathy an emotional response to someone else's feelings or situation (p.214)

enrichment something which stimulates cognitive development (p.144)

equilibration restructuring schemas into new structures (Piaget) (p.187)

ethics desirable standards of behaviour towards others (p.56)

ethnocentric viewing other cultures through your own cultural lens and seeing them as inferior to one's own (p.36)

ethology the study of animals in their natural environment (p.105)

exchange theory the idea that we consider our interactions with others on the basis of rewards and costs (p.82)

experiment a research method in which all variables are controlled except one, so that the effect of that variable can be measured (p.33)

experimental condition/experimental group the group of subjects who experience the IV (p.42)

extinction when a response to a stimulus is no longer seen (p.10)

formal operational stage fourth stage of cognitive development (Piaget) (p.185)

frustration-aggression hypothesis the proposal that frustration always leads to aggression (p.107)

gender the psychological or cultural aspects of maleness or femaleness (p.148)

gender concept a full understanding of gender, including its permanence (p.148)

gender constancy the understanding that one stays the same sex despite changes in appearance (p.150)

gender identity the knowledge of one's own and others' gender label (p.149)

gender stability the understanding that one stays the same sex throughout life (p.149)

generalise applying information from one situation to other situations (p.43)

genetic due to the action of genes (p.5)

graph a way of representing data to show change (p.48)

halo effect the tendency to assume that someone with an attractive quality has other positive qualities (p.232)

heredity anything we inherit through our genes (p.5)

heteronomous morality moral standards imposed from outside the individual and based on the consequences of actions (Piaget) (p.204)

hypothesis a prediction of what will happen, an expectation (p.40)

id part of personality which contains our instincts and desires (Freud) (p.122)

identification the process by which the child comes to take in the ideas and behaviours of the same sex parent, according to Freud (p.152)

impression formation making inferences about people on the basis of little information (p.228)

inborn any characteristic we are born with (p.3)

independent measures a design of study which has different subjects in each group (p.41)

independent variable what the researcher manipulates (p.40)

inference filling in the gaps in information, an assumption (p.22)

information processing viewing cognition by looking at the processes and strategies we use in cognitive activity (p.20)

ingroup-outgroup the division of people into two groups, the ingroup is the group to which we belong, the outgroup is all the others (p.92)

inherit to be born with something passed on through our genes (p.5)

innate part of our physical make-up at birth (p.3)

instinct an inborn need and the drive to satisfy that need (p.3)

interaction the effect which two or more people, or things, have on each other (p.61)

internalise to feel that a behaviour or idea is part of us, that we own it (p.16)

IQ intelligence quotient, a person's score on an intelligence test (p.133)

labelling identifying people as different in a certain way, and then treating them accordingly (p.175)

learning a relatively permanent change in behaviour which is due to experience (p.8)

libido the life instinct (Freud) (p.107)

longitudinal study a study which follows the same subjects over an extended period of time (p.35)

matched subjects a design of study in which each group has different subjects but they are paired on the basis of their similarity in several characteristics (p.42)

maternal deprivation having no attachment, or a damaged attachment, to the mother (Bowlby) (p.65)

maturation a genetically programmed progression of changes towards full development (p.4)

mean average (p.46)

model whoever the individual copies behaviour from (p.12)

monozygotic twins twins from the same egg – identical (p.6)

nature or nurture debate the discussion as to whether human abilities and characteristics are inborn or the result of experience (p.17)

negative correlation a relationship between two variables in which as one increases the other decreases (p.32)

negative reinforcement anything which stops an unpleasant experience (p.10)

norms the beliefs or expectations which members of a group share (p.86)

object permanence a child's understanding that although it can no longer see an object, the object still exists (Piaget) (p.182)

observational learning human learning which takes place by observing others, social learning (p.12)

observation research which involves watching and recording behaviour (p.29)

operant conditioning learning which occurs as a result of reward or punishment (p.9)

opportunity sampling selecting whoever is available to be a subject (p.44)

partial reinforcement reinforcement which only follows some responses, only given once in a while (p.10)

perception the process of interpreting sensory information (p.189)

personal construct the individual patterns we have for interpreting our experiences (p.235)

personality the pattern of individual characteristics which combine to make each person unique (p.121)

phallic stage the stage of psychosexual development when the libido is focussed on the genitals and the Oedipus or Electra conflict occurs (Freud) (p.123)

pie chart a way of showing data by proportions (p.50)

positive correlation a relationship between two variables in which as one increases the other increases (p.32)

positive reinforcement anything which is rewarding to the learner (p.10)

practice effect when subjects do better on a task the second time they do it, occurs in a repeated measures design of study (p.42)

pre-operational stage second stage of cognitive development (Piaget) (p.182)

prejudice an extreme attitude against a group, or a member of the group (p.91)

primary reinforcement anything which satisfies basic instincts (p.11)

pro-social behaviour behaviour which helps others (p.214)

psychoanalytic theory theory based on the idea that behaviour is caused by unconcious forces (Freud) (p.3)

psychometric tests standardised tests which measure characteristics such as intelligence, personality or attitude (p.34)

punishment anything which weakens behaviour, makes a behaviour less likely to happen (p.11)

quota sampling calculating what proportion of particular characteristics there are in the target population and selecting subjects in the same proportions (p.43)

random sampling selecting subjects on the basis that all members of the target population have an equal chance of being selected (p.43)

range the difference between the highest and lowest scores (p.47)

reflex an automatic physical response (p.4)

reinforcement anything which strengthens behaviour, makes a response more likely to happen (p.10)

repeated measures a design of study in which the same subjects are in each group (p.41)

response the activity which results from a stimulus (p.8)

role-taking in a social setting, the ability to take the perspective of someone else (p.216)

sampling the method by which subjects are selected for research (p.43)

scapegoating the process of blaming someone else for your problems (p.92)

scattergram a way of showing the degree to which data is related (p.50)

schema a mental framework which is based on experience (p.24)

script the sequence of events, in a social setting, which go together (p.24)

secondary reinforcer anything which strengthens behaviour but does not satisfy basic instincts (p.11)

self-concept the set of views and beliefs we have about ourselves (p.163)

self-efficacy expectations and feelings of competence about one's abilities (p.127)

self-esteem how we feel about ourselves (p.165)

self-fulfilling prophecy the process by which a person's expectations about someone else may come true, because they treat this other person according to their expectations of them and so bring about the expected response (p.172)

self-image what we know about ourselves (p.163)

self-perception theory the idea that we discover what our feelings are by watching our own behaviour (p.98)

sensitive period the time when an aspect of development is particularly responsive to certain experiences or influences (p.5)

sensory anything related to the senses (p.19)

sensory motor stage first stage of cognitive development (Piaget) (p.181)

separation distress unhappy response shown by a child when an attached figure leaves (p.61)

social categorisation classifying people as members of either the in-group or the out-group (p.92)

social cognition the explanation of social behaviour in terms of cognitive abilities (p.24)

social comparison theory the idea that we compare ourselves with others in order to evaluate ourselves (p.168)

social conformity following the actions and opinions of others rather than one's own (p.86)

social impact theory an explanation of the influence others have on our behaviour (p.89)

social identity theory the sense of who we are which is gained from membership of a group (p.166)

social learning human learning which takes place by observing others, observational learning (p.12)

social norms the behaviours and beliefs which members of a group are expected to show (p.15)

social roles the parts we play in society (p.16)

stereotyping categorising someone on the basis of one feature and therefore assuming they have certain characteristics or abilities (p.93)

standardise to make consistent so that results are comparable (p.34)

standardised instructions the identical instructions given to each subject in a study (p.45)

stimulus anything which creates a response (p.8)

stranger fear distress shown by a child when a stranger approaches (p.61)

subject the participant in a study (p.43)

subject variables ways in which indiviual subjects differ from each other which might affect results (p.45)

superego the part of personality related to the kind of person we want to be (Freud) (p.122)

survey a way of gathering information by asking a lot of people to answer standardised questions (p.30)

temperament a style of responding (p.128)

thanatos human instinct for self-destruction (Freud) (p.106)

trial a rehearsal or practice (p.9)

unconditioned response behaviour over which one has no control, e.g. a reflex (p.8)

unconditioned stimulus anything which causes an automatic response (p.8)

valid to measure or test what is supposed to be measured (p.34)

variable anything which varies (p.33)

vicarious learning learning from the way others are encouraged or punished (p.111)

Index

Abelson, R 236
abstract thinking 185–6
accommodation 156, 187, 189
achievement tests 137
adolescence 124, 217
adoption studies 142–3
Adorno, T 91
affectionless psychopathy 65, 70
affiliation 14–15, 16
aggression 4, 9, 13, 30, 92, 105–17, 157
aims of research 39
Ainsworth, M 62–3
Allen, M 157
Allport, G 92, 232
altruism 214, 217–19, 220–1, 222
anonymity 88–9
anxiety 14, 123, 124
Argyle, M 165
Aronfreed, J 215
Aronson, E 99
arousal 218, 219–20, 222
Asch, S 86–7, 88, 89, 229, 230–1
assimilation 156, 186, 187, 189
attachment 5, 15, 45, 61–71, 73–4, 77, 114
attention 21, 115, 221, 223, 234–5
attraction, social 80–3
audience effect 84
authoritarian personality 91–2, 98
autokinetic effect 86
autonomous morality 204

Bandura, A 12–13, 30, 101, 109–11, 126–7, 152–3, 157, 167, 202, 209, 211
bar charts 48, 52, 55
Baron, R 115, 116
Batson, C 219, 220
Baumrind, D 113, 213
Bayley Scale of Infant Development 136–7
Bee, H 144, 146
behaviour
  and gender 150–2
  human 11, 83
  innate 8
  moral 200, 210–13
  pro-social 214, 225–7
  shaping of 10, 83
Bem, S 101, 149–50, 156
Bem, D 98, 164, 171
Berkowitz, L 107–8, 115
Berstein, B 143
bias 30, 34–5, 94, 137–9, 164
  in sampling 31, 66, 72, 144
Bierhoff, H 224
Binet, A 133–4
Birch, H 128–30
blind spot 20
Block, J 153
Bouchard, T 146
Bower, T 192
Bowlby, J 5, 24, 64–71
British Ability Scales (BAS) 135–6
British Psychological Society 56
Broman, S 137
bullying 116
Burgner, D 158–9
Buss, A 130, 131
Byrne, D 80
bystander intervention 221–5

Campos, J 193
case studies 29, 65, 66
categories in cognition 22–3, 96 *see also* cognition
centration 184 *see also* decentring
Chess, S 128–30, 131
child rearing style *see* parenting
Clarke, A 70
classical conditioning 4, 8–9, 107–8, 201–2, 214–15
clinical interviews 29, 31
coaction effect 84–5

cognition 20–1, 116, 136
cognitive development 4, 114, 131, 164, 181–9
  and moral behaviour 203–6, 210, 217
  Piagetian 5, 80, 144, 181–9, 216
compliance 88
concepts 23, 24–5
concrete operations stage 184–5
conditioned
  responses 8–9, 201
  stimuli 8–9, 201
conditioning
  classical 4, 8–9, 107–8, 201–2, 214–15
  operant (instrumental) 9–12, 108–9, 126, 201, 202, 220
confidentiality 57, 72
conformity 86–90, 102
conscience 122, 201
consent of participants 56, 149
conservation 184
consistency of care 63, 73–4, 113
control groups 41, 67
Cooley, C 164, 165
co-operation, social 99–100
Coopersmith, S 167
correlation 32–3, 81, 111–12, 130, 139, 140, 142–3
correlational studies 31–3, 40, 50–1, 53
cortex, visual 20
Cottrell, N 84
counterbalancing 42
cross
  cultural studies 18, 36–7, 131, 150, 195–8, 213
  sectional studies 35–6, 72
Crutchfield, R 88
culture, effect of 131

Darley, J 174, 222, 224
Darlington, R 145
data
  collection 45–6, 52
  drawing conclusions from 53–4
  presentation 46–52
Davey, A 95–6
debriefing 45, 57
decentring 184, 189, 204
defence mechanisms 92, 123–5
deindividuation 88–9
delinquency 65, 70
demand characteristics 34, 87, 108
dependent variables (DV) 40–1, 110
depth perception 197
development
  cognitive *see* cognitive development
  moral 200–10
Diener, E 88–9
Dion, K 232
discrimination 91–3, 95, 97–104, 175
disobedience 114
displacement 92
distinctiveness 234
distress 14, 56, 72, 149, *see also* separation distress
divorce 71–5
Dollard, J 107
drives 3
Duck, S 80
Dumaret, A 142

Eagly, A 82
Edwards, C 213
ego 107, 122, 125
  defence mechanisms 123
  ideal 200
egocentricity 76, 182, 183, 216
Einstein, A 139
Eisenberg, N 207
Electra complex 152, 201
Emerson, P 35, 45, 63, 64, 66–7
empathy 15, 22, 116, 214–7, 219–20, 222, 239
enrichment 144–6
environment 4, 6, 17–18, 131,146, 195–8
  enriched 144
  social 16, 69, 74–5
  in twin studies 141, 142–3
environmental developmental views 194–99 *see also* nature/nurture debate
equilibration 187, 189
equity 226
Erikson, E 125, 126
  psycho-social theory of 125–6
Eron, L 112, 114
estimation of own ability 158
ethics 56–8, 72, 73, 149, 194
ethnocentrism 36–7, 95, 206, 239

ethology 105–6
evaluation apprehension 84–5
event schema 24
exchange theory 82
exemplars 25
expectations 161, 172–5, 214
experimental
control 33
designs 41–2
experiments 30, 33–4
extinction 10, 202
Eysenck, H 201

Fagot, B 151
familiarity in attraction 80–1, 82
Fantz, R 191–2
fathers, role of 66, 73
Fazio, R 174
fear of strangers 62
Festinger, L 168
Fiske, S 21, 235
fixations 123–5
formal operational stage 185–6
Freedman, D 131
Freud, S 3, 106–7, 114, 121
psycho-dynamic theory of 3, 122–5, 152
friendship 77–80
frustration-aggression hypothesis 92, 107

ganglion 20
gatekeepers 237, 240
gender 13, 148
acquisition of 152–6
and behaviour 150–2
and cognition 154–5
concept 148–51, 155
constancy 150, 155, 156
differences 156–9 *see also* sex differences
identity 149
schemas 156
stability 149–50
generalisation 29, 43, 53
genes 5, 6
genetic programming 4
Gibson, E 192, 194
Goffman, I 16, 169–70, 172, 175
graphs 48, 49, 52
Gregory, R 194, 196
group
norms 88, 89
tests 136, 137
guidelines, ethical 56–8, 149, 194

halo effect 82, 129, 175, 232, 233
Halverson, C 156
Harper, L 77
Harris, P 217
Harter, S 166
hereditarian developmental views 189–94, 199 *see also* nature/nurture debate
heredity 5–6, 17–18, 142–3, 146
Hess, R 161
heteronomous morality 204
Hetherington, M 73, 74, 75, 76
Hewstone, M 158–9
Higgins, T 168–9, 235
Hodges, J 67, 70
Hoffman, M 209, 210, 216
Holloway, S 161
Huie, K 77
human behaviour 11
Huston, A 160
hypotheses 25, 39–40, 53

id 107, 122
ideal self 168
identity 15
identification 124, 152, 200, 207
illusary correlation 23, 238
impression formation 228–33
independent
measures designs 41, 42
variables (IV) 40–1, 110
individual tests 136
inferences 22–4
information, organisation of 19, 20–5, 88, 136
information processing 20
in-group-out-group 92
inheritance 5, 136 *see also* heredity; nature/nurture debate
innate
abilities 3, 17
behaviour 8 *see also* reflexes
innateness of temperament 128–30

instincts 3, 4, 65, 106, 122
instructions, standardised 45
instrumental conditioning *see* operant conditioning
intelligence 6, 7, 34, 69
  environmental view of 143–6
  hereditarian view of 140–3
  quotient (IQ) 17, 69, 133–6
  tests 129, 136–40, 157
inter-observer reliability 30
interaction 61, 63, 114, 131, 199
internalisation 16, 88, 96, 124, 153

Jacklin, C 150, 156
Jacobson, L 173–5
Jensen, A 139
jigsaw technique 99
judgement of distance 192, 197–8
justified self-interest 226

Kagan, J 213
Kamin, L 141
Kelley, H 82, 231
Kelly, G 235–6
Kelly, J 73
King, G 235
Kohlberg, L 18, 149, 154, 203
  stages of moral development of 205–6
Kohler, W 195
Krebs, D 216–17

labelling 136, 139, 149, 175–7
Lamb, M 66
Langlois, J 157
language codes 143–4
LaPiere, R 98
Latané, B 84, 89–90, 222, 224
law of effect 9
Lazar, I 145
learning 8–11
  social 12–13
  vicarious 12, 110, 127, 202
libido 107, 123, 124
Linville, P 172
Lloyd, B 153
Loftus, E 235
logical thinking 184
Londerville, S 114, 210
long-term memory 21
longitudinal studies 35, 67, 72, 100, 112, 128–30
Lorenz, K 6 105
Luchins, A 229–30

Maccoby, E 113, 150, 156
Main, M 114, 210
Markus, H 165, 172
Martin, C 156
Martin, J 113
mass media 96, 101, 109, 111–12, 237–40
matched subjects designs 42, 100
matching hypothesis 83
maternal
  deprivation 65–71
  privation 68, 70
maturation 4–5, 189, 195
mean scores 46–7, 52, 55
measures 45
memory, short-term (working) 21
mental
  age 134
  images 24
  representation 23–5
Merluzzi, T 236
Mischel, W 153
modelling 126–7, 152–3, 209
  and aggression 114–15
  and social learning 12–13, 109–11, 160, 202
models 12, 73, 95, 101, 124, 210–11, 220, 238
monotropy 65, 66–7
moral
  behaviour 200, 210–13
  development 200–13
morality principle 122
Moriarty, T 33
Muller-Lyer illusion 196
Murstein, B 40, 50

nature/nurture debate 5–6, 17, 36–7, 105
  and aggression 112, 114
  and intelligence 133, 146
  and perception 189–99
  and temperament 129
needs 3
negative correlation 32

negative reinforcement 10–12, 108, 126, 153–4, 202
Neisser, U 21, 234
Neuberg, S 21
Newcombe, T 80–1
normal distribution 134, 140
Norman, D 235
normative influence 88, 90
norms
  group 86, 88, 89
  psychometric 34, 134
  social see social norms

object permanence 182
observation schedules 30, 45, 48
observational
  learning 12, 97
  studies 29–30, 48, 108, 129, 150
Oedipus conflict 123–4, 152, 200
operant conditioning 9–12, 108–9, 126, 201, 202, 220
Operation Head Start 144

pairing stimuli 9
parental influence 161, 167–8, 207–10, 220–1
parenting 113–14, 131, 144
Parke, R 66
partial reinforcement 10, 126
participants in experiments 43, 44, 56–7
  consent of 56, 149
Patterson, G 108, 114
Pavlov, I 8, 201
peers, influence of 210–13
perception 182
  visual 5, 18, 20, 189–99
personal
  attractiveness 80–3
  bias 164
  construct theory 80, 235–6
  responsibility 224, 226
personality 91–2, 121–32, 228–33
Pettigrew, T 98, 101–2
phallic stage 73, 123, 152
physical attraction 82
Piaget, J 4, 24, 25, 80, 139, 144, 154
  ideas on moral judgements of 203–5
  theory of cognitive development of 5, 80, 144, 181–9, 216
pie charts 48, 50, 52
Piliavin, I 222–3
Piliavin, J 30, 44, 218, 219, 222–3, 226
play 76–7, 187–8
pleasure principle 122
Plomin, R 130, 131, 140–1, 144
pluralistic ignorance 222
positive correlation 32
positive reinforcement 10–12, 108, 126, 153–4, 202
practice effect 42
pre-operational stage 182–4
prediction 39–40, 140
prejudice 31, 91–104, 175
primacy effect 82, 228–30
primary reinforcers 11
pro-social
  behaviour 214, 225–7
  reasoning 206–7
programming, genetic 4
propaganda 96
Pryor, J 236
psychoanalytic theory 3, 121–5, 152
psychometric tests 34–5
punishment 9, 11–12, 109, 126, 153, 202, 208

questionnaires 31–2, 46
questions 31

racism 102
Ramey, C 146
ranges of scores 47, 52
Raynor, R 9
reasoning, pro-social 206–7
receptors 19–20
reciprocity 225
Rees, J 67, 70
reflexes 4, 8–9, 182
reinforcement 126, 151, 153–4, 208
  internal 203
  negative 10–12, 108, 126, 153–4, 202
  partial 11, 126
  positive 10–12, 108, 115, 202
  vicarious 111, 202
reinforcers 11
reliability 34, 129
repeated measures designs 41–2
report writing 52, 54

representation, mental 23–5
research, aims of 39
responses
  conditioned 8–9, 201
  unconditioned 8–9, 201
responsibility, personal 224, 226
responsiveness, sensitive 63, 67, 113
reversibility 185
right to withdraw 57, 72
Robbers' Cave experiment 99–101
Robertson, J 69
Rodin, J 222–3
Rogers, C 168–9
role
  of fathers 66, 73
  models 160, 161 *see also* models
roles 15, 89, 116, 169–70, 172
  social 16, 169–72, 236
  taking 216
Rosenberg, M 231
Rosenhan, D 176
Rosenthal, R 173–5
Rubin, J 161
Ruble, D 150, 155, 164
rules 212
Rutter, M 68–70, 74, 131

Sameroff, A 176
sampling 41, 43–4, 53, 55
scapegoats 91, 92, 107
scattergrams 48, 50–2, 53, 81
Schaffer, R 35, 45, 63, 64, 66–7
schemas 229, 236
  and information 21–4
  innate 182, 186
  and stereotypes 93–4, 156, 323–3
Schmitt, B 85–6
scripts 24, 236–7
Sears, R 109, 113, 161
secondary reinforcers 11
security of attachment 62–3 *see also* attachment
Segall, M 196
segregation 99
self
  awareness 88–9
  concept 16, 163, 166, 169–72, 174
  discrepancy theory 168
  efficacy 13, 127, 153–4, 166–7, 202–3
  esteem 15, 93, 163, 165–6, 168–9, 172
    and labelling 175, 176
  fulfilling prophecy 102–3, 139, 157, 165, 172–5, 176–7, 233
  image 163–5, 166, 176
  perception theory 98, 101, 171–2
Selman, R 79
sensitive
  periods 5, 65, 71
  responsiveness 63, 67
sensory
  information 19 *see also* perception
  motor stage 181–2
separation distress 61–2, 69–70
seriation 185
sex differences 156–9, 160–2 *see also* gender
  and friendship 78–80
  reinforcement of 160–2
  and self-efficacy 153–4
  and social learning 73, 109, 111–12, 150, 154
Shallice, T 235
shaping behaviour 10
Sherif, M 86, 99–101
short-term (working) memory 21
Siegel, M 211–12
similarity
  and attractiveness 80–1, 82
  and helping behaviour 218–19, 222–3
Skeels, H 69, 70
Skinner, B F 9–11
sleeper effect 145
Smetana, J 209, 210, 212
Smith, C 153
Snyder, M 174, 175
sociability 130
social
  categorisation 92–3
  class 143–4
  cognition 24, 165, 172, 217
  comparison 15, 168
  conformity 86–90, 102
  co-operation 99–100
  justice 226
  facilitation 84–6, 89–90, 224
  impact theory 89–90, 224

social learning theory 12–13, 160
and aggression 109–12, 114
and moral development 201, 202–3, 210
and personality 126
and sex 73, 152–3, 156
and stereotypes 94–7
loafing 84, 89
norms 15–16, 86, 169, 206, 210, 218
changing 101–2
and labelling 175
and prejudice 96–100
and pro-social behaviour 214,. 225–7
responsibility 224, 226
roles 16, 169–72, 236
Spitz, R 65, 66
Sroufe, A 63
standardisation 34
standardised, instructions 45, 55
standardised, tests 34
Stanford-Binet test 134–5, 140
stereotypes 23 174–5, 232–3, 239
and gender 151, 154, 156, 160–1
and prejudice 92–101
stereotyping 92–4, 95, 232–3, 239
stimulation 64, 69, 71
stimulus
conditioned 8–9, 201
pairing of 9
unconditioned 8–9, 201
Storey, R 211–12
stranger fear 61–2
Stratton, G 195
studies
correlational 31–3, 40, 50–1, 53
cross-cultural 36–7, 18, 131, 150, 196–8, 213
cross-sectional 35–6, 72
longitudinal 35, 67, 72, 100, 112, 128–30
observational 29–30, 48, 108, 150
Sturrup, B 216–17
subjects *see* participants
superego 107, 122, 124, 200
surveys 30–1, 96
symbolic thinking 183
Szasz, T 175

tabulation 46–7
Tajfel, H 92, 93, 166
Taylor, S 164, 235
temperament 63, 74, 114, 128–31, 144
tests 34–5, 136, 137
Thibaut, J 82
thinking 183, 184, 185–6
Thomas, A 128–30, 131
Thorndike, E L 9–10
Tizard, B 67, 70
traits 230–1, 233
transduction 19
twins 6–7, 128, 130, 140–1,

unconditioned
responses 8–9, 201
stimuli 8, 201
unconscious mind 122, 124
understanding 21

validity 34, 139
van Dijk, T 101
variables 31, 33, 35, 40–1, 45, 55
vicarious
learning 12, 110, 127, 202
reinforcement 111, 202
visual
cliff 192–4
perception 5, 18, 20, 189–99
vividness 235
von Senden, M 194

Walk, R 192, 194
Wallace, J 194
Wallerstein, J 73
Watson, J B 9
Wechsler, D 135, 139
Wechsler Scales 135, 137, 140, 142, 157
Weinberg, R 167
Whiting, B 213
withdrawal, right to 57, 72, 149
Wolf, K 65, 66
Word, C 102
working memory 21

Zahn-Waxler, C 220
Zajonc, R 81, 84
Zimbardo, P 88–9, 170–2, 176